"It would be hard to match the charge that courses through the stories of those who fought and bore witness to the ongoing wave of protests and uprisings in the Arab world. The authors are to be commended for their wise and far ranging-choices and for rendering them eloquently. A powerful answer to those who despair for the future of the region."

–James L. Gelvin, author of *The Arab Uprisings: What Everyone Needs to Know*

"This book is essential reading for all those trying to understand an Arab world in profound transformation. It provides a fresh approach on a fundamental and often misconceived reality that affects everything and everybody."

–Manuel Castells, author of *Networks of Outrage and Hope: Social Movements in the Internet Age*, Wallis Annenberg Chair in Communication, University of Southern California

"Young eyes looked across their region and found each other— over the past ten years they had fought together in small groups or large demonstrations—in solidarity with the Palestinians; against the rising price of bread; arms linked against the impending war on Iraq; against the depredations of IMF-driven financial polices; inside Syria's *maframa* torture program and outside Mahallah's factories; shouting slogans to deplore violence against women . . . . Of such struggles were made experienced organizers, wise beyond their years. Of these voices is *Demanding Dignity* made, a captivating read."

–Vijay Prashad, author of *Arab Spring, Libyan Winter*

# DEMANDING
# DIGNITY

## A Note about the *I Speak for Myself* series:

*I Speak for Myself* is an inclusive platform through which people can make themselves heard and where everyone's voice has a place. ISFM's mission focuses on delivering one core product, a "narrative collection," that is mindset-altering, inspiring, relatable, and teachable. We aim to deliver interfaith, intercultural titles that are narrow in scope but rich in diversity.

Please be sure to check out our website, www.ISpeakforMyself. com, to learn more about the series, join the conversation, and even create an *I Speak for Myself* book of your own!

Sincerely,
Zahra T. Suratwala and Maria M. Ebrahimji
Co-Founders, *I Speak for Myself*

Books in the Series

Volume 1: *I Speak for Myself: American Women on Being Muslim*

Volume 2: *American Men on Being Muslim: 45 American Men on Being Muslim*

Volume 3: *Demanding Dignity: Young Voices from the Front Lines of the Arab Revolutions*

# DEMANDING DIGNITY

## Young Voices From the Front Lines of the Arab Revolutions

*edited by* Maytha Alhassen and Ahmed Shihab-Eldin

WHITE CLOUD PRESS
ASHLAND, OREGON

*The views and opinions expressed by each contributing writer in this book are theirs alone and do not necessarily represent those of the series' editors or I Speak for Myself, Inc.*

White Cloud Press books may be purchased for educational, business, or sales promotional use. For information, please write: Special Market Department, White Cloud Press, PO Box 3400, Ashland, OR 97520
Website: www.whitecloudpress.com

Cover photo by Reuters / Amr Dalsh
Cover and Interior Design by Confluence Book Services

First edition: 2012

Printed in the United States of America

Library of Congress Cataloging-in-Publication Data

Demanding dignity : young voices from the front lines of the arab revolu-tions / Co-Editors: Maytha Alhassen and Ahmed Shihab-Eldin.
p. cm. -- (I speak for myself series)
ISBN 978-1-935952-71-8 (pbk.)
1. Arab Spring, 2010- 2. Arab countries--Politics and government--21st cen-tury. 3. Revolutions--Arab countries--History--21st century. 4. Youth--Politi-cal activity--Arab countries. I. Alhassen, Maytha. II. Shihab-Eldin, Ahmed.
DS63.1.D457 2012
909'.097492708312--dc23
2012027791

This book is dedicated to all the martyrs of the revolutions including our dear mentor and friend, Anthony Shadid.

# Contents

# Note on Transcriptions

In transcribing Arabic words and names, we have followed the Modern Standard Arabic system, although we have chosen not to use diacritical marks as found in scholarly literature.

# Introduction

The Arab world has forever changed. After decades of oppression and dictatorship, a revolutionary spirit, led primarily by the region's youth, has risen across the Middle East and North Africa/Maghreb (MENA), challenging the governments in power, their relations with the West, and the roles of religion, women, and democracy in society. Millions of protesters have taken to the streets across the region, sharing one central demand—to live in dignity, and in doing so, to reclaim their right to self-determination, rather than life through subjugation.

For many, particularly in the West, the civil unrest that swept across the region in 2011 came as a surprise. The United States, like much of the world, was shocked to find Hosni Mubarak, whom they had supported for the last three decades with 1.3 billion dollars of annual military aid, fall in just eighteen days. Yet the Arab world has been ripe for the revolutions we have now witnessed for far longer than many Arab elite circles or the Western think tanks and media might like to admit, or could have predicted.

Since 1975, the United States has pumped more than 28 billion dollars in military and economic aid into Egypt, but it has turned a blind eye to the government's pervasive corruption, human rights violations, and decades of election rigging. While corruption was largely assumed and suspected, empirical evidence was often missing. Wikileaks changed that.

In each Arab state that has experienced civil unrest, if not full-fledged revolution, the story is a familiar one: Western-backed dictators ruled for decades, capitalizing upon the growing class divide and seldom displaying transparency in governance. Despite token gestures by these dictators to bring democracy and opportunity to Arab citizens, the widening wealth gap prompted episodes of civil unrest, including sporadic food protests that were quickly crushed by the regimes. Civil unrest was equated with terrorism, and the West continued to prop up the authoritarian leaders in pursuit of oil deals and geo-political convenience. But a trend was emerging.

Whether in Tunisia, Libya, Egypt, or Morocco, a growing awareness that these governments represented the interests of others, rather than their own citizens, manifested itself in society. With each election, instances of voter intimidation, fraud, and vote rigging grew rampant. After Egypt's presidential election in 2005, for example, it was publicly announced that Mubarak won by securing 88.6% of the vote. As the years passed, little changed. Arab leaders often used the word "democracy"—even Mubarak's political party used the name National Democratic Party—but political participation and social equity had been largely ignored for decades.

Many turned to religion to find purpose or answers. The hope behind endorsing a unifying Islamic identity rested on a desire to return to a moment of civilizational greatness that preceded Western colonization. The 1970s witnessed an Islamic Revivalism that quickly replaced the dashed dreams of a collapsing Nasserist pan-Arabism. Many of these movements were either brutally crushed by the state or forced into hiding. As the region's cultural and social fabric grew more conservative, those who had enough money or privileges left to study abroad, and few returned. The long-standing brain drain robbed the region of its real natural resources: not oil and gas but a skilled, youthful workforce and a rich cultural past.

Arab youth, who make up the majority of the population in the region's countries, were inheriting false promises and broken societies.

As the economy worsened across the Middle East and North Africa/Maghreb, millions of unemployed but educated youth found that the opportunities of living a fulfilling life were narrowing. This basic lack of opportunity punctuated by staggering humiliation might have atrophied hope, but it paradoxically appeared to propel spirits—inciting widespread revolts we've seen catch fire from one country to the next. Young, educated graduates transitioned from universities to encounter closed doors in terms of gainful employment and free public expression. With unemployment on the rise and inflation in the double digits, the youth grew more hungry, frustrated, and disillusioned. Eventually the barrier of fear that had subdued previous generations broke.

It is only fitting that the young Arab named Mohamed Bouazizi would come to symbolize the frustration of a generation. He was his family's sole breadwinner, supporting them on a meager income, and he was frequently harassed by corrupt officials. His self-immolation— resulting from an altercation with a policewoman who confiscated the food cart on which his entire family relied—epitomized his generation's hopelessness. And it sparked the series of political fires that in the West is referred to as the "Arab Spring."

As the protests spread from Tunisia to Egypt to Algeria, governments attempted to stave off and co-opt the unrest. In response to bread riots in the beginning of January 2011, Algeria cut taxes on sugar and cooking oil and imported a million tons of wheat—and also arrested over a thousand protesters. Soon after, Jordan's government announced a delay in raising fuel prices. Yemen scrambled to modify its constitution, and in Kuwait, the government gave each of their citizens a $3,500 (US) bonus and subsidized certain food purchases.

With the exception of Bahrain, the Gulf has so far remained largely immune to the "day of rage" protests seen in countries across the region. Still, governments in the Gulf seem to be intimidated by voices calling for change and reform. In April 2011, five activists in the United Arab Emirates were arbitrarily arrested for signing an online petition calling for reform. They were kept in custody for months before being offered a pardon on National Day.

In each of these instances, the government seemed to be responding to an intellectual and activist ripple effect moving through the

Arab world—quite opposite the image of that world popularized in the West after September 11, 2001. In the ten years since then, the West has associated Arabs and Muslims with images of destruction, killing, and sectarian conflicts on its television and movie screens. Today, images of young Arabs and Muslims fighting for their right to determine their own future stream online and on TV. One could even conclude that the Arab revolutionary youths' formula for protest—an ostensibly leaderless movement that linked cyber and public spaces by tweeting and YouTube video uploading from occupied public squares—has been the inspiration for cascading protests globally, including the rise of the Occupy Movement and the Chilean Spring that same year. In many ways, the protest movements of the Arab world have re-inspired Americans to challenge corruption at home. One of the United State's most provocative public intellectuals, Cornel West, who has spoken at different Occupy events across the United States, acknowledged, "We will send a message that this is the U.S. fall responding to the Arab Spring."[1]

The message is now clear: citizens of the Arab world are no longer to be feared by the West, just as they no longer fear their own leaders or shy away from the right to practice free speech. New generations of Arabs are reclaiming what it means to be Arab. Through the democratization of media and technology—specifically new disruptive publishing platforms and social media—this connected generation of Arabs has found power in numbers online and ways to translate those numbers into the streets.

For decades, civic engagement was hardly tolerated and more often brutally oppressed in public life. In fact, the very notion of challenging authority in any Arab country was rarely imagined, let alone carried out. Technology has challenged that notion. When the Internet arrived in the Middle East and North Africa/Maghreb in the early nineties, the region's youth found a platform to escape but also to connect. They confronted their challenges, their dreams, and each

---

1. "Democracy Now" interview with Cornel West, September 29, 2011.

other in the virtual realm. In some countries, blatant censorship of Internet content became an explicit reminder to youth of the tentacles of dictatorship reaching into their lives. It even inspired this tech-savvy generation to work around web restrictions through innovative and entrepreneurial projects.

During the uprisings, Arab leaders quickly recognized the role of the Internet in mobilizing protests and documenting police and military brutality. On January 27, 2011, just as President Obama appeared live on YouTube to answer questions submitted from the American public, Egypt's President Hosni Mubarak shut down the Internet in an attempt to crush the popular uprising in his country. Despite that, the advent of civic engagement eventually spilled from the virtual realm to the streets and public squares as well as across the full spectrum of society. Revolutions proceeded, equipped with posters, avatars, chants, community created clinics, and hashtags.

As the protests spread through the Arab world, Western governments and media were unsure what to make of them, let alone what to name this unprecedented movement. The *New York Times* called it "Al Jazeera's moment." True, this moment may have been to Al Jazeera what the first Gulf War was to CNN; however, it was not Al Jazeera's moment. It was the people's moment. Al Jazeera, like social media, played a crucial role in amplifying the voices of those who had finally come out in large numbers to be heard—connecting them with millions of others in the region and billions more the world over. Yet it was the people's voices that were echoing from rooftops and public squares across the region chanting: *Allahu Akbar* (God is Great!) and *Ash-sha'ab yureed isqat an-nizam!* (The people want the fall of the regime!).

## Why We Care
### Maytha Alhassen

My involvement in this project started years prior to the uprisings. In 2008, I was approached to contribute to a collection of writings about

Muslim women from the United States on the relationships among three identities: being a woman, being a Muslim, and being an American. Since 9/11, Western media's preoccupation with Muslim women and Muslim American women—who were frequently represented as either veiled, silent, or invisible—had grown exponentially. But strongly missing from that representation were the voices of the women who were being spoken about. Co-edited by Maria Ebrahimji and Zahra Suratwala, *I Speak for Myself: American Women on Being Muslim* showcases essays by forty American Muslims under the age of forty from different racial, class, political, and professional backgrounds.

After the success of this book project, the co-editors decided to brand the concept and launch an "I Speak for Myself" series. The second book in the collection, *All-American: 45 American Men on Being Muslim*, presents the voices of American Muslim men. The mission of the third book in the series—this book—is to provide a timely intervention: personal stories by Arab youth from the Middle East and North Africa/Maghreb who were intimately involved in the uprisings of their respective countries and who used social media in some capacity to aid in their activism. It is only fitting, then, that my involvement in co-editing this book was the result of uploading pictures onto my Facebook page.

In the summer of 2011, I planned to attend a two-week academic seminar in Granada, Spain on Critical Muslim Studies. In keeping with my travel philosophy, I decided to augment my Granada trip with other trips around the region. I began in Tunisia, documenting a hip-hop tour by American artists Remarkable Current and their musical collaboration with Tunisian rappers (whose lyrics are included in this book). In the process, I met a young grad student, Achref Aouadi (who has also contributed an essay), who helped organize the tour and doubled as an activist and bridge to multiple communities in Tunisia's youth scene. He also provided me with a critical background in the socio-political history of Tunisia, the revolution, and the work of youth organizers.

After heading to Spain for the seminar, I added trips to Morocco, Egypt, and Lebanon to my summer itinerary. In Morocco, debate was heated around the upcoming vote on King Mohammed VI's proposed constitutional referendum, which did not seem to quell protests by the February 20 Movement. As I landed in Cairo, demonstrations re-erupted over frustrations about the postponement of trials for high-ranking police officers. The day I arrived in Beirut to visit my family, the U.N. Special Tribunal for Lebanon submitted the indictment and confidential arrest warrants of the four suspected assassins of Lebanon's Prime Minister Rafiq Hariri in February 2005. My efforts to enter Syria, where my mother and father are from (Lattakia and Aleppo), were dashed by the unpredictability of violence and border control.

In between visits with my family, I spent my time in Beirut regularly catching up with *New York Times* journalist Anthony Shadid at Gruen Café in Hamra. We spoke about the final touches he was making to his upcoming book and about my professional journalistic and academic trajectory. We also imagined what impact these revolutions would have on promoting a borderless Middle East and Maghreb, one free from the arbitrarily drawn colonial borders now blurred by entering and exiting refugees. During my travels, I met with more youth organizers in each respective country, visited public squares where protests had taken place, attended music festivals and weddings, conducted oral history interviews for my doctoral project, and posted my musings and photos from my excursions on Facebook and Twitter.

Two days after I returned home, I flew to Washington, D.C. to appear as a guest on Al Jazeera English's show *The Stream*, a highly interactive show that harnesses global discussions with a social media community launched in the Spring of 2011. During the taping, I became re-acquainted with a friend from the Arab journalism community, Ahmed Shihab-Eldin, digital producer and co-host of the show. He managed the online conversation between the social media community and guests in the studio or on Skype as well as the digital vision for the show. A couple of weeks later, I was approached by the *I Speak for Myself* editors about co-editing and curating a collection focused on the Arab uprisings and the use of social media by youth organizers. They reasoned that I would be a perfect fit to carry on the legacy of the brand because of my connection to the region and the recent trips I had taken. Honored by their trust in my capabilities and intrigued by the project, I accepted.

Honestly, I must admit that I was slightly reticent at first. There was something unsettling about my position as an Arab *American* woman taking a lead role in collecting, organizing, editing, and having an extensive hand in the production of a book aimed to represent youth activists in the Arab world. I have visited the region never for more than a couple of months at a time; I haven't truly *lived* there. Thus even though I feel strongly connected to the region, there is an inescapable politics of representation that is frequently ignored by those in the West, even those with ties to the region.

I didn't want to be that person who exploits her connection to the region by pretending to "speak for them" in her Southern-California-bred English, thereby promoting her own voice in the mainstream media conversation—as many have done before me and continue to do. Although I was unfathomably inspired by the young Arab generation's imagination-defying bravery, this was their story, not mine. That said, if I could use my skills as a facilitator, writer, and educator to assist in exposing the English-speaking world to their story, then I would gladly offer my services. And so I did.

As I began work on the book I became caught in a cobweb of awe and amazement at the youth generation—my own generation—who toppled dictators installed years before they were born and envisioned a new way of treating humans through their demand for dignity. For me—a budding academic with ethnographic training, a student of decolonization and Third World (non-alignment) movement history, an aspiring journalist, and a woman still cogently connected to the region with family in Syria, Lebanon, Tunisia, UAE, and Saudi Arabia—staying stateside during this profoundly transformative historical moment was a challenge.

I had initially designed an ambitious plan to complete my five-year degree in four. That plan was quickly derailed by the events unfolding in my ancestral homeland. I made the resolute decision to be witness to this moment. This meant delaying my doctoral progress. Yet this was the very kind of moment for which I combed through archives, conducted oral history interviews with elders, and about which I taught my students. Something deep in my gut told me this one would be worth stopping for.

My awe was amplified in the case of Syria, a country I visited for much of my adult life. I remain in disbelief that the Syria I knew —a country bursting with culinary, artistic, and musical culture, ridiculed by the omnipresent paternal posters of the Assads, and gripped by collective fear of publicly stating one's political opinion—had become a nation in which many of its own dissidents and discontents had RISEN UP! And we were all shocked that the brother we regionally neglected as a significant player in pan-Arab affairs, Tunisia, started it all.

This book would be my contribution from afar, my attempt to "bear witness" (as Anthony would call it) to this moment. If I could not be on the front lines in each country, I would assist in weaving together narratives from people on those front lines so they could speak not only to the world, but also to each other.

My first task as a co-editor was finding my counterpart. Although I did not know him beyond two or three interactions over the span of a couple of years, I could not think of a better fit than Ahmed.

## Ahmed Shihab-Eldin

When Maytha approached me to join her as co-editor on this book, I was immersed in a series of chaotic and fateful events that deprived me of sleep, catapulted my career, but most important, connected me, at times intimately, to my shared generation of Arab brothers and sisters fighting for their freedom and right to self-determination.

I re-joined Al Jazeera in January 2011, after having resigned from a previous post at its Doha headquarters. Al Jazeera was ready to develop a truly innovative program that would tap into the power of social networks to find underreported stories, and I was invited to be a central part of it.

When I arrived in Washington, D.C. for my new assignment, all I knew was that Al Jazeera's aim was to create a live daily talk show that would tap into conversations already happening on social media. The plan was to leverage those voices through curating and aggregating tweets, Facebook posts, and You Tube videos to generate a truly global discussion involving a multitude of voices.

Stephen Phelps, who I had the pleasure of working with in Qatar, was tasked with launching our show, *The Stream.* In my first week on the job, he asked that I search online to find stories with impact that were generating a lot of discussion. In doing so, I stumbled across the hashtag "#Sidibouzid." Immediately I called up hundreds of photos and videos showing students protesting, police abuses, and sporadic gunfire.

Tunisia's revolution appeared first on social networks, marking its place in history, weeks before the world's mainstream media woke up to the story. Tweets and videos popped up on the Internet from Tunisia, warning of trouble to come in the region. Protesters called for help from hacktivist groups. Tunisia's government began hacking into and deleting Facebook accounts. And soon enough, another hashtag appeared across the networks, "#Anonymous."

Within a matter of hours, Anonymous launched "Operation Tunisia," paralyzing the president's website, several key ministries, and the stock exchange.

Reports from netizens revealed that 1.5 tons of gold went missing from Tunisia's Central Bank, and photos of a young man who had slit his wrists in Gafsa over unemployment circulated online. For a full week, I watched the story unfold, speaking to activists using Facebook, Skype, and Twitter, as protests turned bloody. On January 12, 2011, with Ben Ali's regime on the verge of collapse, *Time Magazine* reported the story. But the story was already out there online, documented in photographs shot with mobile phones and streaming video.

As the messages went viral, protests broke out across the world expressing solidarity with Tunisia. I began speaking and connecting with those staging solidarity protests in London, Berlin, Switzerland, Egypt, and Algeria. The beginning of a revolution was unfolding, and I had a front-row seat. The mainstream media was only beginning to catch up.

I had grown up in Egypt for nearly a decade, having moved there with my family in the summer of 1992. Even then, disillusionment and widespread poverty as well as soaring food prices suggested to me that change was inevitable. The Internet arrived in the country exactly one year later. It would be just under two decades later, in January of 2011, that the Internet in Egypt would be shut down by President Hosni Mubarak.

Although I followed almost all the uprisings, including in Yemen, Bahrain, and Syria, it was Egypt's revolution that struck a nerve, depriving me of sleep as I eagerly watched the people mobilize and then circumvent Mubarak's decades-old oppressive tactics to eventually unseat him from his throne.

On February 11, 2011, the day Mubarak stepped down, I was traveling on an Amtrak train from Washington, D.C. to New York City to speak on a panel at Google's headquarters for Social Media Week. The topic was the use of social networks in Egypt. There I was, sitting in the quiet car of the train, as the voices of hundreds of thousands of Egyptians celebrating the downfall of a dictator echoed in Cairo's skies, through my laptop, and into my earphones. Thanks to Tweetdeck and Al Jazeera's live Internet stream, and the fortuitous though unreliable Internet connection on the train, I was able to witness a day millions of Arabs would have never conceived possible.

When I got off the train, as I walked from 34th Street to Google's downtown offices, I was overwhelmed with emotion. I was physically and emotionally exhausted. I was also frustrated that I could not be there in Egypt. Tears streamed down my face.

In the Arab world a new power structure had emerged, and eventually protests had spread to other countries. The anger that fueled the protests had much earlier rooted itself inside Arab minds. My own mind was spinning as I tried to keep up with the influx of tweets as country by country people took to the streets, demanding dignity, demanding change.

Many activists and netizens who played crucial roles in the many uprisings eventually appeared on *The Stream*—some by Skype, and some in person. I learned intimate details of their stories. Some had watched helplessly as their fathers and brothers were beaten and dragged from their homes. Some were tortured themselves after sneaking across borders to mobilize and support sister revolutions. They all shared the scars of damaged dignity.

As the world struggled to understand and contextualize this unprecedented wave of revolt in the region, I was invited to travel and speak at conferences around the globe, only to meet more activists, human rights advocates, victims of oppression, and sympathetic entrepreneurs. Although our show was designed to cover the entire world, the stories from the Arab world were dominating much of the discussion online, as well as my own attention. My seat on the orange couch of *The Stream* set in Washington, D.C. gave me a platform to interact virtually with many of the protagonists in these epic stories—a chronicle of the human struggle for self-determination and dignity. The experience both inspired and humbled me. It also began to affect my health.

When I was invited to the Google Zeitgeist conference in September 2011, I had been ill for several weeks. I continued doing the show but was popping Tylenol like candy. It was only after two weeks of night-sweats and perpetual fever that I decided to see a doctor. The week after returning from the Google conference, I learned that I had glandular fever. I needed rest, but when members of the Arab Development Initiative called me to emcee their inaugural event in Montreal, I felt compelled to say yes.

As it turned out, this proved to be the most rewarding event I attended in 2011. The group, made up of young, driven Arabs living in Montreal and elsewhere in the diaspora, made it their mission to assist and promote highly skilled, educated Arab youth in the Middle East and North Africa in their efforts towards development. I was consumed by their compulsion to get involved and wondered how I might help share the Arab youths' stories as a way of participating in the development of the region.

Just as these youths were battling the cancer of corruption and inequality plaguing their governments and lives, my mother, living in Vienna, Austria, was two years into her battle with cancer, which threatened her life. Being immersed in one of the most professionally and personally chaotic and impactful periods of my life, I was worried that I would not have the time to give this book the attention it deserved. Still, I could not say no to Maytha.

Aside from attending panels and conferences, and squeezing a few vacation days in order to visit my ailing mother, I have had little opportunity to travel to the Middle East and North Africa region. Working on this book has given me the opportunity to identify and collaborate with Arabs as they joined together in demanding their dignity. It has has enabled me to partake in the pursuit of a more just future for the Arab world and be as close to the agents of change and their stories as possible.

As time passes and the struggle for freedom and dignity continues, I am grateful for the opportunity to learn from these brave men and women, and to help share their stories. The truths and the lessons they reveal about the human condition will stay with me for a lifetime.

## Why You Should Care

The essays in this book are written by Arab youth who have collectively sparked a revolutionary spirit that has toppled governments—the consequence of decades of repression and resistance. Contributors from ten countries across the Arab world meet within these pages.

Their essays fall somewhere between journalistic first-hand reports and intimate journal entries. Inspired in part by universal human aspirations, each story captures the changes that are impacting this revolutionized region and that are uniting like-minded citizens through civic engagement. Their voices are as varied as the stories they tell, but their destinies are shared. They are a connected generation, and by reading their stories, you are connected to them too.

You will read of a Moroccan journalist's witnessing public school teachers immolating themselves as they protested in front of their ministry in Rabat. You will be reminded of suffering in daily life. You will follow along as a young Egyptian navigates his way through social and political upheavals from Egypt to Syria. You will hear the voices of relentlessly silenced and tortured Bahraini human rights activists. And you will witness how hope can rise from the ashes of destruction.

These stories of our fellow global citizens—chants, cries, and songs proclaimed from rooftops far away—continue to be heard to this day through this book. They point to a vision of pan-Arab identity, expressed in their shared spirit and connected struggles. Their voices together culminate in a call for contesting political, religious, and conventional authority. Yet perhaps the most revolutionary of their demands is for the principle that undergirds democracy everywhere: for *karama*, dignity.

# A Young Man's Spark (Bouazizi)

## by Anas Canon

**ANAS CANON** is a man of profound words and immeasurable talent whose expertise in audio production, sound engineering, and as a DJ are recognized and requested worldwide. The breadth of his body of work testifies to the distinct ingenuity and inspiration he infuses into his projects.

Anas is firmly committed to advancing social awareness and promoting diversity through art and continues to explore new channels for his creative expression. He serves as the artistic director and executive producer for the independent media collective Remarkable Current, which he founded in 2001.

As an extension of Remarkable Current, Anas developed the Hip Hop Ambassadors program in hopes of presenting positive examples of African American musicians to the international community, as well as spreading the messages of peace and love through the universal language of music. One of the Hip Hop Ambassadors' recent tours to Indonesia, sponsored by the U.S. State Department's Performance Arts Initiative, broke U.S. Embassy press records and was an unprecedented success in the region, reaching millions of viewers. Often sought out by the media for his opinions and perspectives, Anas has been published in the Washington Post and on CNN.com, as well as interviewed by countless newspapers, magazines and media outlets including PBS, BBC, and MTV.

## Azeem

It ain't
Easy in the land of Muhammad Bouazizi
Real revolutionaries here—Tunis-ie
Azeem ismee mush Young Jeezy
One man died …
So the whole world could be—free

Ya Allah,
my Lord my liege
We don't want to see police shoot young teens
There has been enough death and blood in the streets
Let's get together
For the Father
Of Unity…

## Nizar T-Man

Salam Aleykoum,
I am starting off with the name of Allah
La ilaha illa Allahu, Muhammad Rasoul Allah
Tunisia, this country
Tunisia, the star and the moon
Tunisia, my country and your country
With our hands, we will build our country
We built the present and our future is ahead
Today, hand in hand, we will build our dreams
We endured more than fifty years under the oppression
We opted for the freedom and questioned for the truth

## Weld-Michel

Tunisia is free, free, free
Tunisia is free, free
Raise you head up, you, Tunisian (x3)
Tunisia is free

## L'Empire (Arabic)

People are crying
Bouazizi drown into these tears
Bouazizi set himself in fire, died
From there a nation is born
In fact, the people forget the hate and the pain
Over time, all changed
I slept and I woke up
Now after a long time of silence the nation is free
Streets recovered by the blood of martyrs facing rifles
Here, people came out from the darkness to the light with pain
Prostrated (sujud), Bowed down (roukou') because of the hunger
The Head up

## L'Empire (French)

Twenty-three years of dreams
Jan. 11, 2011, Tunisia explodes
Bouazizi, go, trigger the revolution
The guerilla shouts for revenge
We call on for democracy, as usual
Tunisia, today, awakes

## Kumasi

Salaamul Hub from Tunis to the Hub
City of Compton
Revolution and mobbing
the mark us like Garvey
the spirit is starving
crying and Wailing Bob Marley
Sekou Touré, Patrice Lamumba
Malik Shabazz
revolution freed me like Muhammed Bouazizi
Unity and Peace
Victory Ya AZIZI

# Serendipity in Syria
## by Muhammad Radwan

**MUHAMMAD RADWAN** is an Egyptian American industrial engineer with a B.Sc. from Texas A&M University. He has lived in several Middle Eastern countries including Egypt, Syria, Saudi Arabia, Bahrain, and Morocco, and has also traveled extensively throughout Latin America, Europe, and Asia. Currently, Muhammad is pursuing a master's degree with a focus on renewable energy and sustainable development at Stellenbosch University in South Africa. He has worked in several industries including food manufacturing, textiles, and pipe coating, and has written articles for Al Masry Al Youm English and Campus Magazine. Muhammad is passionate about world politics, social justice, and the quest for knowledge that offers an alternative perspective. He aims to respect cultural similarities, celebrate the differences, promote positivity, and pursue universal truths.

When I first learned about the events in Cairo in January 2011, I was paralyzed for a few brief moments. I was living in Syria at the time, working as a branch manager at a geosciences company. Without debating the issue, I decided to go to Cairo, and I purchased a plane ticket to leave within hours of making the decision. For three weeks, starting on January 28, the Day of Anger, I was in Tahrir Square on a daily basis. I witnessed police forces being over-powered by thousands of freedom-demanding Egyptians. I witnessed millions in the square demanding their rights. I witnessed protesters sacrificing for themselves and their fellow countrymen. I witnessed the downfall of one of the longest-serving and most reviled dictators in the Middle East. The events of those weeks overshadowed all my previous travels and experiences around the world.

During my time in Egypt, my employer inquired about my whereabouts, future intentions, and possibility of returning to my post in Damascus. My answer was always concise: I would return when Egypt was liberated. The ousting of Hosni Mubarak was a milestone in the struggle for liberation, and a few days after his fall in February 2011, I did indeed return to Damascus.

At the Damascus International Airport the company driver awaited my arrival. On the way home, I asked him if he thought being an Egyptian during these turbulent times would be a problem in Syria. He responded with conviction, assuring me that Syria was experiencing no turmoil and that the government media was extolling the youth of Egypt's historic revolution. Yet my doubt lingered. I knew the Syrian government was not so different from the governments of other Arab countries whose people had begun the struggle against oppression.

In the following days, I closely monitored the events unfolding in Egypt, Yemen, Bahrain, and Libya. Qaddafi was in the midst of losing half the country to the rebels of Benaghazi. His response was brutal and swift. The international community responded to the deaths of thousands of Libyans by staging protests all over the world at Libyan embassies. Even in Damascus, a city that outlawed gatherings of this kind, activists organized a silent protest. Having gone from the extreme of Egypt's volatile atmosphere to the subdued Syrian capital, I decided to join Syrians supporting their brothers in Libya in front of the embassy in Abo Ramaneh in central Damascus.

The scene at the Libyan embassy could have been one of the hundreds that took place in Cairo during the past five years. Just as in Egypt, the number of security personnel exceeded the number of protesters. After a few hours, and with a lot of strangers walking up to our faces and taking photos, I decided to leave.

A few weeks later, Syrians began to prove the company driver wrong. Not all Syrians were content; far from it. The events in the southern Syrian city of Daraa were not immediately covered by the press, but the activists on Twitter had successfully relayed the news of mass marches and deaths of protesters. It had taken a little longer, but Syria was beginning its revolution. Until this point, all the events centered around Daraa, isolated in the south near the border of Jordan. This geographical isolation delayed the revolution's spread to other parts of the country. Yet opposition figures and activists decided there was no better time to push ahead with their calls for freedom, justice, and equality. Every Friday they tried to organize a protest, but every Friday only a few would arrive. On March 25, the dissenters organized a protest in the Ummayad Mosque in the Old City of Damascus in support of their countrymen in the town of Daraa. By this time, international media had begun taking an interest, and Syria had finally become "newsworthy."

The Facebook group explained the details of the event: location, time, objectives. That morning, I ate at my favorite *foul* (a traditional breakfast fava bean dish) restaurant and recalled a tweet I had just read from a Syrian activist: "I do not know if I will come home, get arrested, or die today, Freedom to Syria." I thought to myself: I went home to Egypt and did not get arrested; by attending this event, am I positioning myself to get arrested in Syria? I decided that I would not chant, I would not participate, I would merely witness an event so strange to Syrian culture: a protest.

When I arrived at the Old City, I decided to take the Hamadeyaa Market route to scope out the surroundings and gain a sense of how urgent this event was in the eyes of the people and the state. Numerous parallels between Egypt and Syria could be drawn at these times. I scanned the corridor market as I headed towards the mosque at the end, but I did not see the black leather jackets or other conspicuous signs of the Mukhabarat, Syria's infamous security services.

As I approached the square in front of the mosque, a group of men near the entrance began chanting in unison, "God, Syria, Bashar, and that's it!" This slogan was to become one of the symbols of the pro-Assad regime in the coming months. A camera crew was already set up and began filming the demonstration.

Walking into the compound of the mosque, I could now hear the Imam giving his sermon for the Friday prayer. However, this sermon differed from all other sermons I had ever heard. It lauded the Damascenes and their proud heritage of not succumbing to *fitna* (meddling with malicious intent to cause chaos).

People in the prayer hall were unusually attentive, staring directly at the Imam. He continued to explain that the Facebook groups that attacked the regime were Israeli agents attempting to sow unrest in the country. Suddenly, people among the crowd began to stand up and walk to the back entrance of the prayer hall in what appeared to be disapproval. Within minutes, a crowd had formed and was chanting anti-regime slogans. The Imam stopped the sermon. The feeling in the hall sent shivers down my spine. Another group formed within moments and began chanting pro-regime slogans. I looked around me and saw a row of people with their mobile phones recording the events. I did the same.

The two crowds faced each other and began to pour out into the complex right outside the prayer hall. I rushed to find my shoes and followed the crowds outside. I wanted to tweet about this, but I also began to feel that it was time for me to leave. Events were escalating fast, and sooner or later I could find myself in a difficult position.

As I tweeted, a short man walked up to me, looked at my mobile screen, and asked what I was doing. I told him I was writing a message to a friend and was on my way out of the mosque. He grabbed my phone. Another man appeared behind me and, holding my shoulders, led me to a room inside the mosque. I asked them what the problem seemed to be, but no one was answering my questions. I found myself surrounded by twenty security service men, and every few minutes, another protester would enter the room. All of them showed signs of distress; perhaps they were not as optimistic as I was. But once they asked for my identification and saw my Egyptian passport, my fate was sealed.

When there were about ten protesters in the room, the security officers tied our hands together with plastic and put tape around our mouths. We were led to the door, where a van waited to transport us unlucky ones. The van did not have chairs and all the protesters were piled on top of each other, including me. The security men stood inside the back of the van, blocking all the windows so that no one could see either from the outside or the inside. I began to have an anxiety attack. My optimism had completely faded, and I realized that I was in dire straits. One young Syrian tapped me on my knee to comfort me. His gesture indeed reassured me, though it was fleeting. We had arrived at our destination.

Once we were in the security station, the guards, now safely concealed behind the walls, could act with no concern for public scrutiny. I was now in their territory and they immediately let me know the score. I was in their eyes an equal of the anti-regime protesters and could not explain myself without risking a beating. They began to abuse the detainees by punching them and hurling insults. Walking down a set of stairs, the security men barked orders at the detainees: "Look down. Sit on your knees. Stand up. Look down!" Eventually, each person was called before a man sitting in front of a cardboard box. "Take off all your clothes." After I stripped down to my underwear, the guard started shouting at me, "All your clothes!" As I stood in the nude, they checked my belongings and I signed a document. I was ordered to take my clothes and follow the guard, eventually ending up in a holding cell. It was a small (1.8 by 0.70 meter) off-white-colored cell with nothing but a few thin blankets on the floor. The metal door included a small sliding window that the guards could whip open at any time to check on the hapless guest inside.

I remained there for a few hours wondering what my fate would be. These thoughts were often interrupted by the loud shrieking of what I assumed to be my fellow detainees. The door was finally flung open and I was called into an office, but not before they placed a blindfold over my eyes, not so different from the sleeping masks given to passengers on planes. As the officer questioned me about my nationality, occupation, and reasons for being in Syria, I still felt I might have a way out of this situation. Within minutes, I was proven wrong. He said, "Son, we are Mukhabarat. Your stated reasons for being at the mosque are unacceptable." And then: "Take him away!" Apparently, going to Friday prayer at the central Umayyad mosque one last time before flying back to Egypt did not qualify as an acceptable answer.

I was transferred to a small room nearby, the one from where the loud screams of pain had emerged earlier. The guard instructed me to lie down on the ground on my stomach, still blindfolded, then to raise my legs in the air with the bottom of my feet facing the ceiling and to hold my hands together behind my back. I heard a loud smack and then an excruciating pain shot up from my feet, causing my whole body to convulse. Before I could utter a sound, the guard struck my feet with his stick multiple times. At this point, I was the one every other prisoner could hear. I decided to make as much noise as possible and to begin crying. The plan was to show them my low threshold for pain so that the *falaka* (as this practice is commonly called in Arabic) session would end in the shortest possible time. The pain was unbearable after the first few minutes of continuous strikes on the bottom of my feet. I expected my feet to become numb, but the sensitivity of the bottom of one's feet is so high, the pain just kept increasing. Eventually, my feet fell to the ground and the guards started beating my back and legs. Luckily they had not asked me to remove my leather jacket, but in order for them to feel they were succeeding, I screamed in pain even though the jacket took the brunt of the blow.

Once they deemed I was ready for my follow-up interrogation, they carried me to another room. It was here that I met Abu Tarek, as they called him. Abu Tarek spoke softly and stood out from the others. I could not see him, but I understood the others respected him. He began to ask me the usual questions in his soft tone, but he quickly became violent when I denied having gone to Israel. He threatened to remove all my clothes and douse me with water at which point they would administer electric shocks to my genitals. My anxiety levels were reaching a new peak. I explained that the electricity would not be necessary, and I understood at this point that they were looking for a scapegoat. I offered to go along with the suggested narrative to avoid the unimaginable pain that appeared to be the only alternative. Abu Tarek said if I were to help him, then he would help me. A bad film director would have loved this scene. He began discussing the details of this chimerical journey, suggesting random incidents that could form a story that fulfilled his objectives. I denied what he was saying many times, each time followed by a threat that would cause me to capitulate once again until he was finally satisfied.

I spent a few hours in the holding cell and was then taken up to the second floor of the building to meet Abu Tarek again. He asked me if I remembered the details of our last discussion and explained that I would repeat the story in front of a camera crew. In the next room, the crew was already set up, and they began asking questions that were obviously tailored for the answers Abu Tarek and I had prepared. The *ma'alem* (chief and superior of Abu Tarek) watched as this carefully orchestrated farce played out. At the end, he made some amendments to the story line that were so absurd, they were edited out of the final video.

Unknown to me at the time, they immediately began airing this video repeatedly on Syrian National Television, and the word quickly spread to the outside world. My family and friends were shocked to learn of my incarceration by watching me on television admitting to very damning actions. I would find out later that everyone quickly mobilized to use any resource available to secure my release. My cousins set up a Facebook group, Free Mohamed Radwan, which gathered thousands of members within days. My mother and brother went on Egyptian and international news programs like CNN and FOXNews to plead for my release. My father traveled to Syria and met with Syrian Mukhabarat and with the Egyptian and U.S. embassies. Protests in Cairo, London, and Beirut were organized by friends and family. The media attention was far beyond anything the Syrians anticipated, stirring up much commotion. The Egyptian Foreign Minister at the time, Nabil El Araby, intervened directly. It was the first time in Egyptian history that so much attention and effort had been concentrated around an Egyptian national abroad. During Mubarak's time, Egyptians did not expect, and definitely did not receive, any such help while living in or visiting other countries.

Meanwhile, I sat in my room at the detainment site oblivious to all the efforts of my family and friends. And their efforts did not impact the behavior of the Mukhabarat for a few days. Apparently the story had seemed so amateurish and obviously concocted as a propaganda tool for the regime that their subsequent interrogations of me demanded more extreme confessions. The interrogator would ask for my real name and when I said my name would claim that I was using a pseudonym. I would deny these false accusations and in return would be threatened with the *maframa*, or grindhouse. The answer I received about the practices of the grindhouse was summed up very simply: "It is where we sit you on the ground, open your legs wide, and continuously hit you in the genitals until they "pop" so that you cannot have any children in the future."

It is conceivable that the *maframa* was only a threat, designed to cause psychological torture, but at the time the threat seemed very real. I understood what the Syrian Mukhabarat are capable of. At the last moment, as I stood waiting to lose my future children forever, a man walked up to me and took me back to my room. Until today, it remains a mystery who that person was and why he did that.

For the following two days, my hosts seemed uninterested in concocting any more fanciful tales. No one requested to see me while I sat in solitary confinement contemplating if I had satisfactorily lived my life. This time offered a rare opportunity to reflect on the person I had become, my life goals, and how to find beauty in the darkest of places. My thought patterns were circular, reminding me of my thoughts during days I'd spent at the top of the Andes mountains and one late night in a shady Houston underground. The familiarity of this combination of anxiety, clarity, and uncertainty against a backdrop of faith and trust filled my world with positivity.

Late on Thursday night, the 31st of March, my last night in prison, they remembered me again. I was handcuffed, blindfolded, and led to the structure adjacent to the one where I had spent the previous six days. Since I was still limping with bruised and swollen feet, the guards carried me up the stairs. I ended up meeting a man who, by the guards' tone of voice and servile attitude, commanded respect. Again, I was accused of spying for Israel or the United States because "the story does not make sense unless you work for someone." I was told that Syria could do whatever it wanted to me since "the U.S. and the international community have already shunned us, as you already know. So it makes no difference to us whether you live or die." I sincerely believed this was the end of the line and figured there was no better way to approach this situation than providing the truth. I wondered, "Will it set me free?"

At the end of the conversation, the man asked me if I would like anything besides the water I practically begged for, such as returning to Cairo this moment. I was broken down, and suggested he do whatever he saw fit. They returned me to my cell.

The next day was a Friday. My cellmate of the first two days had told me they empty out the jails every week to make room for new detainees captured in the weekly protests. "But you must be able to walk well," he said. I tried walking on my bruised feet as much as possible so it would not appear that I had been abused, hoping this might help. Around noon, the guards called me to gather all my belongings and sign a paper that I had received them. They even returned my mobile phone with the very videos for which I had been arrested a week earlier. This proved to me that they were not after photos, videos, or foreign agents. The reason for my incarceration was to create an illusion of foreign agents, to counter the revolution with baseless propaganda that unfortunately had the desired effect. The guards blindfolded me once again and took me and three others away in a car. The route to the Damascus airport was on a long empty highway and the trip took about forty-five minutes. After twenty minutes in traffic, I began to worry that I was not getting deported, and that maybe I wasn't to be released at all. But where else could I be going? Flashbacks of documentaries of Tadmor (Palymra) prison raced through my head. The guards in our car were arguing about the traffic. It was Friday and the whole city was apparently in turmoil, forcing the driver to take alternate routes to our destination. When we arrived at our destination, I was asked to wait while the four guards rushed to sign a document so they could leave. With their departure, the sense of normalcy began to return.

Everyone was amiable. No yelling or shouting, no barking orders. Calm voices. No blindfolds. I was led into a room where I saw two men sitting. One stood up and introduced himself as the Egyptian Ambassador to Syria. He introduced the other as a major of something or other in the Syrian branch of I don't care anymore. The only thing on my mind was when I would get to leave the country. We left this place immediately after the introductions, and finally it was sinking in that I was being set free.

We arrived at the Ambassador's residence to find my father waiting for me. The consul was there as well, and I began explaining the details of the whole experience. A reservation was made for the next day to Cairo, since I had just missed this day's flight. The consul told me to check out Facebook while I was relaxing at home and to think about the fact that no one in Syria's modern history had been arrested and released in such a short period. "This is record time, and trust me, we know. It's our job to know," the consul explained.

The next day I landed in Cairo to a hero's greeting, with my mother standing in front of a crowd of friends, family, and cameramen. The event was highly publicized, and the media was relentless. I wondered how strange it was for someone like me to get all this attention when there were Syrians losing their lives and Egyptians a few months earlier had done the same, though no one had ever heard their names. Then I thought that those people would probably not care about their names anyway, that the real issue for them, and for myself, was: When will our countries be free?

*Ash-sha'ab yureed isqat an-nizam!* The people want to bring down the system!

# Bahrain Cartoon
## *by Carlos Latuff*

**CARLOS LATUFF** is a Brazilian political cartoonist whose work largely deals with anti-globalization, anti-capitalism, and anti-US military intervention. Although he is best known for his cartoons highlighting the Israeli-Palestinian conflict, he played a central role in documenting the Arab uprisings and revolutions, circulating and sharing his cartoons for activists.

Much of his work appeared at protests across the region and was replicated as graffiti on street corners across the Arab world. Carlos was born in Rio de Janeiro, Brazil and is of Lebanese ancestry. Carlos visited Israel and Palestine in the late 1990s and the injustice he witnessed on his travels inspired him to create his cartoons.

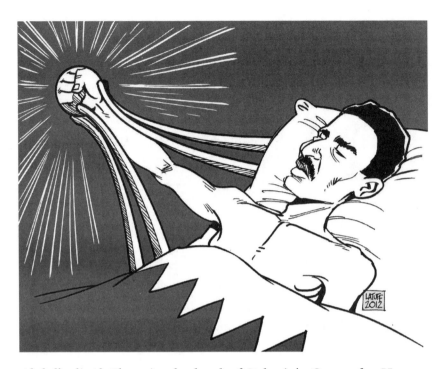

Abdulhadi Al Khawaja, the head of Bahrain's Center for Human Rights, who was tortured, was detained, and staged a hunger strike for more than 100 days in prison, is depicted in bed. His sling is held together by Bahrain's Pearl Roundabout, where protesters first gathered to challenge the government and demand reforms on February 14, 2011. The monument was destroyed by the government on March 18, 2011. Al Khawaja is the father of Maryam Al Khawaja, who has yet to see her father, as she has not returned to Bahrain where he remains imprisoned.

# Another Flight
## by Maryam Al Khawaja

**MARYAM AL-KHAWAJA** is the Head of Foreign Relations for the Bahrain Center for Human Rights, and a former Fulbright Scholar at Brown University. In Bahrain, Maryam played an instrumental role in the democratic protests taking place in the Pearl Roundabout in February 2011 that triggered a government response of widespread arrest, discrimination, and the spreading of fear. She is the daughter of Abdulhadi al-Khawaja, founder of the Bahrain Center for Human Rights, who was among a group of high-profile activists and opposition leaders recently sentenced to life imprisonment and severely tortured. Four other members of Maryam's family were also imprisoned and tortured.

Although she has since left Bahrain to play a role as international advocacy officer and also to avoid arrest and/or imprisonment, Maryam remains very connected to events on the ground and has emerged as a leading voice for human rights and political reform. She has been influential in shaping official responses to the atrocities in Bahrain around the world by engaging with prominent European and American policymakers.

"Hello?"

"Hi, is this Maryam Al-Khawaja?"

"Yes, how can I help you?"

"Hi, I'm a journalist and I wanted to know what your reaction is to your father's sentence."

I opened my eyes and tried to awaken my still-half-asleep brain and body.

"Excuse me?" I said.

"I wanted to know what you thought about your father getting the life imprisonment sentence in Bahrain. And about your sister getting arrested too."

"I'm sorry, can you call me back later?"

I felt my voice get shaky, and I hastened to end that phone call so I could call my family. I texted my sister; she was supposed to let me know as soon as the verdict was read. She didn't answer, so I called my mother.

"Mama? What happened?" I asked her.

"Your father got life imprisonment, and as soon as the verdict was read he said, 'The struggle will continue,' so they beat him and dragged him out of the court room. Then your sister said 'Allahu Akbar,' so they arrested her too."

"What?"

I kept hearing the call waiting tone on my phone. Several news outlets were calling me—probably to ask what I thought of my father's sentencing.

"I have to go, Mum. I'll talk to you later. Please let me know as soon as anything happens."

"Of course, *mama*. Be strong," she responded.

With that, I ended the phone call. I took a deep breath in and slowly let it out. I felt the tears streaming down my face. I am not one to cry, but this time I could not control it. It was as if at that moment my eyes had decided they needed to renew my vision by cleansing my view with tears. I took another deep breath as I heard my phone ring, and I thought, "This is not the time to get emotional. Pull yourself together."

I started answering phone calls and also writing an email about the government's sentencing of twenty-one people, including my father, that morning.

The date was June 22, 2011. I was turning twenty-four in four days, my first birthday away from my family. I had left Bahrain in the beginning of March that year to give a speech at the Human Rights Council in Geneva, and had not been able to go home since because of the political unrest in my country. I had been living out of a suitcase, traveling from country to country trying to make sure the international community knew what was taking place in Bahrain. It had been difficult, but, as always, I derived strength from my mother.

My mother has been the backbone of the family for as long as I can remember. She is the strongest human being I know. Despite overcoming some of the most difficult of situations, she continues to tell me never to lose hope. If I ever manage to become at all like my mother, it will mean I have done well in my life.

On April 8, 2011, my father was beaten unconscious in front of my family. I was not there, but I will never forget that phone call. I was sitting on the train traveling from Washington, D.C., after extensive meetings with the U.S. administration, to stay at a friend's place in a nearby city. It still struck me how, prior to the revolution, it had been very difficult to get meetings with the U.S. government, but now in my capacity as head of foreign relations for the Bahrain Center for Human Rights, I was able to do so. While I was on the train, my phone ran out of batteries. I had forgotten my charger at the hotel, so I decided to take a nap instead of panicking about being disconnected from the world.

A heavy feeling woke me up, and I asked a girl sitting close to me if I could borrow her charger. As soon as my phone turned on, it started ringing.

"Maryam, I need to tell you something but you must take a deep breath and just know it's going to be okay, all right?" my friend said.

"What is it?"

"Your sister called me. They just arrested your father and your two brothers-in-law."

Silence.

"Maryam, are you okay?"

In that moment I became oblivious to my surroundings. I was no longer on the train. The people around me, staring at the mascara-filled tears running down my face, no longer existed. The only thing that brought me back to reality was my friend's voice.

"Maryam?"

I cleared my throat. "Yes, I have to go."

It was afternoon in the United States but after midnight in Bahrain. I started reading my sister's tweets about how my father had said he would go with the security forces voluntarily, how they had beaten him unconscious, then taken him away with my brothers-in-law. How she had tried to intervene when all she could hear was my father saying, "I can't breathe." How they threatened to arrest her too. How my mother tried to stop them but was thrown against the wall. I felt angry and sad, but worst of all, I felt helpless.

Logically, there was very little I could have done to stop this from happening, but the fact that I was so far away was eating me up inside. I couldn't stop crying. With my hands clenched into fists, all I could think was "I need to buy a ticket and go home." I kept reminding myself of what my father always told me: "Do not hate people, hate actions."

That night, my friends saved my life. My best friend convinced me that I would only make the situation worse for my family if I went back to Bahrain and then was also arrested. A few other friends came over, and we spent countless hours that night writing emails and calling the media and international NGOs to let them know what had happened. It was as if my American friends had suddenly turned multi-lingual, conversing in French, Spanish, Arabic, and English.

I pushed the thought that my father might not be alive out of my head. There was work to be done.

From my father's arrest until September 2011 I was able to speak to him only once, for less than a minute. He was on the phone with my mother, so they phoned me and put us both on speaker. I told him to stay strong, that we were all there standing by him. He responded: "No, it is more important to stand with the people."

As a young activist with an official role in support of human rights in Bahrain, I was able to bring some attention to the atrocities in my country: speaking at top universities, meeting with high ranking government officials, receiving invitations to conferences around the world, and even managing to speak to the President of Switzerland, U.S. Secretary of State Hillary Clinton, and the High Commissioner for Human Rights at the UN, Navi Pillay. During this time, it was not unusual for me to travel to more than four countries in a span of only a month and a half, staying only a few days in each country.

Nevertheless, I always felt like I was not doing enough. Despite all my traveling, all the meetings, the people of Bahrain continue to suffer on a daily basis, and the Western governments, to a large extent, continue to ignore what is happening.

Whenever I wanted to take a break, I would think to myself, "The people of Bahrain do not take breaks from the situation they're in, the Bahraini government is not taking a break from committing constant violations, so how can I take a break from fighting them?"

One of my challenges was choosing what to speak about during all these meetings. Should I speak about the more than three thousand political prisoners, most of them subjected to the severest types of physical, psychological, and sexual torture? Or about the hunger campaign run by the government as they sacked more than three thousand people from their jobs? What about the three hundred students dismissed from their universities and unable to finish their education? What of the countless peaceful protesters blinded as they were violently attacked by riot police?

Or the fifty-four people killed in cold blood?

Do I speak of the government's targeting of the Shi'a in an attempt to inflame sectarian divides, the demolishing of Shi'a mosques, and desecration of graves and religious places? How can I explain that simply releasing prisoners does not mean everything is now fine? The toll that the severe torture takes on people haunts them the rest of their lives.

Systematic torture was not new to Bahrain (with the exception of the period between 2001 and 2007). Since the 1990s there has been no time when accountability was granted or rehabilitation provided for torture victims. In this latest crackdown, starting mid-March 2011, four members of the royal family were allegedly involved directly in torturing protesters. This includes the King's own sons, Nasser and Khalid bin Hamad Al-Khalifa.[1]

Human rights violations in Bahrain are so serious and so prevalent that I could never cover the entire topic in one meeting with a US government official. What to speak of mentioning the larger story of what had been going on in Bahrain for the past 240 years, which caused the February 14th uprising, and continues to influence events.

It didn't surprise me that the Bahraini government had chosen to respond to the uprising with such violence and disregard for basic human rights. What did surprise me were the actions of some of those I used to call friends during the crackdown from March to November 2011.

I respect people when they have opinions different from mine, and I have friends who disagree with the protests and think people should have just stuck by the status quo. But I cannot respect people who come out to insult, defame, and attack others because they have decided to take to the streets to demand their rights. I was hurt when

---

1. Bahrain's ruling Al Khalifa monarchy are a Sunni family that came to power in 1961 under British colonialism (which did not end until 1971). Although the majority of Bahrainis practice Shi'a Islam, all high-ranking government position are reserved for Sunnis, with the exception with a few token Shiîs. While Bahrain's civil unrest is often attributed to sectarian divisions, it is important to note Britain's colonial policies that contributed to this division. Approximately two-thirds of Bahrain's population practice Shi'a Islam.

I noticed that one of my close friends had written on Facebook and Twitter that "all the protesters should be killed, and if the government does not do it, then we should do it with our own hands." What baffles me the most is how, under any circumstance whatsoever, can anyone justify or publicly call for the torture of another person.

I can understand people's frustration due to the closed streets and the overwhelming number of security forces in the streets, preventing them from going to work or shopping in the malls. People complained about protesters closing the streets, failing to realize that this was to prevent security forces from running over young protesters with their cars, which is what happened to Ali Badah. Shouldn't the blame be placed on the regime, not the protesters? When an ambulance is unable to reach an injured person or get someone to the hospital, is it the fault of the protesters who are being shot at or the fault of the police who are shooting at them?

The refusal of some people to come out from their comfort zones to demand dignity and to be seen as citizens rather than subjects—or if they choose not to then to at least respect those who do—is beyond me. Unfortunately, the double standard of those who say they want democracy then stand against those who fight for it is not limited to Bahrain.

It is obvious to me through my work around the world that there is a clear double standard when dealing with the so-called Arab Spring—as the West has come to call it. Some politicians are honest and straightforward and tell me that Bahrain is different because it is in the Gulf, home of oil and strategic allies to the world's superpowers. Whereas Libya has received a direct intervention to save its people from a ruthless dictator, Bahrain receives another type of intervention: Gulf Cooperation Council troops entering the country to help quell the protests. Not only was the arrival of Saudi and other GCC troops into Bahrain not condemned by the international community, U.S. Secretary of State Hillary Clinton went so far as to say that Bahrain has the sovereign right to invite foreign troops in—thereby legitimizing the action and making it geo-politically impossible for other governments to criticize the move.

There are different ways to cope with the stress and insanity of dealing with such a situation. You keep yourself busy. God knows there's always enough to do. You make sure you do not go to bed unless you are extremely exhausted so your mind has no time to wander. You do not deal with cases as if they are people you know and love, but rather as if they were all mere strangers, none more important to you than another. Sitting on planes, where you have no Internet access, you either write or sleep.

Yet even sleep can be problematic. In the realm of dreams, you cannot control things. As my body lies sleeping, my brain works at its highest capacity, bringing back images I've seen of the people killed, people injured in the hospital as I walked around documenting cases. My mind replays the night of February 17, 2011, when I struggled to pick up a child who was watching her mother scream as she held on to her other child, trying to get out of the Pearl Roundabout as security forces mercilessly attacked peaceful protesters who just minutes before were sleeping in their tents.

In some of my dreams the security forces catch up to us, and my imagination runs wild with vivid details of torture that I've previously written down from testimonies of those released from Bahraini prisons.

I wake myself, take deep breaths to slow my heart, and then open my laptop to continue the fight for human rights in Bahrain.

This line of work also takes an extreme toll on one's health. The stress causes abnormal hair loss, weight loss, insomnia, and exhaustion, not to mention the effects of post traumatic stress disorder, which I think most people in Bahrain have by now. It also has a negative influence on one's personal life because you find yourself without the time to be there for your family and friends. Your work trumps all else because the stakes are too high. Your life is not yours anymore.

I am blessed with friends and family who are very understanding, and support me in my work at all times. I do have one outlet for venting: writing rants. Here is snippet from one Skype conversation with my best friend:

> they call it the arabspring
> they beautify
> the bloodshed
> the spilt brains
> the torture
> the arrests
> spring
> people losing their arms
> spring
> people shot in the chest
> spring
> people electrocuted in their ears
> spring
> people with their jaws broken
> spring
> if this is spring
> what will winter be like?

When I meet with government officials, I explain the gravity of the human rights violations taking place in Bahrain and how important it is for their governments to take a stand on the issue. I tell them that they needn't send armies to "liberate" the people of Bahrain. They need only exert enough international pressure to stop the human rights violations in the country. The Bahraini people can do the rest.

But unfortunately Bahrain is an inconvenient revolution. The United States' Fifth Fleet is stationed there. It is in the backyard of Saudi Arabia.

Of course, the Gulf monarchies viewed a revolution in their midst as a threat. What if people in other Gulf countries also decided they were entitled to more rights and political involvement? If the Bahraini monarchy fell, it could mean the end of the other monarchies as well. Unfortunately, these are not monarchies that are willing to progress and change, to reform.

The Minister of Justice, Mr. Al-Khalifa (I do not need to know his first name, as I can say the Minister of anything and it would be an Al-Khalifa family member), says that because Bahrain has a monarchy and a constitution, that automatically makes it a constitutional monarchy. The Bahraini regime treats the country like a family business. People living inside Bahrain are their subjects, not citizens, and everyone works for the family.

The regime, time and time again, calls the King "the father," and everyone his children. This, in a way, implies that he, as your father, can control your personal freedom, can choose to take away that freedom, can beat you because you did something he doesn't like. This was one of the reasons for this revolution; people are reclaiming their dignity and their God-given rights as individuals, as humans.

Despite many calling the revolution in Bahrain the "failed revolution," I disagree. It is ongoing despite everything everyone has done to try and stop it. And most important, it has brought people together.

I felt very anxious when I first heard that a group of government thugs posing as Sunnis attacked a Shi'a religious mourning proceeding while others had a musical party next to the mourning proceeding to instigate violence. I thought to myself: This is it … this might be the beginning of a tidal wave of sectarian violence washing through Bahrain.

But then, I was astonished that Sunnis and Shi'is had not only stood side by side that night against the government thugs and riot police, they started a hashtag on Twitter called "SuShiBH," where they spoke about the unity between Sunnis and Shi'is in Bahrain. We are still on thin ice, though. The threat of sectarian violence exploding in the streets is very real because the government is pushing for it to happen.

I remember the last time I was on a plane leaving Cairo. It was right after I had left Bahrain in March of 2011. I was very worried because as I was boarding, I was receiving messages about a huge demonstration in Bahrain, which I knew would be hit hard by the security forces.

This was before the GCC troops were sent to Bahrain, while people were still gathering in Pearl Square. Because I could not possibly find out what was going on in Bahrain, I sat and wrote a poem. This poem symbolizing the monument in the square, in which five pillars hold up a pearl. The pillars represent the Gulf Cooperation Council countries, while the pearl represents Bahrain. But this monument became an icon of freedom for the people of Bahrain. Ironically, I had not known at the time of writing this poem that the monument would be torn down only a few days later. Here is an excerpt:

## The Pearl's Pillars

Five arms stretched from the ground
Each palm embraced the pure limp bodies in shrouds
Their reflection was a wide glow in the dark night
Shining down on the peaceful crowds
Five arms stretched from the ground
Each palm held a cry of *Allahu Akbar*
Held a revolutionary song
Held a poem of defiance
Held a scream for freedom
Five arms stretched from the ground
Palms covered with a grave of flowers
Fingertips pointing towards the heavens
A mother's tears celebrating a wedding's last hours

Five arms came down with vengeance
But heroes stood their ground
Flowers in hand
Bullets were the only answer they found

Once when I was sitting on a panel at an event with activists from other countries, my friend from Libya spoke about how he carried a gun to fight for his freedom against Gaddafi. I could see the audience's faces glowing with respect as he described how he had put his life on the line to fight for a better future for his country. When it was my turn to speak, I found myself once again having to explain how the revolution in Bahrain is not sectarian, how people were not stooges of the Iranian regime, and how they were not all terrorists. That's when I decided that I had to be blunt.

I said to the room: Do you realize the double standards of this very conversation? Bahrain at one point had around 300,000 people coming out to protest, almost 50 percent of the population. This is like saying 40 million Egyptians came out to protest against Mubarak. Per capita, we have the second highest number of deaths, and the highest number of detainees. Why is the dire urgency of a situation dependent on how many people have been killed? Is one life lost not one life too many? You admire my friend from Libya for carrying a gun to fight for his freedom, yet I have to explain to you why you should support a people who, even after eight months of an extremely violent crackdown, after a campaign of terrorism led by the regime, are still for the most part peaceful. What point have we reached in our own humanity if we are valuing one life more than another based on citizenship?

The Bahraini government uses so much toxic tear gas, which according to the symptoms of its victims, cannot be anything but nerve gas. This has caused a number of deaths by suffocation, like five-day-old Sajida, but also causes pregnant women to lose their babies, and will be the cause of long-lasting diseases and illnesses like cancer. Messages coming out of Bahrain now always say "Help us, they are killing us slowly."

I would like President Obama to visit Bahrain, and go to every single Bahraini family's home, look them in the face, and explain to them why their lives are less valuable than those of the Libyans.

Explain to the fourteen-year-old boy with one of his eyes missing because of a bullet why he should settle for being a subject to an authoritarian monarchy for his entire life.

I wish we lived in a world in which the people deciding on international policies, and the people committing crimes against others, had to face their victims every day. If President Obama himself spent one night in a Bahraini village, I would guarantee his participation in the protests the next day.

Instead of taking a strong stand for human rights in Bahrain, the United States administration has decided to delay, not cancel, the $53 million arms sales to Bahrain. This is despite its knowing that the armored Humvees it is selling have been used by the Bahraini regime against unarmed, peaceful protesters and only after members of Congress opposed the sales. Unfortunately, at this point, because of U.S. policies, I have more hope for the European Union taking a stand on Bahrain than the United States.

My father, Abdulhadi Alkhawaja, was sentenced to life imprisonment on June 22. He has a number of metal plates and screws keeping his jaw attached to the rest of his face due to the torture he was subjected to. My uncle, Salah Alkhawaja, was sentenced to five years imprisonment on the same day. His wife was subjected to sexual assault during his arrest. My brother-in-law Wafi AlMajed was sentenced to four years imprisonment for being related to us. Wafi had to crawl to and from the bathroom during a period in which he could not walk as a result of the torture.

My other brother-in-law, Hussain Ahmed, was sentenced to six months imprisonment and released upon finishing the sentence. My mother, Khadija AlMousawi, was fired from her job of ten years by order of the Ministry of Interior. This is a situation familiar to hundreds of families in Bahrain.

The governments will continue to try and silence people. In Syria, Yemen, Egypt, and Bahrain, they will continue to torture, detain, use excessive force, and kill, as long as the people and political leaders of this world choose to stay silent. They will continue to kill their citizens until Western governments realize that their real interest lies in countries with real democracies, not authoritarian regimes. Until they realize that the best way to create stability is by including people and treating them like citizens, not by silencing them and tying their hands to provide a fake calm in the country.

Until then, I will continue to travel from one country to another, appealing to both people and governments to stand by human rights, and to support all people putting their eyes, arms, backs, legs and lives on the line to say, "I am an equal human being, and I refuse to be a subject anymore." I will continue to support everyone out there screaming, "Dignity!" Another flight, another report, another conference, another meeting. Be patient, people of Bahrain, Yemen, Syria, Egypt and everyone else in the world fighting for freedom; one day you will reach your aspirations, and build a better country for your families and your children.

# Flying into a Revolution

*by Abubakr Al-Shamahi*

**ABUBAKR AL-SHAMAHI** was born in Birmingham, United Kingdom, and is of Yemeni origin. He is a freelance journalist and the editor of CommentMidEast.com, a platform for young people's writings about the Arab region. Abubakr has written for publications including Al Jazeera English, the *Guardian*, and the *Yemen Times*. He has also provided analysis and commentary on the Arab world for BBC World Service Television and the Islam Channel (UK). Abubakr received his bachelors degree in politics from the School of Oriental and African Studies, University of London, where he is currently pursuing a graduate degree in Near and Middle Eastern Studies.

I'll be honest. I am no revolutionary hero. I have never seen myself as a future leader of Yemen. I have never dreamed of myself as a Yemeni Che Guevara. The masses chanting for freedom in the land of my parents did not inspire me to buy the first tickets I could find to return to Yemen. I bought my tickets back in November 2010, a month before the start of the Tunisian revolution.

Initially, I had planned to go to Yemen in April 2011 for an internship with the *Yemen Times*. The the largest English language newspaper in Yemen, the *Yemen Times* was founded in 1995 to provide an independent voice in the Yemeni media scene. It has always been a useful barometer of Yemeni political and cultural life for diplomats and foreigners living in Yemen. The newspaper is progressive in many ways. For example, the editor, Nadia al-Sakkaf, is a woman who holds her own despite the patriarchal grip on Yemeni society.

Don't get me wrong. While I might not consider myself a revolutionary, I have always disliked the Yemeni government. Growing up in the United Kingdom, being British as well as Yemeni, has made me automatically distrust any ruler who serves for more than ten years, let alone the thirty-three years the Yemeni ruler has been in power. On trips to Yemen through my teen years, I was always perplexed by the presence of huge photos of President Ali Abdullah Saleh ("His Excellency the Brother President Ali Abdullah Saleh, may God protect him," as the state TV announcer would always say). I tried hard to imagine huge billboards of Tony Blair grinning at people from every building as they faced their daily London commute, but it seemed too preposterous.

The pro-Saleh members of my family tried to explain to me the basis of their support. They reasoned that Saleh had united the country and given the Yemeni people stability and prosperity. They spoke of going to protests in support of "the father" and his candidacy for the elections. They also mentioned that all the students in their school were forced to go to these protests. Other cousins (the cooler side of the family) offered a different view. I remember hearing one of my cousins refer to Saleh sarcastically as "Uncle Ali," satirizing the patriarchal image that Saleh fostered.

For years, I watched family members struggle to find jobs—Yemen is a country where unofficial unemployment statistics put the figure at 60–70 percent. There were educated young people from good backgrounds who simply could not find a job that would give them the money to put food on the table. Meanwhile, Saleh and his cronies sat in their mansions on the edge of town, their houses fully lit while the rest of Sana'a went without electricity, enjoying running water in a town where many had to source their own water for their tanks.

As 2010 passed into 2011 the tides of revolution began to flow into the Arab world. The Tunisian revolution and the fall of Ben Ali was a momentous occasion, but one that many people, myself included, viewed as perhaps unique to Tunisia. The Tunisian revolution sparked protests in Yemen, but these protests were heavily organized by the opposition parties and merely called for reform of the system. The protesters quickly dispersed once midday approached—going off for dinner and then the *qat* (a mild narcotic chewed by most Yemenis).

Then came Egypt. The events beamed live from Cairo and elsewhere in Egypt—protesters facing the police, people praying on a bridge over the Nile while being sprayed by water cannons, camels charging into Tahrir Square. These images were seared into the minds of millions, myself included. As a final-year undergraduate student, I was predominantly in my university's library during this time, yet I found myself with Arabic television feeds on one side of my screen and Twitter on the other, class essays and revisions long forgotten.

I began to hope that we would see the same happen in Yemen as in Egypt, though I was also pessimistic. I could not imagine a prolonged Yemeni sit-in. Certainly, there were ample reasons for Yemeni anti-government protests. However, Yemen lacks a sizeable middle class. Received wisdom tells us that the rich are comfortable and do not welcome the instability that a revolution would bring, and the poor are more concerned with putting food on the table than changing the government. There was also the very real fear of a civil war. Yemen is one of the most weaponized societies in the world, with an estimated 75 million firearms in a country of 25 million people.

Yet it happened. The deposing of Hosni Mubarak on February 11, 2011 provided a  spark for the Yemeni revolution. That night, a couple of hundred people went out onto the streets of Sana'a and

Ta'iz to celebrate the Egyptians' victory, and in the midst of their celebrations another chant started breaking out: *ash-sha'ab yureed isqat an-nizam* (The people want to bring down the regime). With that, our revolution started.

In the early weeks of the protest, I followed news of young protesters being attacked by pro-government thugs. The government mobilized its supporters in Sana'a's Tahrir Square, hoping to prevent a repeat of the Cairo sit-in. The protesters simply went to the gates of Sana'a University and put up their tents there. This became *Taghyir* Square—Change Square.

As the weeks went by, the protests grew, and I began to hear of family members and friends taking part in the protests. I was unbelievably proud of them.

The days passed in March, and my departure date neared. Emails came from the *Yemen Times* asking if I was still coming; my answer was, "Of course." In reality, then chances were fifty-fifty. My parents, especially my dad, were the worrying sort. Their son going to Yemen two weeks after fifty-two protesters were killed at Change Square was not the most enticing proposition. A number of foreign journalists were also deported from Yemen in the weeks before I was set to travel. With the large camera I would be carrying, I was fearful of being stopped at Sana'a airport and sent back to the UK on the first plane. Very few of my friends even knew that I was on my way to Yemen. Those who did know only ever heard my constant qualifying statement, "I'll believe I'm there once I'm driving out of Sana'a airport."

My dad tried to convince me not to go. Various people "in the know" told him that it was not safe for me to go. My dad knew that the government would target independent newspapers. He feared that I would go to protests, and he knew that those protests would be under attack by the regime.

In all honesty, I was not afraid. But this was not some extreme bravery. I simply thought that the imagined risks were exaggerated. I was also not particularly enamored with the idea of participating in political protests in a country where people were shot for speaking out. Sure, I supported the protesters, as I have explained. I considered those in the anti-government sit-ins heroes. I wanted to see Change Square. But was I prepared to die for the cause? No.

I understood the grievances of the anti-Saleh protesters. I wanted true democracy in Yemen. I wanted an end to the corruption and poverty that accompanied this regime. But I hadn't lived that. I was raised in Birmingham, not Sana'a. I wasn't the one living in a country where the population struggled in poverty while the rulers lived in palaces. I wasn't the one living under a dictatorship. I wasn't the one struggling to find a job and put food on the table. I wasn't the one attacked for protesting. I wasn't with those killed for protesting. I was lucky.

So my departure date came, and I flew out. By the end of the day I was in Yemen, revolutionary Yemen.

I was shattered when I arrived. Driving through opposition-controlled parts of the city and seeing anti-Saleh graffiti everywhere was bizarre. As soon as I dropped my luggage at my cousin's house, he asked me if I wanted to go to the Square. This was not even a question, and we got in the car.

I remember my first visit to Change Square quite clearly. Bouazizi's flame had really had its effect, lighting up this amazing part of Sana'a and creating hope for a better future.

The first thing I spotted as I entered the Square was a banner placed across one of the entrances: *marhaban bikom fi awal kilomitr karama* (Welcome to the first kilometer of dignity). The area included several side streets and main roads, all entirely covered in tents, and resembling a bustling shantytown more than a protest square. There were small tents, colossal tents, and make-shift tents that were simply a piece of fabric across two posts. People sat cross-legged watching Al Jazeera evening news either on little television sets in their tents or on a giant screen that had been set up. They cheered when the news anchor managed to turn the Yemeni government spokesman into a stuttering wreck. I saw a tent with "Youth of Facebook" on it and even two guys playing on a playstation. How everyone was able to wire up their tents to the power supply was beyond me. Yet, with the typical Yemeni ability to make the most out of a situation, they had managed to turn this tent city into a buzzing, exciting place to be.

I had arrived in Sana'a a little more than two weeks after the March 18th killing of fifty-two protesters, labeled the Friday of Dignity massacre. This was the first time the government had killed such a great number of protesters, and evidence of that fateful day was still easy to find. I was shown the house from which snipers fired and where groups of protesters retreated in an attempt to take the snipers on. All that was left now were randomly strewn military uniforms that the snipers were apparently wearing, and a wall of pictures of the martyrs who fell that day. Nearby, a couple of rocks were placed around a patch of bloodstained road. In the middle was a bloodied beanie hat. This was where one of the protesters fell after being shot in the head. The hat was left exactly where it had fallen. A few meters away was a memorial for the martyrs of the revolution full of flowers, pictures of the deceased, and candles. Knowing, in retrospect, that so many more protesters would die in the months to come is sobering.

This simple trip to Change Square altered many of my perceptions of the protest movement and what it would mean to be a part of it. My university, the School of Oriental and African Studies in London, was a hotbed of revolutionary talk that never particularly enticed me. Yet one night of walking around a protest camp did more to shift my perceptions on how change could be brought about than three years at the UK's premier revolutionary outpost. When you see a street-vendor selling *shahi al-hurriya* (freedom tea), it is particularly hard not to want to be part of such a movement.

I decided that I would attempt to help the protesters in whatever way I could. Yemen doesn't have many English speakers, at least relative to other Arab countries, so I offered to provide my services to translate and write. I started writing articles for my own website and for Kabob-fest, an Arab American blog that was kind enough to reply to my offer of reporting from a frontline of the Arab uprisings. My role would be to document in order to inform those on the outside. I wrote, shot photos, took video, anything I could to get the simple message out there: The Yemeni people want their freedom. Don't ignore them.

Soon enough I was on my first protest march—exactly the kind of event that I specifically promised my family (and myself) I would not be going to. I suppose there aren't many better excuses for disobeying your parents then attempting to help bring down a dictator, and a revolution certainly changes your opinions.

The march was scheduled for April 13th, and everyone knew it was going to be big. State television had been broadcasting announcements the night before that protests were forbidden—a very clear warning. The people still went out. When I arrived at Change Square, I saw cars haphazardly parked anywhere (some things never change) and streams of people going through the many checkpoints. Huge billboards above carried revolutionary slogans, the most succinct being the giant *irhal*! (Get out!)

Mixing in the vast crowd, I came across all sections of Yemeni society. The youth, the country's ticking time bomb, were present, but so were their parents and grandparents. I saw the poor and the well off. I saw men in traditional Yemeni clothing, daggers on their belts, and men in suits and ties. Clearly, people in every stratum of Yemeni society wanted the downfall of the regime.

I began to interview people, asking them why they had come. Ahmed, a teenager walking with his friend, told me he was present because "corruption has reached terrible levels, and there is one man to blame." That man's name was in graffiti all over the city: *irhal ya Ali* (Ali, leave). I managed to take some fantastic photographs, one of my favorites being a man in full Yemeni attire holding a picture of Che Guevara.

On one of the city's main overpasses I met Khaled, a middle-aged man in traditional Yemeni clothes. He narrated to me the beginnings of the Yemeni revolution. "We came here on February 11, when Mubarak was deposed. You could count with your fingers [the number of people

Inspiration, Yemeni man holds up picture of Che Guevara, Sana'a, Yemen

present]. People laughed at us, and told us that nothing was going to happen here. Look at us now. Look at the people now."

On we went. Reaching a high point I looked back to see if I could spot the end of the protest. All I could see was the stunning backdrop of one of the many mountains that surround Sana'a and an apparently unending sea of people. Turning a corner off the one of the main highways, we started passing through a busy shopping street. Here the protesters chanted for the shopkeepers to close their stores and made a general call for civil disobedience. Some of the shopkeepers heeded their call, closed their shutters and, fists pumping, joined the march. Others stood outside their stores, cheering in support and raising their fingers to display the "V for victory" sign. Families watched from the windows, with children waving Yemeni flags and cheering. One family poured confetti on us, eliciting applause from those passing by.

By the end of the protest that day, I was tired, dirty, and hoarse. But most of all, I was proud. Proud of my people, who had finally risen up against the regime that had robbed them for three decades and left them in poverty, proud that they had found their voice, proud to be Yemeni.

What people had forgotten, however, was that in a revolution, especially one that drags on, there are lots of non-revolutionary moments. Not everything involves protesting, watching the injured arrive at field hospitals, or fighting the regime. Of course, the presence of hundreds of checkpoints means that you always know that something is not quite right, as does the nightly ritual of channel-flicking to keep up to date with the news. However, there were strange moments when this was like any other trip to Yemen: wandering around the beautiful Old City of Sana'a to take photographs, eating at the latest chic café, even missing an evening at Change Square to watch the finale of "Arab's Got Talent." People were living their lives, or trying to; it was just that they were trying to overthrow the regime at the same time.

The slight sense of normalcy could go away in an instant. Power cuts had become unbelievably regular, and candles were my new best friend. The lack of power was particularly frustrating as I was attempting to complete my undergraduate dissertation (oddly enough, on the effects of the Arab media on democracy and free speech). While driving through the streets of the capital it was now normal to see people protesting with empty gas canisters the fact that, at this time, gas was either nowhere to be seen or prohibitively expensive. Many felt that this was all punishment from the state, and that is probably true.

Normalcy disappeared at other times as well. I learned to distinguish between fireworks and bullets one night when what I thought was the sound of the former near my house turned out to be the latter.

Towards the end of the month, the situation developed quickly. The youth had initially thought the revolution would be over soon, and they wanted escalation. Every Friday after prayers the crowds chanted their plan to march on the presidential palace. They expected to be met with brute force, as had happened before.

On April 27 one such escalation march took place and, with my cousin Hamza, I joined. The beginning of the march was largely uneventful, the only memorable moment being the tearing down of a large billboard of Ali Saleh. However, as the march passed the Amran roundabout, an area with a large security deployment, protesters began to chant directly at the security forces, accusing the regime of being the cause of their poor wages. The soldiers stood passive. Did they know what was waiting for the protesters around the corner? Passing by the flyover, we began to approach the May 22 Stadium.

Just as the front of the march began to pass by the stadium, shots started to ring out. At first the shots were sporadic, but soon it became clear that this was a sustained attack. Within minutes the first casualties were being carried out, bloodied.

When the protesters first heard the sustained gunfire, many turned to leave, myself included. However, a few men shouted for everyone to stay, saying, "Hold your ground. Don't run." They explained that if the crowds split up it would be easier for the regime forces to attack them. The words seemed to have an effect. Instead of running away, the protesters kept moving forward.

I could not quite believe what was going on. Here I was, a third-year politics student at a British university, born and raised in Birmingham with a planned flight to return to the UK in just over a week, in the middle of an anti-government protest in the land of my forefathers and being attacked by the guns of the state. My head told me to run. I understood the Yemeni people's problems and supported their aspirations, but was I prepared to die for them? I was doing well at university, had my family and friends in the UK, and in all honesty was worried for my mom's health if anything should happen to me. This is not your fight, my head reminded me.

My head demanded I leave, but I couldn't. I did not see one person run away, including Hamza, age seventeen. Run away while all these people bravely moved forward? The shame would have been too great. Thus I decided, on the basis of shame, to carry on. The main thought going through my head was, "You're an idiot." I could see the snipers on the rooftops all around us, calmly deciding who they were going to shoot next. I could hear the sound of heavy artillery being occasionally used against the protesters. I could see the pro-Saleh thugs behind the gates of the stadium with their guns and sticks. I could see the blood on the ground, on the walls, on the people. And truthfully, for a period, I thought this was going to be it for me.

There is no way to explain the sense of fear in this situation. Those with previous experience were already breaking up rocks and preparing Molotovs. But there were many others afraid, like me. Some were prostrating and praying on the ground. People crushed each other as they tried to keep moving forward, all the while ducking their heads to avoid any shots to the head coming from the snipers.

What has really stuck with me is the fact that people were being shot at from all sides and were seeing others hit, yet they continued to march forward. Never have I seen people sacrifice themselves like that, and I hope never to see it again. To crown it off, they chanted as the bullets whizzed around: *silmiya, silmiya, silmiya miya miya* (Peaceful, peaceful, we will remain peaceful). I was amazed.

Gradually, my fear went away. It was as if I couldn't possibly get any more afraid, and my adrenaline kicked in. Then came the anger. Ignoring a phone call on his cell phone from Hamza's mother, Hamza and I joined a group around a corner to try to figure out what to do next. From that vantage point, I saw a teenager run across the street to a wall that gunmen were hiding behind. In full view of the snipers and other hired killers, he jumped and slam-dunked a stone onto the gunman hiding behind the wall. He then ran back to a hero's welcome. Another young man came and stood next to his friend near me. He calmly said to his friend, "I swear, I heard the bullet whiz right past my ear!" I was mortified. I will always remember that.

We were sitting ducks. But it did not matter anymore. Returning to the main road, the crowd surged forward, the sound of gunfire echoing around. We chanted louder, drowning out the noise of the bullets. Just as I had never been more scared, I was now angrier than I had ever been. How dare these people shoot at us? I could see these men. They were human beings. Why were they shooting at me? What had these unarmed protesters done to deserve being executed by the state? It was then that I realized why the youth could never accept any deal that gave immunity to Saleh or his men. It is hard to forgive a man who has killed your family and friends and put your own life in jeopardy.

The protesters moved forward. Eventually, sections of the crowd managed to flee the shooting. The crowds were angry. Yet as they passed a shack carrying Saleh's picture and ruling party flags, instead of attacking it, they simply kept on walking. I was fuming and could barely control myself when I saw a poster of *him*.

The worst of the rage came as the crowds passed the state television compound. A cameraman could clearly be seen filming the crowds, preparing to piece together another propaganda story. And sure enough, later that evening, state television news described the crowd of thousands as an illegal mob. We walked past armed Republican Guard troops and directed our ire at them, "Oh the shame, the peaceful are getting hit with fire." The soldiers showed no emotion.

News began to filter through the crowd that the security forces had kidnapped some people, their fate unknown. One of the dead was a fourteen-year-old child. All of the dead had been hit in the head or torso, apart from one who had been run over by a water truck.

The protesters were weary as they approached Change Square at the end of a ten-kilometer march during which they had faced snipers and machine guns. However, here was one final act of defiance. As they trudged in they chanted in unison: *la, la, mat'ibnash; al-hurriya mush bi balash* (No! No! We're not tired, freedom isn't free).

Throughout my remaining time in Yemen, I came back often to Change Square and its vast array of activities. The giant tents hosted various talks, conferences, and debates. Poetry nights and other cultural events were held. The tents carried names such as the "Parliamentarian's Tent" or the "Academics' Tent." In them, a cross-section of Yemeni society would sit, listen, and participate as various subjects were discussed. How they were going to get rid of the government was not the only topic. Economics professors gave talks on how the country had ended up in such a dire financial state and what could be done to avoid this in the future. Former ministers explained past misdeeds of the government and the endemic corruption present in certain sections of the regime.

Women played an active role in the Square. The media had focused on one woman, Tawakkol Karman, a principal early leader of the protest movement, but there were many others. Women led chants on the main stage as thousands of men, those of conservative tribal backgrounds included, chanted along. Women sat and recited their own poetry or debated in packed tents. All of this took place while President Saleh was telling the nation that there was too much free-mixing going on in the Square. The reaction of female Yemenis was immediate: A mass march went out the next day, with one protester interviewed for television telling Saleh: *lazem yi'tarim nafsu*, the Arabic equivalent of "Check yourself before you wreck yourself."

Those at Change Square emphasized the peaceful nature of their revolution. Even when they had been shot at and attacked, they did not fight back with weapons. They walked on "with their bare chest," as Yemenis would put it. I spoke to a tribesman who told me that this was the first time that he and his group had ever been in a tent without their weapons. They had left their weapons hundreds of miles away in their villages. Southern tribesmen also spoke of their changing opinions. A group from Shabwa, a city in southern Yemen, explained that they were separatists before the revolution started. They were initially shocked to see Northerners, who they assumed were living the good life, risking their lives to protest against the same regime that the Southerners hated.

This movement was all about change. I was witnessing a change in Yemeni culture, in the way Yemenis thought about issues and in their aspirations. The people in the Square were determined. They believed that their victory was inevitable, that God would bring it, because they were in the right. They were determined to wait as long as it took, for truth always emerged victorious over falsehood.

My opinions also changed. For one, my own stereotypically negative view of tribal people became more positive as I met tribal men who had left their weapons behind, were saying that they would remain peaceful, called for a civil state, backed the youth, and defended the youth when they were attacked.

For another, my opinions about myself and who I was changed. There was no epiphany, or at least it has not come yet. But now I am much more in touch with my Yemeni side. I cannot bear to watch the graphic videos that have come out of the country, but I do so to remind myself, so I never forget. I want the Yemeni people to enjoy the same rights that I have in the UK. The Yemeni people are no worse than the British, a point I emphasized to pro-Saleh people I met in Yemen. I heard people tell me that Yemenis were corrupt and thus deserved a corrupt leader. That Yemenis could not have a real democracy. That it was not in our culture. I know that is not true. Those people I saw risk death for change, freedom, and dignity, as clichéd as it sounds, are worthy of building a new country.

I am proud to say I am Yemeni, and I am even more proud after what I saw during my time there. The Yemenis were finally living up to the greatness of their ancestors, whose stories we had always been told. I also felt newfound pride in my Arab identity. From Tunisia to Egypt to Libya to Syria to Bahrain to Yemen, Arabs, including all those in the rest of the world who have spoken out, were breaking the fear barrier that has prevented the general populace from speaking out against their regimes.

The bullets and the blood, the injured and the dead: they will stay in my memory for a very long time. But once those are gone, and once I am gone, what those people sacrificed for will remain. It may take a very long time to come to fruition. It may appear that the old forces have won. But in reality, with the great educator that is Change Square, things can never go back to the way they were. They must change for the better. As the banner said: Welcome to the first kilometer of dignity. Welcome to the first small steps of a new Yemen.

# From Nowhere to Somewhere

*by Dina Sadek*

**DINA SADEK,** who has a degree in English Literature from Ain Shams University, Cairo, is a Cairo-based freelance journalist who began her career as an Arabic/English translator and fixer for the *Sunday Telegraph* during the Egyptian revolution in 2011. She accompanied the *Sunday Telegraph*'s correspondent to Libya to cover the Libyan conflict in the rebels' stronghold of Benghazi. In Libya, she worked with Agence France-Presse (AFP) covering the front lines of the Libyan conflict. After spending two months in Libya, Dina worked in Cairo as a freelance fixer with the *Pittsburgh Tribune-Review* covering sectarian conflict in Upper Egypt. Dina has written articles for the online magazine *EMAJ* and the German Goethe Institute's blog in Cairo. She works as a reporter for the Global Press Institute and was chosen as a fellow in the 2011 MENA Democracy Fellowship at the World Affairs Institute, held in Washington, D.C. During her fellowship, she interned for *Foreign Policy* magazine and for the Project on Middle East Democracy (POMED).

The last night of 2010 in Egypt passed like every other New Year's Eve. There were those who praised the past year and those who wished for the next one to be better. I did neither. My year hadn't been a good year, nor had I any hopes whatsoever for the next one.

On the eve of 2009 I had been more optimistic. I had plans for 2010, big ones. I had turned twenty-one in the summer, and for a few years I had been preparing myself for a big move. I was in college studying English literature, a major that I neither chose nor liked. I was working in a dead-end job that I despised. But I was always content, because I knew 2010 would be better. I told myself, "2010 is going to be the year for me." I had been preparing for a while to move that summer to a Western country that welcomes immigrants with open arms. If you are not affluent, visas are difficult to obtain for people from my country. I had been familiarizing myself with how to get a visa since I was sixteen. I knew exactly what I had to do: get a few months' tourist visa, which I most certainly had all the requirements for. Once I arrived in the country, I would start the immigration process, as it is a lot easier once you are there. I thought that my chance of getting a tourist visa was 99 percent. I was so sure of my plans that I started shopping for clothes that would suit the weather in this particular country. And I applied.

My passport was returned the next day with a rejection form saying: "You have not satisfied me that you would leave the country at the end of your stay as a temporary resident." Although I did provide documents proving that I was a third-year college student with one more year of study left, this apparently was not enough proof that I had a definite reason to come back. But I had to appreciate the irony of the rejection: they had accurately guessed my underlying intentions.

After a month of being depressed, I realized that I couldn't actually afford to be down for long. I picked myself up and I started the job hunt again. Having had the experience of working in hotels, I got a job in a different hotel. My monthly salary was around $200 a month, including tips, barely covering my rent and food.

I was not one of those people who knows exactly what they want career-wise and strives for it with passion. I just knew two things: I love politics and I enjoy writing, so a combination of these would probably be my dream job. Pursuing such a job in Egypt was basically as dangerous as putting a wet finger in an electricity outlet. You could not discuss or criticize politics in public in Egypt without risking getting arrested, tortured, or even "disappearing mysteriously." Not to mention the difficulty of actually making a living doing it. So I took whichever jobs I could get; the latest was as a receptionist in a hotel.

Since most of my Egyptian friends criticized me for my liberal views, I started surrounding myself with foreigners, usually expats living in Egypt who would leave at some point. I did not hate Egypt. This was not the reason I wanted to leave. I have a deep love and respect for my country and my people. However, sadly, living in Egypt was not easy if one had dreams and ambitions, which I did. Young people in Egypt would graduate from college to begin a jobless life, or worse, to hold a job that pays just enough to cover transportation to and from work. Unless, of course, you are lucky enough to know someone in a high position to get you a decent job that pays well.

All I wanted was to live somewhere where I was treated as a human being, where I could articulate my opinions without being scared for my life. I wanted to get a decent education and a job that would actually pay for my rent. I wanted to have a life. I believed it was my right as a human being—and how strange a phrase this was to utter in Egypt!

At the beginning of 2011, I was in my last semester of college and preparing for my finals. I had quit a job that I hated and started looking for a job that I might possibly hate less, since I was stuck in Egypt while I finished my degree. Who knew, maybe after I graduated something would change. At this time, I had literally only enough money to cover my share of the rent for one more month.

Then came the 25th of January. Days prior, I received Facebook invitations to join in a protest against the injustice of the regime that would occur all across Egypt that day. Seeing the large number of people who had clicked yes on the event, I knew it was going to big, but never in my wildest dreams had I imagined that it would be toppling-the-entire-regime big. I woke up that day like any other day and checked the news. I saw the images of tens of protesters, and then the number rose to hundreds. By the time the number reached thousands, I was in Cairo's now famous Tahrir Square.

The stories about everything being planned and organized are inaccurate. When I went there, I saw people who were just as lost as I was, not only in the square but also in life in general.

As these couple of thousand protesters reached Tahrir Square they were welcomed with central security's best friend: tear gas bombs. With every eye that teared up as the bombs were thrown at us, the numbers of protesters in the square rose. As loud as we could, we chanted: "The people demand the removal of the regime," and other anti-regime chants. I was thrilled to finally be able to say these things out loud. My favorite was *yasqut yasqut, Hosni Mubarak, yasqut yasqut Hosni Mubarak* (Down down, Hosni Mubarak, down down, Hosni Mubarak).

Naturally, protesters wanted to march towards government build-ings such as the ministries and police stations. And the police and the central security had very clear orders to stop that from happening by any means necessary. The tear gas bombs kept coming for a few hours, until they ran out. That's when the water cannons started and a stone-throwing match commenced between security forces and protesters.

Given the fact that the security forces were holding shields and wearing helmets, they were able to keep throwing stones while many protesters, without similar protection, got injured. When a stone hit my back, I realized right then that "this is really happening." It was us versus them, protesters versus the regime forces, and I picked up the next stone I found and threw it as hard as my small self could manage. I was bleeding from what I later realized was a tiny injury. I was in pain, but I understood at that moment that it did not matter. I had been punched metaphorically every day of my entire life by my country's unjust regime, which had never even once treated me, or anybody for that matter, as a human being.

As the day progressed, the violence temporarily halted and the protesters filled the square, surrounded by the Central Security Forces. You could tell that the number of protesters was increasing by how loud the chants had become, and you could tell who had been the longest in the square by how hoarse their voices had become.

People from different social classes, mostly youths, were present in the square. I am never going to forget the face of an older man in his sixties who was standing in the square. He was checking on a young man who had a bandage on his head due to being injured by a stone. The old man cried and apologized to the young protester, "I am sorry, I am really sorry you have to go through this now. If only my generation had been brave enough to do this a long time ago, you wouldn't have to go through this now."

The power of the chants was indescribable—empowering yet surreal at the same time. After years and years of not being able to speak out, I was suddenly standing in a public square yelling at the top of my voice until my throat became sore.

I left the square that evening to get some rest, empowered by the belief that today had changed everything. The people had finally stepped outside of the fear box, and nothing could be done to hold them back. The regime had tried to break us down with weapons, but they could not compete with us, who were bolder, stronger and more determined.

I woke up the next day getting ready to go back to the square. I checked Facebook and Twitter. To my shock, the square had been cleared of protesters, many of whom had been kicked out, chased across bridges, down alleys, and even arrested. I couldn't believe it, so I went to the square to see for myself. I found a large number of Central Security Forces—thousands of them—surrounding the square, blocking it in every direction. To see it, you would presume they were preparing for war, which sure enough, they were.

I walked through the middle of the square, empty except for the cars once again passing through. I was hesitant to take a picture with my cell phone and post it on the social media websites, but I finally did. That's when one of the high-ranking policemen sitting on a chair on the sidewalk within the square ordered one of his guys to "get her." I was yelled at, thrown to the ground, held by the collar of my shirt, spoken to inhumanly. My phone, my purse, and my person were searched. To date, I still don't even know what they were expecting to find--perhaps a sticker reading, "I hate the regime"?

My ID was checked, and I was asked so many questions my head was left spinning. They asked me where I was going. I answered that I intended to meet some friends, which wasn't entirely false. I was in fact meeting friends to go to the protest, wherever it was, together. But apparently meeting some friends was not a good excuse because the officer who had grabbed me turned to his boss and said: "She's one of them." I wanted to ask him what exactly he meant by that? Egyptian? Protester? Someone who has friends?

Having seen many arrests the day before, I decided maybe it was not a very good idea to argue. They finally let me go. Maybe I had convinced them that my photography was completely innocent, or maybe they simply wanted to frighten me out of doing it again. Whatever it was, I was soon free to re-join the protests. Sadly, I wasn't able to find any, as they were dispersed. Flabbergasted by this, I went to find my friends.

The next day passed much the same way, but with an increased sense of anticipation. Friday was now only a day away. People had high expectations, and the events of the next day certainly didn't disappoint. The plan for Friday was for protesters to start marching to main squares across Egypt around noontime, immediately after the weekly Islamic Friday prayer. Thousands of Egyptians had replied to several social media invitations confirming that they would be attending to continue the fight.

The kind of violence used against protesters all through that Friday was brutal. I was in an area called Giza. Immediately following the prayer, hundreds of protesters began chanting with one voice: "The people demand the removal of the regime." They began to march. But as soon as they turned onto the road leading to Tahrir Square, they were hit by water cannons. As they marched towards the bridge their way was blocked by the Central Security Forces, who faced the protesters with batons and countless tear gas bombs. The determination of protesters that day was shown by how prepared they came. Some brought cases of surgical masks and handed them out to protesters. Others followed advice from Tunisians, who had posted on Facebook and Twitter after suffering through similar experiences involving tear gas. They advised us to wash our faces with soda or smell an onion should we be tear-gassed. Some brought cans of soda and bags filled with onions and rushed towards people hit by the gas to help them.

After a long run-in with the Central Security Forces—plus blocked streets, shotguns, and tear gas at the zoo—we reached a square called Al-Galaa. To our collective shock we found thousands of protesters filling the square and four central security trucks on a bridge. In the hands of protesters were signs covered with anti-regime slogans and anti-regime graffiti . One of the most popular slogans was *irhal* meaning "leave," following the Tunisians, who had held signs saying "*dégage*," meaning "leave" in French. Another popular chanted slogan was *ash-sha'ab yureed isqat an-nizam*! (The people demand the removal of the regime). As the word spread about the violent crackdown on the streets, more and more were emboldened to join the protest. As the numbers grew there were enough people to pose a real threat to the Central Security Forces.

It was not only news of the violence of the regime's forces that incentivized people on that day. Friday the 28th marked the date of one of the stupidest decisions in the history of the Mubarak regime: to cut cell phone and Internet connectivity. Taking Internet access away from youth is like putting a fish on dry land, except that a fish would be helpless to do anything constructive with its anger. Even if I were an apathetic young person who could not care less about the political protests, if you took away something vital to my daily life I would go out and protest against that. Many people joined the protests that day only because when Internet and phones were cut off they could not find out what was going on any other way. And once they felt the power of freedom even for a minute, they could not go back.

People arrived in the square from three directions and got ready to march out through the fourth exit, in the direction of Tahrir Square. The distance between the two squares, Al-Galaa and Tahrir, is no more than a fifteen-minute walk under normal circumstances, but when tear gas bombs are coming at you, you get slowed down a bit.

As we finally neared Tahrir Square, the sound of gunshots became louder and louder. For the life of me, I cannot remember how my friends and I made it to the roof of one of the buildings overlooking the square to witness what we did. What I do remember is that I was very scared. We went into one of the hostels inside the building, which had strict orders from the police not to give rooms to Egyptians. The breaking news on TV was that Mubarak was about to give a speech. I also learned from TV viewers that Mubarak had issued a curfew from 6 p.m. to 7 a.m.—ironic, given that it was already almost midnight and clearly nobody was going home. As much as I'd like to say it was a rebellious decision on my part to defy the curfew, in fact, there is no way I could have known about it, being already outside my house with no cell phone connection.

Mubarak's speech demonstrated how out of touch he was with reality. People sitting next to me watching it had hoped that he had learned his lesson from what happened to the former Tunisian President Zine Aldin Ben Ali, and as such, that he would step down. Instead, he called for reforms and assured us that he would continue this term regardless of the protests calling for his resignation. He added that the protesters were, "controlled by political movements that incited them to turn a peaceful, just protest into a violent one." Lastly, he explained that he fired the cabinet, missing the entire point that people were protesting to eject *him* and his whole regime, not just fire his staff. Right after this disappointing speech we went back to the roof, where time passed very slowly.

As injured and dead bodies fell in the square, the military finally came to the rescue. Military cars entered the square from the protesters' side amidst cheers from the people. The soldiers assured the protesters that they were on their side and chased down the Central Security Forces and police. Rain, which is considered a good sign in Islam, couldn't have come at a better time. Right at the moment when the military cars surrounded the area, it started to pour.

My American friend Tamera was by my side the whole day. I could not be more thankful for her presence—comforting me and calming me down. She was noticeably excited about the army's arrival and started cheering me out of the depression I had been in for a few hours. "I wouldn't trust it right away," I told her. "I'd wait."

For the next several days the protesters held a sit-in in the square. I was not there every day. For the first few days I followed events from home while trying to figure out my life. After all, I was jobless and I had rent to pay. Those two don't usually go well together. Then, on TV, I saw camels and horses running over protesters in the square. Molotov cocktails were being thrown from the roofs of the buildings in the square by thugs hired by the regime. I was speechless. I knew that the regime was accustomed to using cheap tricks against its people, but I had not realized how low they were willing to stoop.

My closest friends during that time were, and still are, a group of Americans who lived in Cairo. As expected, they were all asked to evacuate. "Mubarak took away my dignity *and* my friends," I joked many times. After their evacuation, I felt that now I was *really* left with nothing. No friends, no job, no money to pay the rent. The realization that all this meant that I would have to move back into my mother's home was just the icing on the cake.

Then one morning I received a call from a friend, Troy Carter, to whom I will always be grateful for putting me on track to begin my career. "Some British man is in Cairo and he needs a translator. Would you be willing to translate for him?" he asked. Translating for tourists is not my favorite thing in the world to do, but there is a limit to how picky broke people can be.

I went to the square to meet this man. He turned out to be the foreign correspondent for one of the UK's foremost publications. Having given up on being able to talk about politics out loud in my own country, suddenly I was helping to cover the story of people speaking out in just this way, myself included!

At the end of my first day as a fixer/translator, we discussed my daily rate. "Is $200 a day good for you?" the journalist asked. I somehow succeeded in hiding my jubilation, realizing that hugging him and telling him he'd just paid my entire month's rent might not be entirely professional. "Yep, that will do," I responded nonchalantly.

After my financial problems for quite possibly the next few months had been solved, I was able to give my undivided attention to covering the revolution. Every day the journalist and I went to the square. Everyone had a story to tell. I knew people were unhappy with the regime, but exactly how unhappy was beyond what I had imagined. The protest was not just a cry for the redress of socio-economic grievances, as the regime's PR machine made it sound. For many, it wasn't about the money. They were angry that they had never been able to choose their president and their government, or to express their objections about anything. Now they finally had a voice to do so.

The days passed slowly. Mubarak gave two more pointless speeches. People continued to camp in Tahrir Square, and the army continued to stand guard, until finally, on the 11th of February, something changed: Mubarak stepped down. I had the pleasure of being in front of the presidential palace to witness the celebration. Shortly after, we drove to the now internationally recognized Tahrir Square. Everyone was elated and the chant *irfaa rasak fo'a anta masri* (Hold your head up high, you are Egyptian) rang out through the streets of Egypt.

What I really enjoyed the next morning was reading the national pro-regime newspapers. For years they had praised the regime and its leaders. During the revolution, these papers were claiming that there were no protests. According to them, the riots were just the result of thugs bent on destroying the country. The only stories the papers ran were about the pro-Mubarak protests at which attendance never exceeded five hundred people—in comparison to hundreds of thousands in Tahrir Square. Day one post-revolution, this changed. The headline of the biggest national newspaper read: "The people have brought down the regime," and the paper included a supplement filled with protest pictures dedicated to the "revolution." How hypocritical!

State TV was similar. All through the eighteen days of the revolution, State TV's coverage could not have been more far-fetched. Their staff deserves an Oscar for their performance, acting as if there was no revolution. Only calls from pro-Mubarak supporters were aired, who listing Mubarak's so-called "achievements," while just a click away other channels were airing live from Tahrir Square the battles between the Central Security Forces and protesters at the sit-ins. The day after Mubarak stepped down, State TV was playing revolutionary songs. It was just a wee bit too late.

That day, people were consumed by feelings of joy and love for their country. They removed their camping tents from the square, grabbed their brooms and garbage cans, and cleaned the streets that had been their home for two weeks, as if it was a first step forward towards cleaning their bigger home, Egypt.

I couldn't wipe the smile off my face for over a week. And then I went to Libya.

Conflict broke out in Libya in late February, and the journalist with whom I had worked covering the revolution in Cairo asked me to accompany him to cover the Libyan conflict. I never imagined in my wildest dreams that Libya would be the first foreign country I would visit, especially during a war. But there I was.

I expected violence. I expected death. I expected a war. And so it was. I stayed in Libya for about two months, during which time I learned a lot. When I got back to Cairo, Tahrir Square looked very small.

The weeks and months of 2011 passed. Eight months after the revolution, daily life had not changed much for Egyptians. They were back to being angry and pissed off at everything most of the time. The friendly military that was expected to be on our side wasn't always very friendly. Yet efforts were being made to fight and try the businessmen and former regime officials responsible for the corruption.

As of November 2011, Egypt was awaiting what would hopefully be its first fair parliamentary and presidential elections in three decades. With continued pressure by the people, changes were slowly taking place. Egyptians have a long way to go, from learning about freedom and democracy to actually implementing it in their society. Seeing how people react to politics, it's clear that they haven't been a part of it for years, which is one more reason to despise the former regime.

As for me, I benefited greatly from working with some of the most experienced journalists in the world for two months. I worked with several foreign publications in Libya and my contact list grew. I came back from Libya to graduate from college and I am now officially a journalist myself, although I still do translating for other journalists on the side. I also finally received a visa to travel to the West to do a couple of internships. None of this would have been possible if it weren't for the revolution and my active participation in it. I am finally able to follow my dreams, and now I have a job. My life's direction has become clear. Living in Egypt is now a choice, and I choose it every day.

As 2011 comes to a close, lots of things are yet to change in Egypt, but on New Year's Eve I know what my toast will be for myself and for my country. I am going to praise and even brag about my country and the amazing year behind us, and I will hope for the next year to be even better.

# Hopeless Optimism
## By Rami Jarrah

**RAMI JARRAH** is a Syrian-British political activist and citizen journalist who, during the 2011 Syrian uprisings, wrote and spoke under the pseudonym "Alexander Page." Born in Cyprus and raised in London, Jarrah returned to his homeland of Syria in 2004. He later faced house arrest and a travel ban that led to his decision to stay in Syria and find work. In March of 2011, Rami was arrested while taking part in an anti-government protest. His Twitter alias @AlexanderPageSY was often cited by media outlets and as a result, used by Syrian intelligence to his reveal his identity. In fear of his safety, Rami left Syria in late 2011 and currently lives with his family in Cairo, Egypt. He is the co-director of the ANA New-Media Association, an organization that seeks to support citizen journalism in Syria.

## October 2, 2011

It was 3 a.m. when I woke up to the ringing of my computer with an activist on the other side of the call. I had asked him earlier to perform a name check through a connection in the government he knew—something we would usually do to see whether an activist was wanted by the secret police or not.

Over the past four days I had been sleeping fully dressed, with even my jacket and shoes on, worried that at any moment the government might come storming through the door to get me. Maybe paranoia had gotten the best of me, but recently a number of activists I worked with had been detained and put away. The only thing that kept me somewhat positive was the fact that I had been using my pseudonym, Alexander Page, even when meeting activists or journalists, so that only a few trusted people knew my real name.

I quickly jumped up and rocketed towards the computer to answer the call, and after a swift exchange of hellos he got to the point, but was eager to keep me calm by saying: "Don't worry, this doesn't mean there is no way out," and of course I got the picture. But he continued: My name had been found on the list of those wanted by the Military Air Force Intelligence, a notorious security branch in Damascus. The activist told me that it was in relation to my pseudonym and that the government was aware of my real identity. After a few seconds of silence to come to terms with what was being said, I thanked him and agreed to consider his suggestion of fleeing the country.

I took a deep breath and quickly flipped through some possible scenarios. See, the problem was I wasn't just wanted for demonstrating—I had already been through that before—but the fact that my pseudonym had been mentioned meant the government knew exactly what I was up to: speaking to the media, filming demonstrations and crackdowns. It was only a few months ago that I had seen my avatar on state-controlled media accused of being a foreign agent. If I went into hiding, my family might become a target. Even sending them out of the country would leave me petrified of the moment they would go through passport control and what would happen if they were stopped.

It was clear that I had no alternative; I must get my wife and daughter and flee with them over the border. The airport was definitely not an option. An hour later, with three medium-sized bags and a convincing excuse to my wife, we were in a taxi on the way to the Jordanian border. I told her that the situation was getting tense and that I just felt it was vital that we get away for a few days. During the ninety-minute drive we agreed on what we would say at the border: that we were visiting family for an event. Although I was traumatized at the possibility of being stopped, I was confident that my wife and daughter would not be harmed, as it was my name that was on the list.

I now gave a few moments to myself to recall memories of the past six or seven months, and I was outraged at what I was putting my family through. I was now asking myself, "Was it worth it?" As we got closer to the border this question persisted and recollections and memories reverberated in my mind.

## Seven months earlier

Other than the significant income I was enjoying in Damascus at my job as an import/export consultant, there was nothing really to keep me in Syria. The only reason I hadn't left to the United Kingdom was the travel ban that was assigned to me by the British government between 2004-2007, under suspicion of posing as a Syrian and therefore of being a spy of some sort. That period of limbo opened the door to settling down, finding a rewarding job, and eventually accepting Syria as a permanent residency. But the good job element was not enough anymore and leaving the country seemed a more sensible option.

Now, the Arab Spring had begun. We had just seen the fall of dictators such as Ben Ali of Tunisia and we were closely watching the uprising in Egypt, where Mubarak had yet to step down. A mild anti-government atmosphere was evident in Damascus in spray-painted slogans such as "down with Assad." Slogans on walls and leaflets secretly being strewn throughout neighborhoods across the country calling for protests. Even this mild protest activity compared to the events in other countries in the region was quite significant for Syria.

Despite these murmurs for change, Syria's ruler for the past eleven years, Bashar al-Assad, said that his country was immune to all that was happening across the Arab world, insisting that the Syrian people were satisfied with the country's development and progress. I unwillingly believed him. Or let me put this way: Syrians were not "satisfied" but rather there seemed to be an absence of a will needed to bring about an uprising. "Will" was not something I believed existed in Syria. Living in Damascus for the past seven years, I had become amazed how a people could be so quiet, so complacent. Everyone I knew secretly disapproved of the government in one way or another. Most were affected personally by the monopoly that the Ba'ath party had over almost every single element of society, whether it be public or private, political or religious. Yet, all would abide by a seemingly telepathic law that underscored "you can live happily as long as your happiness does not effect our rule." Syrians were so reluctant to voice their concerns or even speak out in their living rooms that when they finally *did*, they would find themselves immediately lowering their voices to a whisper. I was not used to being silent and my independent outbursts of frustration were usually met with someone telling me to shut my mouth or we would "vanish." While some might have considered such a reaction an insult, close friends and family would always stress to me that this was just an ugly reality we all had to accept.

I honestly could not take it anymore. I wanted change in Syria. The only alternative was to abandon this country—one my own parents had fled decades ago as exiles during the war with Lebanon. To me, Syria was a country full of potential but empty of hope. Its people were not lazy in the literal sense. In fact they were rather active. I had met several twenty-something graduates that were simultaneously working three jobs while desperately trying to have a social life. This was Syria, a country full of rich diversity and culture but empty of aspiration and hope for the future. Something had to happen, something really had to happen.

On the February 5, 2011, an anti-government demonstration had been called for in the Friday market area of central Damascus. This Syrian Day of Rage came after plenty of online activism by thousands of Syrian citizens on the popular social networks. I was at work early that morning, eagerly anticipating the possibility of "something happening" in Damascus. I had told my boss that I had to go to a doctor's appointment. The event had been planned at noon and the location was a fifteen-minute walk from my office. When it was finally time to go, I quickly scrolled through Facebook to see if there were any changes suggested to the event. All was intact. A colleague and I finally headed out together. We made it to the Friday market in the Afeef area of central Damascus a few minutes before noon. With no hesitation, we made our way through the starting area of the market.

To our dismay, we saw that two or three secret police bodies had stationed themselves at almost every single shop on the street. The government was obviously aware of the calls for demonstrations and was taking it very seriously. There were so many police that we were clearly outnumbered. We walked through the market, turned around and walked back; this drew some attention to us. We were now being approached by the "hidden" security apparatus. I quickly grabbed some onions at the grocery stand in front of me and asked the shopkeeper to put them in a bag for me. Quite depressingly we began purchasing groceries, as this is what any person who came to the market would do. This kept us safe but did not keep the suspicious eyes of our predators away. We soon left the market and with our heads down and returned to the office silently.

I really didn't have much to say to myself let alone anyone else. I was not only appalled at the lack of attendance at the "protest" but also at my own inability to be an igniting figure that could actually start the protest. The next two weeks were miserable. I gave in to pleas from my wife to discuss living abroad. I had begun to feel hopeless. Syria appeared to be no place for us to live anymore.

I mentioned a miserable two weeks only because on the 17th of February what came as a shock to most Syrians left me gobsmacked. An anti-government demonstration took place in the old Damascus area. It was kicked off by a generous number of shopkeepers who were angered by a police officer's assault of a young man parking his car. Thousands of people eventually gathered in the Hareeka Square where they chanted, "Thieves, Thieves" and "The Syrian people will not be humiliated." Some considered the event just another random dispute between shopkeepers of the area and the traffic police but there was no doubt to many others, myself included, that the possibility of large numbers gathering in Damascus and expressing themselves in one voice had suddenly become a reality. With renewed energy I was definitely back in the game. Friends and I began handing out leaflets in the Muhajrin and Salhiyeh areas of Damascus. Night after night we sensed that the peopler were glad to receive our literature.

The revolutionary spirit didn't break but rather developed itself, as the numbers of online activists multiplied to thousands. With this build up, two more small but morale-boosting protests took place in central Damascus. About one hundred and fifty people took part in each, one in the Hammadiyah market in the old city and the other in front of the interior ministry, calling for the release of fifteen children who had been arrested for spray painting anti-government slogans on the walls of the streets of the city of Daraa. Both protests were dispersed by secret police, most of the protesters were arrested and subjected to interrogation and some were severely abused. Everywhere I went I could hear people whispering and gossiping about what had happened and it became quite apparent that a popular uprising in Syria had become a possibility. On Friday of that same week, the country witnessed a significant change of events. Demonstrations broke out in numerous places across the country. Daraa was in flames.

On the March 18, I made my way to Friday prayers at the renowned Umayyad Mosque in the very heart of the old city of Damascus. The mosque was built in 634 CE but stands on the ancient grounds of a Christian basilica, and before that its history goes back nearly three millennia. It is a treasured symbol to Syrians of their remarkable place in world civilization. On this day, calls had been made for a mass protest here. The small but still significant events that had occurred over the past few weeks renewed my hope that the Syrian people would find the courage to speak out. When I arrived, I made my way through the courtyard to the inner side of the mosque where a few hundred people were attending the Friday speech before prayers. As hundreds more poured in, I sat down and began to listen to what the sheikh was saying. "The West is trying to fiddle with our country," he concluded. "They are the ones telling you to rise." It was only expected that the government would send this man to try to diminish any possibility of a demonstration taking place. Prayers took about ten minutes and ended uneventfully.

Then, an old man walked across the carpet and climbed up onto the steps by the sheikh, staring at everyone in silence. A group of people stood up and began shuffling towards him. With a loud voice he said, "My sons are prisoners and I want freedom!" His spontaneous but emotional statement led to a roar of commotion. Chants broke out. I stood up quickly and ran towards the crowd and finally joined in. "Freedom!!" I screamed with all my might. The atmosphere was intense and an unexplainable rush of adrenaline pushed me to grip my fist and chant even louder. We funneled towards the main door and just as we made it through, a stampede of secret police with batons and tasers came smashing in. Hundreds of protesters were beaten and dragged across the courtyard as more and more security forces came storming in. With streaks of blood left across the courtyard floor, the government had managed to disperse the protest. But it had begun; we had made our voices known.

As one protester from that day put it: "The moment I chanted freedom was the moment I'd found my dignity."

As we fled the mosque and escaped detention, I quickly made my way to a relative's shop in the area. Before I could pull out my phone and show him what had just happened, I couldn't help but notice the huge smile on his face. I was sure that he had heard about what had just happened, but his was news of a different kind—and more promising. "Daraa," he said. "The people of Daraa have shaken the earth, Rami!" It was true. Thousands of people had taken to the streets in a city well known for its contributions to the government apparatus. It was unexpected, but it was here; we could finally call this a revolution. Demonstrations had occurred in a number of places at one time. The Syrian people were alive again.

As demonstrations continued to surge across the country, it was fair to say that everything had changed for all of us. I left my job because I had a falling out with the company owner over my views on what was happening. He, a close companion of the inner circle of the regime, was unconditionally supportive of the crackdown that had been brutally inflicted on peaceful demonstrators. I could no longer handle the brainwashing environment that surrounded him.

Suddenly there was something so much more valuable than anything money could buy. People were hopeful and optimistic; they were thinking of new possibilities, new ways that Syria could develop, new potential that would be seen. The atmosphere during demonstrations was unexplainable and energizing: for the very first time on Syrian soil you could stand in one place with so many other people who felt exactly the way that you did—and were not ashamed or scared to say or show it. The chants represented me in every way. I would repeat them with so much enthusiasm it was an experience so beautiful and so exhilarating. And even though I had grown up in a free country, I too felt like I had tasted freedom for the first time and couldn't believe how on earth someone could live without it.

The months ahead presented a significant growth of civil participation countered by a preposterous and defensive brutality from the Syrian regime. Assad had declared a war against his own people, calling them terrorists. When they were caught, the nightmare was repeated over and over again, where people of all ages—men, women, boys and girls—were subject to conditions we had never imagined. As the crackdown intensified, the determination of those affected deepened. When we sat at home we would now speak, we would now analyze our country, and introduce solutions for problems that we were sure would soon be implemented once the regime was swept away. In a sentiment that really has no explanation, I became a new person, with new thoughts and hence, new expectations on what life should offer me and my family in the little place called Syria, the little place we now called "home."

## Back to October 2nd, 2011

Then came the 3 a.m. call. My euphoria quickly turned into a salty reality. Within months, I found myself fleeing with bits and pieces of our past life from a country that we had just begun to feel that we belonged to. I took a deep breath in preparation for the border crossing making sure I would not alert my wife of the unease I was experiencing in anticipation of what was about to happen.

As we arrived at the border station, the driver asked for our passports. He pulled over, got out of the car and disappeared into the complex. After ten minutes went by, I began to feel frantic. My wife asked me if something was wrong. "Why the hell is he taking so long," I complained, and got out of the car, desperate to see what was going on. A moment later, he came back and apologized for the delay, and we began moving towards the Jordanian checkpoint.

Just as I was packing the passports away, relieved that we had made it, our driver said, "Oh wait, there is another checkpoint, Air Force Intelligence." Ahead was a small building surrounded by armed civilians, full of people representing the very intelligence branch that was targeting me. We pulled up in front of them and instantly one jumped up to begin examining us as though we were fugitives. He then lifted his hand in the air and asked his superior, who was inside the station, whether he wanted to see our documents or not. With one glance we were shaken off and given permission to continue. I held my breath the whole time and silently gasped for air as the car moved forward. We had finally made it; it was a relief like no other. I placed my head down on the back of the driver's seat as we approached the Jordanian border.

Safe and secure and with much recollection to do, I was (and still am) left with my original un-answered question: the loss and pain, the destruction of homes, the blood of the innocent shed on our streets, our personal losses . . . and where we are now? Yet, there is no doubt that we have seen a glimpse of something that we call freedom. So was it all worth it? The question persists. The answer is simple, but asking was selfish.

# Live-Tweeting a Revolution

### by Sultan Al Qassemi

**SULTAN SOOUD AL QASSEMI** is a UAE-based columnist whose columns have appeared in publications within and outside the Arab Gulf region, including *Gulf News, National Newspaper, Financial Times,* the *Independent,* the *Guardian,* the Huffington Post, the *New York Times, Foreign Policy,* openDemocracy, and the *Globe and Mail.* He is also a non-resident Fellow at the Dubai School of Government.

Sultan has topped *Forbes'* list of top Middle East tweeters. He has amassed over one hundred thousand Twitter followers, tweeting often about developments in the Arab world with an emphasis on the Arab uprisings. Widely credited with sharing links that exposed corruption in autocratic regimes across the region, he is known for tweeting live translations of many communiques from Egypt's Tahrir Square, Yemen's Ali Abdullah Saleh, and the late Libyan leader Muammar Gaddafi. Sultan also founded the Barjeel Art Foundation, with the vision of creating a space where artwork drawn from diverse corners of the Arab world can appear together in an interactive communal setting.

For those who had faith, it was always meant to be so. The fate of Arabs couldn't be to forever live under oppressive regimes, and it shouldn't be. The Arab uprisings started from none other than Tunisia, one of the worst police states and the seat of the Arab Council of

Arab Interior Ministers, who are responsible for monitoring their populations. It was ironic, but it was also very fitting. The collapse of the Tunisian regime was a message to all Arab dictators that sooner or later, no matter how hard they tried to oppress their populations, they would not be able to stand in the face of destiny.

Like millions of young Arabs, I was fortunate to be part of this phenomenon, mainly through the wonders of technology. Just five days before the death of Mohammed Bouazizi, the man who self-immolated himself and one of the major icons of the uprisings, I had finished my term as chair of a pan-Arab nonprofit organization in the UAE whose mandate was to empower youth. Despite numerous requests for me to continue as chair, I decided to set an example and leave the post after my term expired (a concept that is foreign to our region's leaders).

The day before Bouazizi died, I wrote my last article for *The National* in Abu Dhabi.[1] It began with the following: "The Arabs are a patient lot. Twenty years after a wave of democracy swept through Eastern Europe, Arabs are still waiting for their own wave. In the past few weeks a series of setbacks have pushed their dreams even further away. They haven't lost hope though, as the latest protests in Tunisia have demonstrated."

As Um Kalthoum, one of Egypt's most beloved songbirds, famously sang, "Patience has a limit." When Bouazizi died the next day, it was clear to me that this would be a monumental event that would not go unnoticed. I tweeted "Avenue Mohammed Bouazizi 1986–2011." A few weeks after Ben Ali was toppled, the authorities did in fact name a road after Bouazizi.

I continued to tweet speeches and updates from Tunisia, a small country I had never been to before, until Ben Ali fled. Tunisia is far removed from the geo-political challenges of the Arabian Gulf, yet I was so proud of its people, along with millions of Arabs who had also rallied to show their support.

---

1. Sultan Sooud Al Qassemi, "Change we can believe in'? Not for the Middle East," (January 9, 2011) http://www.alarabiya.net/views/2011/01/09/132737.html

A few days after Ben Ali fled the country he had ruled with an iron fist for decades, many of us were struggling to fully come to terms with the end of one Arab dictator. I had returned to Sharjah, my home emirate, from a night out in Dubai. It was around midnight and the Arabic satellite news channels were carrying breaking news that a statement was forthcoming from another Arab dictator, Libya's Muammar Gaddafi. Online social media forums carried reports of a security build up in Benghazi and along the Tunisian border.

A few minutes later, the "King of Arab Kings" and "Dean of African and Arab leaders," as Gadhafi calls himself, appeared on TV live and started criticizing the Tunisians for their "audacity."

"You're lucky to have had a leader like Ben Ali," "What did he ever do to you?" "You should wish for him to come back," he said.

I opened my laptop and started live-tweeting. Those days I had well under ten thousand followers, a number that I was and continue to be very grateful for. Trying to live-tweet Gadhafi's tirade was anything but easy. He spoke in colloquial Libyan; some words I did not understand, so I had to look them up online. I was tweeting with such fervor that my fingers began to feel numb.

"Don't believe 'bookface,'" he said, referring to the social networking website Facebook. "Don't believe what you read on Keleeeks" in reference to the WikiLeaks—diplomatic cables on Tunisia that had been released in early December, exposing government corruption and foreign collusion, which many credit with building the critical momentum needed among intellectuals in order to oust the Tunisian dictator. Although it was winter, I was getting hot, laughing intermittently and tweeting away. Occasionally I would press the Twitter's Mention button and see tweets to me that read "Check out this guy @ sultanalqassemi, he's tweeting mad-dog Gadhafi," while others said, "For some comedy you must read what Gaddafi is saying now via @ sultanalqassemi's timeline." Journalists, diplomats, writers, and most importantly, regular folks, Arab and non-Arab, started to follow and retweet me, sharing my tweets with their own followers.

This activity reflected an interest not in me but rather in what was happening in the Arab world. By the end of that night my followers had increased exponentially. One friend calculated that throughout Gaddafi's rambling speech I tweeted on average once every 45 seconds.

A few days later, Egyptian social media was abuzz with a possible protest on the national "police day," January 25th, when Egypt celebrates the police force's resistance against British foreign occupation. I had followed the tragic case of martyr Khaled Said, another icon of the Arab people's emancipation movement. Egypt's Khaled and Tunisia's Mohammed could not have anticipated the tsunami that would be unleashed upon their martyrdom. With their deaths, a few months apart, more resulted to change the face of their nations and the Arab world than in several decades combined. I still recall the photo, published in June 2010 in *The National*, of brave young Egyptians standing in Alexandria, wearing black from top to bottom to mark their protestation. The group included Muslims and Copts, liberals and socialists, standing together on the beautiful Mediterranean coastline of Egypt's second largest city. I have not seen that photo since then, yet it lingers in the back of my mind. To see it, all I need to do is shut my eyes.

The protest on January 25th was the most dignified I have ever seen. In order to bypass the draconian martial law imposed almost throughout Egypt's military dictatorships since the 1950s and avoid persecution, intelligent Egyptians made sure not to chant or gather in large groups. As I have noted in openDemocracy, at this protest the people knew why they were there and so did everybody else.[2] That is what mattered most: that people knew why they were there even if they were not causing a ruckus. A momentum was swelling, one that translated into more and more people joining the *ash-shaheed* (martyr) page (as the

---

2. Sultan Sooud Al Qassemi, "Egypt: from revolt to change," in openDemocracy (February 8, 2011), http://www.opendemocracy.net/sultan-sooud-al-qassemi/egypt-from-revolt-to-change

"We are all Khaled Said" Facebook page has become known in Arabic).

I felt compelled to continue covering the Egyptian uprising, so I took time off from work. I didn't know what would happen; all I knew was that this was essential for me, as a secularist, as a liberal, but most importantly as an Arab. I had been writing for years about empowering young Arabs to determine their own fate, and in Egypt I found my raison d'être.

I had been in Egypt merely a few weeks before the uprising on January 25. Egypt is also where I chose to take my sister and her kids in 2002 on their first break after her husband passed away, because I knew it so well. Egypt was the land from where all the music, the films, and the TV shows that I grew up on had come from. Egypt was the hope, and my home away from home.

Egypt was, for me, larger than its 85 million inhabitants or one million square kilometers. Egypt is an idea. There is a sense of responsibility towards this land whose sons travelled to fight for the Gulf in 1991—a debt that must be repaid, as I wrote for Al Jazeera.[3] Free these sons, let them and Egypt's daughters enjoy the freedom and dignity they have been denied. When #Jan25 (as the uprising was called on Twitter) started, it was my chance to take part. I knew then, in my gut, that this was no ordinary protest, this was no ordinary country, these were no ordinary people. I tweeted my heart out, translating, switching like lightning between channels, breaking the news, relaying anecdotes from the ground when Internet access was shut down.

"Noor DSL is still working," I recall tweeting, referring to Egypt's Internet service provider.

(I eventually met Noor DSL's CEO and founder, as I have met all the activists and intellectuals who to me were truly heroes. When I flew into Cairo towards the end of 2011, I tweeted "Meeting the Egyptian activists is like meeting the characters from your favorite novel." They were the protagonists of the revolution.)

---

3. Sultan Sooud Al Qassemi, "Gulf states must repay Egypt favor," in Al Jazeera online (February 17, 2011),
   http://www.aljazeera.com/indepth/opinion/2011/02/2011214151229281695.html

One afternoon during the eighteen-day revolution, my friend Bassam, who had been with me in school, called me and told me to stop tweeting because I was "spreading panic." I tweeted that. "You have a lot of followers here," he said. My followers on Twitter had grown to over twenty-five thousand by then. Among them, many urged me to ignore Bassam. "Don't listen to him, we need to know what's going on." Nor was I alone. Many others were also doing what I was doing. But the bravest of all were those on the streets in Cairo. Most were tweeting in Arabic and others in English, but few had access to the multiple TV channels and web portals, both Arabic and English, that I had. Some of these portals were subscription based, and I had a password from work through which I could access the latest news and tweet it.

I tweeted, "I'm going to apologise to my friend and turn him down."

Bassam told me, "I saw your tweet!" I apologized once again to him and shut the phone off and returned to my laptop. I felt confident that my tweets were not gossip or rumors. When Habib A. Adly, Egypt's despised Interior Minister, withdrew the police from the streets, it was announced live on TV, and in the crucial minutes after the announcement, the dissemination of this information to the people meant the difference between safety and danger. Most activists were on the streets, and they did not know that there would be no police to keep things under control. One tweet I recall vividly was "Thank you for letting me know the police are no longer in the street, I will warn my sisters who are out to come back home." In other instances, thugs (known as *baltagiya*, axe-wielders, in Egyptian from the original Turkish word) roamed the street, many loyal to Mubarak and his cronies. More dangerous still were the prisoners who had fled their cells, prompting civilian neighborhood protection committees to form along the streets in noncommercial districts. As the uprising spread beyond Cairo the names of the towns became more known to me. I tweeted estimated sizes of each protest, population of the town, the location, the distance from Cairo in kilometers and miles and as many anecdotes as possible to give context to the revolution.

Some people have long assumed that those of us who come from the Gulf are not sympathetic to political progress, to reform or to change. But this was our chance, too. Many other Gulf social media bloggers and activists started writing and supporting those in Egypt. I maintained, as much as I could, an objective eye by reporting news rather than commenting on it. Mubarak spoke on several occasions, with many of us hoping that he would step down, but he didn't. In those instances, I may have let a few tweets loose that included some "adult" language.

I remember going to visit my cousin and discovering something called *Trendsmap*. Apparently my name was trending in North America, South America, Western Europe, and in some parts of East Asia as well as the Arab world. Clearly, the world had a vested interest in what was unfolding rapidly in the streets of Egypt. For weeks on end, I was up for twenty hours a day, translating and typing. I became online "friends" with dozens, scores, and perhaps even hundreds of people in a short period of time, cultivating relationships online and eventually in actuality.

When Wael Ghonim, the famed Internet activist and Google employee, was released after eleven days in detention that felt more like eleven weeks to us, that was an emotional pinnacle for me. I was tweeting his interview on Dream TV (the *New York Times* used my translation in their coverage), happy he was out and uncertain how things would develop in these crucial days.[4] At the end, the TV presenter played a video showing all the faces of the martyred protesters and asked him, "Was his worth it?" Wael broke down crying, and so did I. There I was, thousands of kilometers away, in my low-lit room in Sharjah, not far from where Wael administrated the El Shaheed page (in the UAE).

I shed tears partly because of what I saw but also because of the build-up of emotions that I had experienced over the preceding

---

4. Robert Mackey, "Subtitled Video of Wael Ghonim's Emotional TV Interview," *New York Times* (February 8, 2011), http://thelede.blogs.nytimes.com/2011/02/08/subtitled-video-of-wael-ghonims-emotional-tv-interview/

few weeks, reading endlessly about Egypt, interviews with martyrs' mothers, sisters, fathers, and brothers. "I want my son back, bring him back to me," said numerous mothers dressed in black. I still recall one mother's face as she wept in her house in one of Cairo's many poor neighborhoods. But he'll never be back. The best that could happen would be for this evil empire run by the NDP to end and a system based on "bread, freedom, and social justice" (the slogan of the Egyptian uprisings) to take its place.

As the uprisings spread from country to county, I gradually returned to the "real world"—my life and my commitments. I spent the next week reporting on and sympathizing with what transpired in Yemen, Libya, Syria, Bahrain, and elsewhere, but I could not offer to these equally just causes the same level of dedication I gave to Tunisia and then to Egypt.

As I write this, more than a year after Mubarak's ouster, I remain hopeful. Despite the political setbacks and politicking, despite the numerous challenges and the plots to hijack what brave young Egyptians did with their own hands, I remain hopeful. Today, for us in the Gulf, it is crucial for the Egyptian uprising to be completed and finally turned into a revolution—for the leadership to change, the laws to change, the mentality of those governing to change. Egyptians, Arabs, and the rest of the world must remain optimistic. As I view the developments in the Gulf—from the social media McCarthyism I have written about to the rise of the Islamists, some of whom threaten to scale back our freedoms—I am reminded that if Egypt succeeds, it will be better for all of us. If Egypt succeeds we will have a new standard of freedom to emulate. We can show those in the Gulf that Islam and freedom can co-exist, that the choice need not be either authoritarianism or chaos. But for all of us to succeed, Egypt—the mother of the world, as it is referred to in Arabic—must succeed first. Egypt the country, Egypt the people, Egypt the idea.

# A Journey
# to Activism
## *by Yasmin Haloui*

**YASMIN HALOUI** is the product of two different cultural understandings and perceptions of reality. Her Tunisian father and Dutch mother taught her to identify with each of their cultures, allowing her to transcend the perceived barriers of both. At the age of twenty, Yasmin's curiosity pushed her to leave Tunisia and go to the Netherlands, where she completed a bachelors degree in Cultural Anthropology and Development Sociology, followed by a master's in Conflict Studies and Human Rights.

In February 2011, after the Tunisian uprising had unfolded, Yasmin returned to Tunisia for several months to conduct her master's research on the uprising. It was during this period that she re-discovered Tunisia, its other realities and its hidden worlds. Since then, Yasmin has been involved with human rights and development organizations, as well as cultural clubs and initiatives working on democracy building and towards a better Tunisia. In September 2011, Yasmin returned again to Tunisia to fully dedicate herself to achieving this goal.

As I walked into the small square I could hear female voices talking and laughing. I approached the open door, knocked, and was welcomed inside. Three young women were sitting on the floor in a small living room. They were gathered around a square of black fabric that was pulled and held tight by four pieces of wood, assembled into a hollow table. They were sewing a traditional black and red *jubba* (dress) by hand, shaping round and flowery forms with golden thread and glitter that covered the the fabric of the jubba.

I presented them with a flyer with information on the program of the Democratic Modernist Pole (PDM), one of the many political parties in Tunisia taking part in the election of the constituent assembly. I asked them whether they intended to vote. Insha'llah (If God wills it), they answered. "But how to vote when there are so many parties? And who to trust?" I explained what the Pole is and what its positions are. I pointed their attention to what had convinced me to support the Pole: not a promise but deeds.

A few months earlier, political parties agreed to a principle of gendered equity. Women had to be part of the constituent assembly that would be tasked with writing the Tunisian constitution. This meant that half of the candidates would have to be men and the other half women. But because of the system by which the election was organized, generally only the head of the candidate list of each party in each region would be elected into the assembly. And in most parties, these heads of the lists were men. According to analysts, a very low number of the 128 individuals in the assembly would be women. Thus the system was already failing.

Only the PDM had acted according to the promises made by all parties, as sixteen of the thirty-three heads of candidate lists of the Pole were women. I asked the three young women to reflect upon this. I asked them to read all the flyers they had received and on Sunday, when they intended to go to the election bureau and tick the party of their choice, to reflect upon the messages. I asked them to take into account when they voted the party's position on women's emancipation, freedom, and rights.

A few days before the election, the feeling of emergency increased; there was the silent and continuing fear of the loss of freedom and democracy, of insecurity and a counter-revolution. People were preparing for violence on Election Day, the 23rd. People made food reserves, and shops announced that they would be closed that day.

My experience of the emergency situation and the fear of loss had been accentuated after an acquaintance recounted his encounter on the previous day with a man lobbying for the Nahda party, calling men to vote for it. His argument? Nahda was going to give employment priority to men and all men's salaries would be doubled. This followed a similar statement made a few months earlier by the leader of the party, Rached Gannouchi. After the revolution he had returned from a long exile in London. He proposed a solution to unemployment in Tunisia; priority of employment had to be given to men. Men had to work, and women could and should stay home. Gannouchi and the party later retracted this statement, but only in the hope of gaining more votes. The argument was re-used on the street, unofficially, in "men-to-men" talks. Perhaps this was a hollow promise, a manipulation of the masses in an intensifying election campaign, and perhaps Nahda had no intention of cutting back women's freedom and rights. But I was not prepared to gamble on it, nor was I willing to see a party that was lying to the people during the campaign have a leading role in writing Tunisia's new constitution.

I felt the need to act. The struggle for women's emancipation in Arab societies had been mainly led by men. The same was the case in Tunisia. It was men like early-twentieth-century author and scholar Tahar Haddad who had attempted, through cultural artistic expressions, to raise awareness concerning gender equality. It was men like former leader Habib Bourguiba, who through his powerful position and his rather unique position as dictator pushed through for reform and laws that would secure women's rights. Yet decades later, Tunisian society was struggling once again with the same issues. Religious and cultural perceptions of femininity resurfaced as topics of contention. The state was going to decide on the appropriate spaces, values, and conduct for women. The body of women was being re-appropriated by men in the populist discourses of political parties. But this time, I believed, it was not up to a Tahar Haddad or a Habib Bourguiba to stand up for women's emancipation. Women would have to lead the struggle for their rights themselves. The means now was informed voting.

Informing people about the PDM and fighting for freedom, democracy, and equality were what initially motivated me to join the campaign. Yet I encountered a challenge I had not foreseen. When I started discussing elections with various individuals, I realized that many doubted that they would vote or had no intention of voting at all. Democracy was to them an illusion, unattainable. According to some, the counts had already been made. They assumed the imperialist and colonialist super powers had already decided who was going to be president. The new leaders would merely become new dictators.

Riding in a cab one day, my friend Imen and I initiated a discussion about the elections. The cab driver shared his thoughts on the matter; he was very pessimistic. All parties were the same according to him: not trustworthy. But this time it would be different, Imen offered: "We the people have changed and we will no longer accept dictatorship. We are more critical and less fearful. We know what we can do." Imen explained that as soon as she noticed that the PDM was deviating from its democratic and human rights principles, she would be the first one to go to the street. The cab driver warned us and told us about stories of torture and rape of women who had dared to challenge the previous regime. We shouldn't resist, according to him. But sitting in the cab, full of hope, Imen and I could not accept the thought of going back to an oppressive dictatorship.

When the Tunisian uprising had initially gained in momentum and evolved into a revolution at the beginning of 2011, I was living in Holland. As a master's student enrolled in the Conflict Studies and Human Rights program at the University of Utrecht, I had been preparing for fieldwork research. During the last few days of a two-week holiday in Tunisia in December 2010, I had heard the first whispered stories about the events taking place in the southern cities of Tunisia. Very quickly, Al Jazeera and France 24 became the main sources of information about what I believed was a protest movement that would quickly be crushed by the government. At the same time, I thought that the protest was the first sign of an unavoidable and forthcoming struggle for democracy in Tunisia. Stories were told about Leila Ben Ali's preparations for a takeover of her husband's regime. Ben Ali was sick, and should he die, she would take over. I was convinced that the Tunisian people would not accept this and that as soon as this scenario started to unfold, conflict and revolution would become inevitable. Yet what I thought would happen in a few years took place much sooner, right at the beginning of 2011. I changed my research topic to focus on Tunisia. My aim was to try to be of some significance in the unfolding post-revolutionary period, as well as tell the stories of Tunisian people living the revolution. So I traveled to Tunisia.

The Tunisair plane landed at Carthage International Airport in Tunis the afternoon of February 26, 2011. Walking out of the plane, I was struck by an unusual scene that challenged all notions of freedom and liberty: a soldier was standing in front of the airplane, at the level of the cockpit. Walking down the stairs, I realized that next to each plane stood a soldier. Four planes and four soldiers were lined up. The soldiers were armed. I observed the weapon of the nearest one. It looked similar to the toy guns my cousin used to receive on Eid. It seemed harmless. The seeming harmlessness of what was a killing instrument was striking. Had all the weapons used to crush the protests during the uprising looked so harmless? On the videos that had been shared on Facebook, the instruments that caused death had always been invisible, as if reinforcing their power to frighten. Death, on the other hand, had been visible. It struck men in their backs while walking in funeral corteges. It struck in the midst of protests and staged chaos. It was indiscriminate when it hit bystanders. It was terrifying when it hit a man in Tunis sitting on his couch watching TV or when snipers on rooftops targeted civilians going about their everyday activities.

The revolution had transformed a nation from silent observers and objects of oppression into active subjects of change. The main tool of this transformation was social media, mainly Facebook. A thousand kilometers away from Tunisia, seated at my computer in a small student's room in a city in the middle of Holland, I joined in the collective Tunisian patriotic activity of sharing information on Facebook. We shared information on groups of armed men moving from place A to B, information on potential threats, information on organized protest marches, information on organized citizen activities. But I also came across videos of courage. Violence, blood, and fear coexisted with hope, pride, and freedom. Life continued, abnormal as it was. Thousands of Tunisians and I watched and shared a very brief video on Facebook. It was titled, "Marriage in Mahdia despite the curfew." Amidst conflict and insecurity, two families were celebrating life, and a young couple was being united. Tunisians were fighting for life by other means than violence.

And yet, what I realized while I was observing the soldiers and their weapons at the airport, and re-imagining the video-scenes of the revolution, was that more had changed in Tunisia than merely the overthrow of the dictator. The experience of violence had changed everyday life. Normalcy had been newly defined.

Riding in the car from the airport with my brother and sister, we passed the Habib Bourguiba Avenue. I could see the tear gas from miles away, the obvious sign of protest and confrontation taking place in the avenue. The street also bore witness to the fact that change had taken place, and that revolution and change were still in motion.

Those first few hours in Tunis were the beginning of months of intertwining experiences of change and continuity. The reality of revolution, as I lived it, was not fundamental change, as many politicians and academics seemed to believe. If it was, then Tunisia had experienced only a partial revolution. Living in Holland, far from Tunisia, had given me a mythical perception of the revolution. But seeing the soldier standing by the plane had pulled me into reality.

Freedom came with a price: death, blood, violence, and insecurity. The videos I had seen online were digital, but now it was all real.

While the revolution had been a national matter, soon after my arrival in Tunisia, I discovered that political interests, translated into local dynamics, dominated the post-revolutionary period. Pieces of the newly framed reality fell into old, existing patterns. Old conflicts lingered and hidden ones came to the surface. New division lines intertwined with past ones to change yet at the same time continue the socio-political relations and reality of life in a small town such as Hammamet. At the end of February, I attended meetings of the Local Assembly for the Protection of the Revolution and the Association for the Defense of the Revolution. The different ideological backgrounds of these two assemblies, the first Islamist and the second secularist, put them in conflict with each other. I found myself caught in the crossfire.

A friend wrote to me on Facebook explaining that a group of people, who she described as ignorant and dangerous, were trying to gain control over the Association for the Safe-guard of the Medina (ASM). She was not clear on what was going on, and I disliked her stereotypical description of this group of men. So I preferred to stay out of it. That Sunday, I attended the second meeting of the Local Assembly for the Protection of the Revolution. I was early, and the two men sitting next to me were discussing the situation of the ASM. They asked me whether I had heard of it. I said I had but all I had heard was that some dangerous people wanted to become members in order to take part in the election. The men answered that those people were not dangerous and that it was time for these thieves and the Constitutional Democratic Rally (CDR the political party of former dictator Ben Ali) people to be kicked out. I realized that these men were the people my friend was talking about. What nonsense. They were not dangerous. Or was I wrong?

The previous week, during the first meeting of the Local Assembly for the Protection of the Revolution, the attendees were assured that the assembly had no political affiliation and that it was meant as a civilian organization to control the further political and social evolutions. It would represent and incorporate all ideologies, as it was of the people and for the people. I was called to come sit next to the organizers, as I was one of the only two women present. Then the organizers of the meeting announced that the assembly needed some sort of legal framework. Apparently a few of them had already decided upon the identity and rules of the organization and the conditions of membership. No discussion, no debate. They announced that the assembly would be guided by Islamic religious guidelines. The organization wanted to create a platform of critique and control and aimed at spreading religious knowledge and raising the number of *kottab* (Islamic schools) in Hammamet. They also wanted to control the transition to democracy. Also, one condition of membership was being Muslim.

As these rules were read out, I felt my face turn red. I could not believe it. The organizers quickly moved on to the next topic on the agenda. There was no time to discuss. At the end of the meeting when people asked for more information and some expressed their disagreement, they were told that if they agreed then they were welcome and if they didn't then they could leave. The Local Assembly for the Protection of the Revolution, which ought to represent all Tunisians, had been given a specific orientation and identity by a minority through an undemocratic decision-making process. I could not take it. I expressed my disagreement, directed their attention to points I thought were unacceptable, and left with a deep inner struggle. Could I act? What could I do? The following week I tried to assemble a group of people who could join me in contesting the claims and legitimacy of the assembly at their next meeting. But I failed to mobilize people. Hammamet appeared to already have two constituencies for the protection of the revolution: one dominated by secularists and one dominated by Islamists. I simply had to choose a group; I had to choose my side. We had inherited the struggles of the past. The struggle between Islamists and secularists that had taken place in the '70s and '80s, which had been resolved through dictatorial measures, reappeared after the revolution. And we young people had failed to dominate the debate and change it. Instead the ideological and normative differences that were to my generation irrelevant became, in the post-revolution period, sites of contention and conflict. We inherited the words, the descriptions, and the language of hate of our fathers, professors, and peers. This language was increasingly present in political speeches and in local politicized meetings. We were in a crisis of framing. And the organization of socio-political life in the post-revolution period was pressuring us into choosing sides.

In one of the meetings of the Association for the Defense of the Revolution, dominated by secularists, well-known and respected Tunisian movie producers were present to discuss the role arts played in the dictatorial opposition and the role it ought to play in the present construction of democracy. Soon these movie producers expressed their fears about the growing Islamist movement and the growing popularity of political parties they deemed to be danger-ous. A Tunisian version of the Iranian scenario was, to them, an approaching threat. A friend of mine, Mohammed, was present. He was a supporter of the An-Nahda, the moderate Islamist party. He walked away, and I went after him. He explained his anger at the way people like those present in this room were talking about the Nahda. I explained to him that this was fear—fear of censorship on future artistic expressions and fear of a returning dictatorship. These people feared the Nahda. It was the same fear that veiled girls had expressed to me when talking about a possible future secular state that might order them to take off their veils in public spaces, just as Ben Ali had done. The fear was being translated in increasingly intensifying hate speech. When studying conflict, I read about fear, wrote about fear, and witnessed, firsthand and through the testimonies of others, the effects of fear. Violence has to be imagined before it is enacted, and this hate speech was imagined violence. Physical violence was the next step. We had to act. I told Mohammad about the meeting I had organized with a number of other friends and acquaintances. We wanted to denounce hate speech, and we would start with raising awareness. I asked him to join us. He was not sure. It was a lost battle, he said. But he would think about it. And he came.

Our first meeting took place in May 2011. A few weeks later our plan was set. We were going to organize a small conference about hate speech and its presence in Tunisian politics and society. Two human rights activists would be present as well as representatives of all po-litical parties. We intended to confront them and ask them to abide to a moral contract stipulating they would not use hate speech. Mean-while, tension was growing between various members of our group because of the use of hate speech by some. The continuing struggle to change the language and representation of the Other within the members of the group itself, as well as retractions from those who had offered help with the conference, culminated in the annulment of the conference. We failed. In the upcoming months, tension grew between what were now socio-political groups in Tunisia.

Moreover, justice had become the concern of a few. On Sunday, the first of May, 2011, in the center of the city of Hammamet, the fam-ily of Zouheir Souissi and the more than four hundred people who had ticked on Facebook that they would take part in the event were supposed to gather for a protest, demanding justice and the prosecu-tion of the police agent who killed Souissi while he was watching the uprising unfold in Hammamet on the 12th of January. Yet only a few dozen came: political activists, Souissi's family and friends, and few others. We stood there, raised our flags and signs, and watched people pass by, read the boards, and continue on their way. After a while a police car passed by, paused to watch, and drove on as well. Justice had become the concern of a minority and a populist tool in politi-cal discourses, but all the while impunity continued. Politicians often started their speeches with mentions of the martyrs who lost their lives in the revolution and the freedom we enjoyed today because of them. A politician would say that the deaths of the martyrs should not be pointless, and as such we should all vote for his party. But this apparent sincerity was merely a performance, a reflection of the nationalist discourse as it is used worldwide. These were empty words, since almost no politician cared to tackle the charge of impunity, to discuss police reform, justice, or reconciliation. On that Sunday morning, the son of Zouheir Souissi joined the protest. In the midst of a group of friends he cried.

By October 2011, nine months had passed since Ben Ali fled Tunisia. Freedom had been gained, but with time the people had lost faith and grown more pessimistic. Their patience had been put to the test. While politicians sought a way to gain seats in the government at the upcoming elections, food prices rose and unemployment spread wider—yet politicians remained silent. "All they want are the seats," people frequently remarked when talking about politicians. Many added, "We are headed into a wall." Sit-ins by workers at factories gave voice to their social demands but conflicted with their economic needs.

A few days before the elections on October 23, a video was shared on Facebook. An immense picture of Ben Ali was hanging on a wall in Tunis. People passed by, looked at the picture, and wondered what this meant. A group of men approached the picture and decided to take it down. As they did, another statement appeared on the second layer: "Dictatorship can come back, so go vote." It was part of a campaign to raise awareness about the necessity of voting.

Elections took place on Sunday October 23, and Nahda won the elections. That morning, friends and I celebrated the first free, fair, and democratic elections in the history of Tunisia. But in the afternoon we discovered that these first free elections were stained by old undemocratic habits. At voting centers people had been either paid or ordered to vote for such and such party. Some voting centers had been organized in such a way that all its personnel belonged to one political party, and with this particular loss of neutrality came scandalous transgressions of the voting process. On Tuesday, I joined a protest movement in Tunis denouncing the election transgressions and demanding the rule of law.

While I was standing among the protesters, a man passed by and criticized the protest movement. He claimed that we were being paid by the CDR to orchestrate chaos. On Facebook we were described as a group of immoral young people, unbelievers and undemocratic. Yet all we asked for was free and fair elections. All we asked for was justice.

The number of those joining the protests continued to decrease. Those organizing the demonstrations decided that everyday protests should be ended. We needed organization, structure, and a plan. Those who refused to remain silent and merely observe the reinstalling of dictatorship had to decide how best to act. After our rather spontaneous intifada and people's revolution, resistance needed to be organized and remain a people's resistance.

Forming a people's opposition, one that combined the feeling of urgency and the needed patience to organize resistance, was challenging. It became even more challenging when we realized that dictatorship was already in the making, in the political sphere as well as in the everyday. Standing in a bakery, discussing politics with a friend, criticizing Nahda, I was ordered by this friend to shut up when a woman walked in. This woman was a neighbor, and we knew she had voted for Nahda. Old mechanisms of fear were taking a new hold on our social life. Nahda was the now ruling party, and as with the old CDR party, people feared criticizing it. Stories of intimidation and threats followed. Fear was becoming more present. On Facebook people shared stories of female professors being intimidated by their students, who ordered them to start to wear the veil. Others, in other universities, demanded the separation of men and women in class via a curtain. Those who expressed these desires were a minority, yet they symbolized the possibility of a new type of dictatorship and a social change many Tunisians had not wished for.

Two weeks after the election, on a Saturday, I went to Tunis to help friends with a judicial action against the transgressions in the elections. We discussed the events that unfolded and the stories or rumors that were being shared, and I asked their advice on what should be done. One friend, Mahdi, argued that we should try to organize one big protest. Yet, he explained, fights and disagreements were beginning to occur within certain groups trying to form a people's opposition movement. Organization was going to be a challenge: "We are all the sons of Ben Ali. We are all little dictators in our own worlds, our own regimes. We believe we have the right to tell people what to say and what not to. Becoming democrats, real ones, will be the only way to beat this system. Otherwise, we are only replacing the old system with the same system but new power holders, ones that will reproduce the dictatorship in more or less extreme ways. But it always remains a dictatorship." Later another friend, Sami, described our struggle: "Yasmin, we are defying power—social and political. We are now moving against the current."

He was right. The revolution was the outburst of an anti-movement, but then the storm calmed down and normalcy took over again. The revolution became part of the system instead of remaining a power outside of it that could defy, challenge, and ultimately change it. Politicians took over. Old discourses ignited from within the old corrupt system framed the everyday, and in the name of our revolution, we Tunisians were now protecting what, months ago, we were fighting.

Yet those who were now standing up again were re-igniting the fire of revolution. We were fighting against the system. The positive aspect of what could be otherwise interpreted as a sad end is that those who are fighting the corrupt system are back at the margins, where every revolution starts.

# Egypt to Libya: Arab Solidarity 2.0

## by Adel Abdel Ghafar

**ADEL ABDEL GHAFAR** was in Tahrir Square from January 25, 2011 (day 1 of the Egyptian revolution) until the fall of Hosni Mubarak. While there, he served as a medical supplies logistics volunteer. He was also a volunteer on the first Egyptian medical convoy to enter Benghazi during the Libyan conflict. Adel is currently a doctoral student at Australian National University and is working on his thesis, titled "A Political Economy of the 2011 Egyptian Uprising." He has written for *Foreign Affairs*, and Al Jazeera English and has appeared on Australian TV to commentate on Egyptian politics.

Before pursing an academic career, Adel worked in the banking industry. He holds both a master's degree in Middle Eastern Studies and a combined master's in International Business and Commerce with a focus on Government and International Business from the University of Sydney. He also holds a bachelor's degree in commerce from Cairo University. Follow him on twitter @dooolism.

Place: Martyrs' Square, Downtown Benghazi

Date: February 28th, 2011 (around 5:00 PM)

The celebratory shots of AK-47s are all around me. Benghazi has just been liberated, and the people are rejoicing in the aptly renamed Martyrs'

Square. I survey the scene: men with bloodied combat fatigues together with their families, children, all ecstatic: after forty-two years, they are finally free from the Colonel's rule.

I walk through the crowd with an Egyptian flag draped over me. People stop me, asking, "Are you Egyptian? Are you part of the medical convoy?" And whenever I answer "Yes," they hug me; some cry, others take pictures with me. Their gratitude is humbling. I feel like a modern-day Arab Che Guevara, even though all I have done is a simple act of solidarity—one that involved entering a war zone.

## Taking Action

The previous week, I had been sitting in my home in Cairo watching Al Jazeera Arabic. The images coming out of Libya were harrowing. Libyans, inspired by events in Tunisia and Egypt, started demanding their freedom from Moammar Gadhafi. Not one exactly known for his compromising skills, Gadhafi responded by unleashing his forces on the general population. From Benghazi to Tripoli, Ras Lanuf to Ajdabya, *akh al-qa'id*, "brother leader," as he was known in Egypt, responded to the unrest by attempting to crush it violently, bloodily, and without mercy.

Only days earlier, we had dislodged our own tyrant, Hosni Mubarak. In eighteen days, faced with millions of protesting Egyptians, his rule had crumbled. I was there on day one, January 25, in the first wave of protests, and I remained there until the end. Emboldened by the downfall of Ben Ali in Tunisia, and long suffering from political, economic, and social injustices, the Egyptian people had said simply: no more.

To me, life in Cairo during the first few months of 2011 felt like the Cairo of the 1950s during the height of pan-Arabism. As an avid reader of Arab history and politics, perhaps I had an over-romanticized view of that period, but that didn't stop me from viewing this period in Egypt's history with a sense of melancholic awe. Some of the Arab world's most inspiring and heroic moments had occurred back in the 1950s, from the nationalization of the Suez Canal and Cairo's hosting of the Free Algeria movement offices to the Voice of the Arabs radio station, broadcasting from the Arab Maghreb to the Gulf, urging the Arab peoples to rise against their local and foreign oppressors. All these historical moments came to my mind when the 1950s patriotic and pan-Arabist song "Watani Habibi" (My beloved homeland) was played in Tahrir the night Mubarak fell, as Palestinian, Syrian, and Yemeni flags flew around us.

It was clear that we were living through historical times, no less pivotal than the revolutionary 1950s. My own experience was incredible, transforming me in eighteen days from a thirty-one-year-old businessman to a revolutionary demonstrator, facing riot police, and becoming a connoisseur of different types of tear gas. After Mubarak fell, my friends and I, along with millions of other Egyptians, celebrated our new freedom and truly felt that we were a moving force of history.

As I watched Al Jazeera at home that day, I knew Gadhafi couldn't get away with crushing his own people. Wedged between Egypt and Tunisia, who had just dislodged their autocratic leaders, Libya seemed ready to follow suit.

My friends and I, emboldened by our revolution, decided to take a direct approach to helping. Libya was not just another Arab country going through an uprising. The cultural, historical, economic, and social ties between Egypt and Libya run deep. Watching the slaughter of Libyan civilians on TV was like watching our own families being murdered. Helping was not optional. It was an obligation. In addition to that, Libya was right next door, so we felt that we should act directly.

I heard about an anti-Gadhafi rally to be held in the posh Cairo neighborhood of Zamalek, so I headed there to find about a hundred people, a mixture of Libyan expats and Egyptians, supporting the Libyan uprising. They carried posters with photos of the Libyans who had died during the uprising, victims of Gadhafi's brutal crackdown. Chanting *yasqot yasqot al-Gadhafi*! (Down, down with Gadhafi!), the demonstrators attracted more and more followers. A window in the embassy building opened, and it was clear that one of the embassy staff was watching us. The crowd jeered at him, and he smiled nonchalantly. To me, that man exemplified the Gadhafi regime's attitude towards his people, the "divine right of kings"[1] to rule and to crush all opposition.

My friends and I discussed what we could do to help the Libyan people. Someone mentioned that Benghazi's hospitals were in desperate need of medical supplies. Perhaps we could collect funds and buy the necessary medical supplies, then drive with the supplies to Libya. My friend Tarek Shalaby and I decided to launch a social media campaign via Twitter and Facebook and via our personal networks raise funds for the supplies. A Libyan friend put me in touch with a contact in Libya, who gave us a list of desperately needed medical supplies. In two days, we were able to gather approximately 60,000 EGP (10,000 USD) worth of medical aid—not a massive amount by global standards, but quite a decent one for a couple of youths to collect in two days' time using social media.

## The People's Crescent

Place: Salloum: The border town between Egypt and Libya

Date: February 24, 2011

Tarek, two other friends, and I meet in downtown Cairo on the day of departure. We fill the two cars with supplies and simply head to the border. In retrospect, this wasn't the best laid plan. Our intention is to drive to the border-crossing point at Salloum and give the supplies to any medical convoy crossing into the country. At this point, Libya is officially a war zone, and my friends and I are heading directly towards it.

---

1. The Divine Right of Kings is a doctrine of political legitimacy used by European Monarchs several centuries ago. It stipulates that a monarch is subject to no earthly authority, deriving his right to rule over his subjects directly from God. It was abandoned in Europe by the 17th and 18th century, but sadly it still exists in different forms it the Arab World. Certain Amirs, Sultans, Kings and Presidents rule as tyrants over their people, hopefully not for long.

Approaching Salloum, we can feel and smell the chaos of war—hundreds of thousands of migrant workers, Egyptians, Africans, and East Asians all attempting to escape the combat in Libya. As we near, we see an endless line of small buses transporting the lucky ones to Cairo and beyond. The unlucky ones, of which there are thousands, are stranded at the border in no-man's land. African and Asian workers with no Egyptian visas are not allowed entry unless collected by their embassies. Some have been stranded for days, and the horrid conditions are apparent.

Approaching closer, I can see a group of Filipino workers resting on the ground, some sleeping, some begging for food. I glance inside our car at all our well-stocked snacks, and I feel ashamed. We park the car outside the border-crossing center and bring out a bag of food. The Filipino refugees scramble and reach out to receive it. I feel like a UNHCR aid worker giving out food in a refugee camp. We give out all of our food supplies, and they dig in gratefully. We speak to them in English; they tell us they have been stranded here for days, and their embassies have yet to collect them. This is what misery looks like up close and personal, but we have yet to see the even greater misery awaiting us on the other side of the border.

The officers at border control naturally refuse our request to cross the border and deliver the supplies inside Libya. I have a conversation with a mustachioed, burly Egyptian army officer:

Officer: Are you a doctor?

Me: No.

Officer: Are you an aid worker?

Me: No.

Officer: Then what the hell are you doing here? This is a refugee disaster area! The other side of the border is a warzone! Are you crazy trying to cross? The answer is NO'

Me (calmly): We are just trying to help our fellow Libyans. It's our duty, as we toppled our tyrant, to help them topple theirs.

The officer mutters, "These Tahrir youth, revolution has messed with their heads," and walks off.

Now we are in a bit of a dilemma. We do not want to leave thousands of pounds of medical supplies on the side of the road for some convoy entering Libya to hopefully pick up, yet there is no one in sight to hand the supplies to. It's been a long day (it is about 3 AM), and we decide to break for the night. We drive around the border town of Salloum to find a hostel to sleep in, but all are full, mostly with foreign journalists and cameramen covering the refugee situation. We finally find a hostel manager who allows us to use his bathroom, and we sleep in our cars in the parking lot outside.

After a most uncomfortable night of sleep, we wake up to our yet unsolved dilemma. We decide to drive close to the border, perhaps to find some inspiration. By chance, I see a man talking on a satellite phone. I hear him speaking in Arabic with a Libyan accent. Thinking this might be an opportunity to solve our dilemma, I approach him and introduce myself. His name is Usama, and he is a Libyan businessman working in Dubai who has left his work and family to come help in any way he can. He has contacts inside Libya and is sending convoys and supplies into Libya. Jackpot.

We show him our supplies. He says he can help us deliver them with a convoy that is arriving shortly. We chain smoke and wait. The convoy arrives, and it's filled with Egyptian doctors and male nurse volunteers, including several doctors who had served at the field clinics in Tahrir Square treating protestors. The doctor in charge of the convoy says he is happy to take the supplies in but he could not get us in even if he wanted to because border control is tight. Nonetheless, we decide to make a legitimate attempt to enter Libya.

We head to the officer in charge, who flatly informs us that we're not crossing without proper authorization. We try sweet-talking, begging, everything, but he doesn't budge. We reconcile ourselves that this is the end of the expedition, and at least the supplies will be delivered. Then Tarek comes up with a simple yet brilliant idea: why not just walk calmly towards passport control, submit our IDs, and try to walk in?

What ensues is the most absurd hilarity we would encounter on this trip. We walk calmly to the passport control booth.

Me: We want to get into Libya, here are our documents.

Chain-smoking border officer: Show me your IDs.

He looks at them and asks: Are you part of a convoy?

Tarek (lying, but trying to keep a straight face): Yes.

Officer: Which convoy?

We look at each other, puzzled; we were doing so well, but no one thought to come up with a name. Suddenly, it hits me; I make up a name and blurt it out to the officer: Al-Hilal Ash-Sha'abi (the people's crescent). In Egypt, the Red Crescent is the most well-known aid organization, and somehow in the labyrinth of my head I have come up with this gem. It works.

The officer looks at me, writes our names on paper with the header "The People's Crescent." Then he says: "Okay, I have to run this by my supervisor."

We are in shock; the supervisor had already refused us, so if he hears of our renewed attempt, he might even accuse us of fraud. In desperation, Tarek says the magic words: *Matkhafsh, yeb'alak ash-shay*, which translates literally to: "Don't worry, you will have your tea." It's effectively the Egyptian code phrase for "We will grease your pocket with a bribe." We slip him a 100 EGP (16.5 USD) note between the papers, and his face lights up.

"No problem," he says. "Let me get this stamped for you." He goes, comes back, gives us our IDs, and says, "The People's Crescent convoy is good to go. Good luck, gentlemen."

We cross the booth and are officially in no man's land. The supplies are loaded onto the Egyptian convoy's buses. Their doctor asks us to join them; he says he needs volunteers. We drive across the border, and are greeted by Libyan revolutionaries holding AK-47s. We get out of the car and they hug us, salute us. One fighter, smiling, says to me: "Welcome to free Libya."

## Into a War Zone

Place: Tobruk

Date: February 25, 2011

Driving in two buses and escorted by Libyan revolutionaries, we head to Tobruk, our first stop, where we spend the night. The next day, we are briefed by the Libyans that we are heading to Benghazi. They explain to us that Benghazi has only recently been liberated, and there are sporadic gun battles across the city by Gadhafi loyalists, but we shouldn't worry as the city is mostly under control.

In the bus, we get to know the Egyptian doctors and nurses, many of whom had served in the Tahrir field clinics during the Egyptian revolution. There are many courageous people, one of whom still strikes me as particularly political and revolutionary, especially at such a young age. Abdel Karim is a nineteen-year-old student and Tahrir volunteer who joined this convoy from Cairo.

(Months after our journey into Libya, Abdel Khalek was captured by Gadhafi's forces near Ras Lanuf, where he was working in a field clinic set up by the Egyptian doctors. He was transported to Tripoli, made to wear military fatigues, and tortured, after which he was forced to confess on Libyan state TV to being a terrorist and one of the instigators of the uprising in Libya. He was tortured throughout the Libya conflict, but luckily he was kept alive and released afterwards—yet another unsung hero of the Arab revolutions.)

Spirits are high as our bus enters Benghazi. We occasionally break into songs and chants made famous in Tahrir, as well as *Misr wa Libya, eed wahda*! (Egypt and Libya are one hand). On the way, we stop for a break at a café and supermarket. I pick up some juice and biscuits and head to the counter to pay with Libyan currency I had exchanged at the border. When I ask the shopkeeper how much I owe, he detects my Egyptian accent, looks outside to see the bus and people wearing their doctor's garb, and asks me if I'm part of that convoy. When I tell him we're part of an Egyptian volunteer convoy heading to Benghazi to deliver aid and set up field clinics, he smiles broadly and says that he cannot accept my money. *Allah ma'ak*, he tells me—God be with you.

This happens over and over throughout the trip. Every time I attempt to pay for food, drink, or accommodation, the Libyans refuse our money, their small gesture of thanks for the convoy. To me it is a profound moment of Arab solidarity in action; complete strangers from across borders caring and helping each other as fellow Arabs locked in conflict with our own repressive and brutal despots. I am excited and overwhelmed by their gratitude and indeed proud to do my part, however small the contribution may be.

We enter Benghazi amid the bursts of AK-47 gunfire. Blackened carcasses of buildings continue to smolder with smoke, their walls filled with shrapnel. Anti-Gadhafi graffiti is scribbled, apparently hurriedly and furiously, on many of the walls. The arid stench of smoke and gunfire surrounds us; the traces of the city's liberation are still very fresh. We could be in Gaza or Fallujah under attack: indeed the city has the classic hallmarks of a resisting town, and it is clear that a lot of people have fought and died here.

We arrive at Benghazi Central Hospital and disembark to an incredible scene. The Libyan fighters have gathered in an impromptu guard of honor to receive us, and as we pass by them, they fire their AK-47s in celebration and welcome, a slightly disconcerting welcome. Together, we chant: *Misr wa Libya, eed wahda!* over and over again.

Once inside the hospital, we are confronted by the true magnitude of carnage that the brave people of Benghazi have suffered over the past ten days. It is a horrific scene, people screaming in their beds, some with blown off limbs, others with deep gunshot and shrapnel wounds, as well as many burn victims. My blood is boiling; it's one thing to see carnage on TV, it's another to witness it up close and personal. It hits me then how easy we Egyptians had it toppling Mubarak, with less than eight hundred casualties during the eighteen days of uprising. Standing here in the hospital, I know the numbers in Libya will be ten times higher; Madman Gadhafi has unleashed hell on his own people to hold onto power, and the evidence is all around us.

We spend the next few days in this hospital and another nearby clinic in downtown Benghazi helping the doctors and speaking to the patients. We are shown large .50 caliber bullets made for anti-tank usage, which we are told were being used on civilians. The stories the doctors and patients tell us are both harrowing and in-spiring. Many had taken up arms after Mubarak was toppled, and Benghazi and Tobrouk had risen against Gadhafi mid-February. There were a few days of relatively peaceful protests, and then on February 17, Gadhafi's forces opened fire on the protesters, killing twenty-four. But still, the people persisted in rising up against him. We spend our days in the hospital listening to stories and deliver-ing our cargo of medical aid to the clinics. One day, my friends and I decide to go see Martyrs' Square. I had brought an Egyptian flag with me to Libya, so I tie it around my neck and head to the square.

## Arab Solidarity 2.0

Place: Martyrs' Square, Benghazi

Date: February 26, 2011

As I walk around Martyr's Square, it feels exactly like Tahrir Square after Mubarak had been toppled on February 11. I meet the grim but smiling faces of exhausted, triumphant, and fiercely patriotic people who have risen up to resist a ruthless and merciless dictator. Revo-lutionary and patriotic songs blare through loud speakers, and cars full of fighters from different neighborhoods stream into the square, firing their AK-47s in the air in celebration. The city is being purged of all Gadhafi loyalists; some are still in hiding and will continue to cause problems even after we leave. But for now, it is time to celebrate.

Benghazi's courthouse is the center of the crowd's congregation and celebration. Its walls are covered with murals and hundreds of photos of the city's fallen heroes. Each photo carries a date of birth and a date of death. Too many young Libyans have died, some during the past few days of conflict, others years before in other attempted uprisings that Gadhafi had brutally squashed. Until now, their families have been unable to grieve and show their images in public as testament to the regime's atrocities. Only now can their memories be honored.

As I walk around draped in my Egyptian flag, many people stop me to congratulate me on the Egyptians' toppling Mubarak. Others thank me and the Egyptian people for inspiring them to rise up against Gadhafi. Their gratitude is both overwhelming and humbling. To them, my presence in their square is a sign of Arab solidarity, something they never really experienced throughout the decades of being isolated from the world, vilified, and trapped in this oppressive dictatorship. It also dawns on me just how much of an impact Egypt's revolution has had on Libya, the Middle East, and indeed the world.

The Egyptian doctors set up a medical tent in solidarity with the Libyans in the square. Flags of Egypt, New Libya (the 1951 flag that was re-adopted after the 2011 uprising), and Palestine fly at the mast of the tent, a truly beautiful sight to see amidst this spirit of triumphant liberation. Locals line up to shake hands with the Egyptian convoy and have photos taken with them, all of whom feel incredibly humbled.

Over the next few days, I spend my time between the hospital and Martyrs' Square, absorbing the atmosphere, talking to people, documenting their stories, and taking photographs. Mobile phone networks are working in Benghazi, but the Internet is cut, so I ask a friend back home in Egypt to access my Twitter account and send out tweets on my behalf. Through my text messages to him, I recount the incredible scenes of the square and the people.

On the last day of our visit, our Libyan friends suggest we make a trip to Gadhafi's compound in central Benghazi, the scene of the bloodiest battles before the city was liberated. Of course we say yes.

## "I Am in Gadhafi's Bathroom #Surreal"

Place: Gadhafi's palace

Date: March 1, 2011

As we near Gadhafi's compound, it's evident from the surrounding structures that this area has seen some of the heaviest fighting. Burnt-out buildings once filled with people now carry the hallmarks of shrapnel and battle. The first thing we see as we enter the compound are the mangled remains of its once fortified gate. The gate was once a five-meter-wide, two-meter-high structure manned by gun towers on each side.

Mohammed, our Libyan guide, tells us that in the days of battle in Benghazi, Gadhafi loyalists eventually retreated to this fortified compound, called Al Kateeba, meaning "the squad" in Arabic. The revolutionaries had tried to breach it several times, but the gate was too thick to break through. They decided that the only solution was a suicide mission to blow the gate apart. Many revolutionaries put their name forward to have this honor, and ultimately Mahdy Zeyo, a forty-nine-year old bespectacled man, was chosen.

Mahdy was an unlikely hero. A father of two girls with diabetes, he worked at the state-run oil company. But something inside of him snapped as he watched the dead bodies of his neighbors pile up, and he decided to do something about it. He said good-bye to his daughters and wife, and headed out on the morning of February 20. He filled his car, a black Kia, with explosives, added butane gas canisters in the trunk, laced the whole car with plastic explosives, and drove off. He drove it at high speed right into the fortified gate, blowing up the car and the gate and losing his life instantly.[2] The revolutionaries streamed through the smoldering walls into the compound, and fought door to door against the loyalists until the whole area was

---

2. Mahdy Zeyo is now revered in Benghazi. His story was covered by the *Washington Post*, *New York Times* and *The Guardian* globally. A short documentary titled 'We Win, or We Die(Slam Dance Cut)' on You Tube explains the events of that day, and gives some background on Zeyo.

cleared. On the walls of the compound, beside the mangled remains of the green gate, two lists are written in black paint: One is *Qaa'emat al omalaa* (the list of traitors) with the names of Gadhafi's henchmen who had fought inside this compound. The other list, a much larger one, is called *Qaa'emat ash-shuhadaa* (list of martyrs) and has the names of all the freedom fighters that had died storming this compound. I count more than two hundred names. Being present on the site of such devastation and loss of life is both surreal and disquieting; again I'm reminded of how lucky we Egyptians had been in comparison, with a much lower number of martyr deaths.

Inside the compound, we visit Gadhafi's residence. What was once an opulent villa is now a blackened structure with only its walls standing. Libyan families have poured into the area, revolutionary tourists fascinated by this once enigmatic and off-limits building. The walls of the villa are laced with anti-Gadhafi graffiti. The villa itself has an escape hatch that leads through an underground tunnel to the outside. No doubt this was used by some of the loyalists to escape when they lost control of the compound.

I come across the master bedroom, which has an en suite bathroom. I go in. I am inside this bathroom that Gadhafi must have used. Most of the room's items have been ransacked and looted, but the toilet and washbasin are still intact. The surreal absurdity of the situation hits me, and I SMS my friend to send a tweet that is re-tweeted around the world: "I am in Gadhafi's Bathroom #surreal." My twitter followers increase by about four hundred after this tweet. That's social media for you.

Standing in front of the toilet, I wonder what exactly I'm doing here. I'm not a rebel or even a Libyan. I'm not a reporter, a doctor, or a human rights worker. In fact, I have absolutely no legitimate grounds to be here inside Gadhafi's bathroom. But here I am, witnessing the slow but unstoppable turning of the tides that, nine months later, would end with the liberation of Tripoli and the death of the Libyan despot.

However, today is March 1, and as of today, Gadhafi may think that he can still retake Benghazi and this compound. And yet it's not him but me who is standing in his bathroom. I relish the thought that this somehow represents a personal victory for me over Gadhafi. Right there and then, I know that his days are numbered.

We continue our tour of the compound. We head next to the conference chambers, where world leaders like Berlusconi and Mubarak had met with Gadhafi. Now all traces of opulence are gone, and only charred debris remains. As more curious Libyans stream in, Mohammed suggests we go visit the "special chamber."

We understand that "special chamber" is code for the torture chamber, where Libyan dissidents were left to rot. We take a hidden stairway to the underground chamber. It's a very eerie, dimly lit labyrinth, where some chains and other "tools of the trade" remain despite the ransacking. Hooks dangle from the ceiling, where people were probably hanged while being electrocuted. The sight nauseates me; in fact, standing in the room is intimidating, as I can only imagine the propensity of horror inflicted on innocent civilians in this very room. It's beyond me how one man can torture and massacre his fellow countrymen, his brothers, his neighbors, all for the sake of a decaying regime. Yet Gadhafi and his henchmen's time has come. Someone has written on the torture chamber's wall "We have come for you, Gadhafi, you dog," and signed it "the grandsons of Omar al Mukhtar."[3]

Once out of the compound, it's time for us to head home. We've delivered our goods, met incredibly brave people, and seen the remains of a war zone. Now reality calls, as do our bewildered and worried families in Cairo.

We say good-bye to the convoy doctors and our new Libyan friends. The Egyptian convoy will head further west to Ajdabiya and

---

3. Omar al Mukhtar is the father of Libyan resistance to colonialism. Born in 1862, from 1912 he actively lead Libyan resistance against the Italian colonialists for 20 years. He was captured and executed by the Italians in 1931, and is still revered by all Libyans to this date.

Ras Lanuf, areas not yet liberated and still undergoing fighting, and finally to Tripoli. Our small act of solidarity doesn't compare to the sheer bravery of these doctors, who continue to volunteer throughout the conflict, setting up field clinics right in the midst of battle scenes.

## Misr wa Libya eed wahda!
## (Egypt and Libya Are One Hand!)

When I'm an old man, I hope to look back upon 2011 and remember it as a definitive year of my life, when I was part of events of much historical significance and patriotic importance to me and millions of Arabs. The camaraderie with the Libyan revolutionaries and the everyday Libyans was profound. The chants Egyptians and Libyans chanted together in Benghazi, such as Misr wa Libya eed wahda! will forever resonate in my mind with pride.

Even though the times have changed since the heyday of Arab nationalism, it's clear that Arab solidarity is alive and well—perhaps not between the presidents, emirs and kings, but certainly between the everyday Arab people. The saying goes, "If America sneezes, the world catches a cold." Perhaps one day we will say, "If Egypt is liberated, the whole Arab world will follow suit."

# I Do Not Read History, I Write it

## by Achref Aouadi

Coming from a family of political activists, **ACHREF AOUADI** has pursued blogging and cyber activism from a young age. In 2009, he was selected to take part in a leadership program in the University of Minnesota, after which he founded the Student-To-Student university club, the first English-speaking university club in Tunisia, which was focused on advocacy and community service. After the Tunisian revolution, Achref founded I WATCH, a Tunisian watchdog organization working on transparency, good governance, and anti-corruption. I WATCH conducted the largest domestic observation mission in Tunisia's last elections.

Achref graduated from the International Anti-Corruption Academy, a pioneering institution that aims to overcome shortcomings in knowledge and practice in the field of anti-corruption. He was chosen by the United Nations to represent the Tunisian civil society in the United Nations Anti-Corruption Convention in 2011 and was also elected founding president of the Lions Club Tunis Pioneers. During the Libyan war, Achref served on the Tunisian-Libyan border, helping rescue and provide aid to over 500,000 people seeking refuge in his country. He is currently pursuing a master's degree in cross-cultural studies.

We talk about the Tunisian revolution as if it started on December 17, 2010, the day when Mohamed Bouazizi set himself on fire, or else on the fateful day January 14, 2011, when Ben Ali fled Tunisia. But the real flames of the revolution were kindled in 2008 by the youth of Rdayef in the Mine Region. The fight for dignity started then and there. Why am I talking about this? I want to tell those who underestimate the power of social media and cyber activists: dictators are, in fact, aware of such a hidden power. In 2008, when the uprising started in Rdayef, a town in the governorate of Gafsa, the government censored Facebook for more than three months, and also censored YouTube, Flicker, and Dailymotion. The government perceived the effect and importance of social media before the people did.

Drawing a comparison between the Tunisian uprisings of 2008 and 2011, one wonders why the former failed while the latter moved from a mere uprising to a revolution that paved the way for many other Arab revolutions. What is the difference between the two? In 2008, social media sites were censored. In 2011, social media was present. In Egypt, one of former Egyptian President Mubarak's first responses to the protests in his country was to shut down Internet access because he knew its huge impact and because he saw what social media and bloggers had accomplished in Tunisia.

My life as a blogger began in 2009. Do you know what it means to live in a country and to not know what is going on in the southern part of it? Do you know what it is like to be in the same country where your brothers and sisters are suffering and not be able to share their pain? One day in 2009 when I opened YouTube and searched for "Rdayef," I felt a bitter feeling come over me. At that time I was participating in an exchange program in the United States. I was one among a group of twenty-three North African students, coming from Egypt, Libya, Tunisia, Algeria, and Morocco, who showed outstanding leadership achievements and skills.

That night I could not really sleep—the videos of the people in Gafsa kept haunting my mind. The videos showed torture. They showed the merciless killing of poor people asking for their right to live. They showed young men and women claiming their right to work. I was very bewildered: how could we be that cruel to one another? But what really made me feel uncomfortable was that I was duped. I was made a fool of. I believed stupidly what the government said about democracy, that the people in this area, the Mine Region, were happy with the government's "wise" policies. In Tunisia, "the government" automatically meant "the President." And according to an official statement by the government, those "who were making trouble" were "a minority and a limited group of mercenaries" paid by "foreign countries jealous of Tunisia who envy us for the prosperity we live in." It was disappointing to discover after all these years just how naïve I was.

The next day, feeling deeply frustrated, I searched for a way to release all the anger that was boiling inside me. I was looking for a way to restore myself and take all the videos I had seen off my mind. Penetrating questions replaced those images: Was I guilty of not paying attention to my own people and country? How can people from the same country, sharing the same language, religion, origin, and dreams, inflict such atrocities on one another? I could not really find a way to regain peace. This was my internal struggle while in the middle of this exchange trip.

During the trip, a journalist from the *Minnesota Daily* approached our group and started asking us questions about our respective countries and cultures, and our impressions about the United States. When she questioned me, I began talking about all the beautiful things associated with my country and its people. Then I stopped. Is this really what the world should know about my country at this moment in history? They can Google its beautiful beaches and palm trees if they want. But people should know that behind the mask of tolerance and democracy that the government has promoted there is an established dictatorship. Behind the five-star hotels there are the "for bread only"[1] people. Behind the sunset there is no hope. My peers go to the beach not to swim but to emigrate to Europe in the middle of the night. Between the lines of the government's pompous slogans exists a bitter tragedy.

I cannot remember what I told the reporter. The only thing I do remember was her asking me, "Can we meet tomorrow and discuss it further?" I spent another night sleepless, but this time it was not because of my solidarity with the people in the South, or even because of the videos of torture I had viewed on Facebook. I was afraid—yes, I was afraid. Only one question kept plaguing my mind: "What kind of trouble have I gotten myself into?" Why did I feel the need to publicly voice my criticism about the government and speak out about the assets they had stolen? The night was long. I had enough time to imagine all the different scenarios that could happen to me for publicly speaking out. None of them had a happy ending. They all ended in the Ministry of Interior, the "temple of human rights," as activists sarcastically referred to it. Should I call the journalist and apologize? Should I pretend I was ill? I was sure I would be in serious trouble for speaking out about the government. I started reciting old Arab war poetry and verses of the Qur'an just to feel tranquil and help put me to sleep.

Daylight finally came. My fear started to subside, replaced by nervousness. The countdown started: eight hours until the meeting. I felt every single second pass, trying in vain to figure out a way to apologize politely and save face.

In such moments you always need some moral support, somebody close to your heart to calm you down and hear your concerns. I needed to talk to my family and hear their support. I needed to hear my father tell me that I had made the right choice and that I should go. But instead, when I phoned them, they started firing an arsenal of

---

1. The name of a Moroccan book famous for depicting the poverty of the marginalized classes.

insults at me. And their concerns that masqueraded as insults were not completely unfounded. They were afraid for their son but also for themselves. Their conclusion: do not meet with the journalist.

Such a reaction did not surprise me, especially from my father, the old politician who had spent eight years in exile. I understood. He was playing the role of a father concerned with protecting his son, and he did not want to see the tragedy he had experienced happen to me. A former member of the Tunisian communist party, my father was sentenced to five years in prison, but instead spent eight years in exile, returning to Tunisia after receiving a presidential pardon.

Regardless of the real and present danger, I decided to go ahead and meet with the journalist, and I ended up telling her more than I had imagined I would.

I guess I was discovering myself. In doing so, I discovered that my frustration with my government was not provoked only by the YouTube videos I had recently watched but had begun much earlier. My frustration dated back to the first time I ever lowered my voice to talk about the president. I instantly started remembering all those moments of political programming: the moment you are asked to change the topic every time you attempt to tackle a political issue, the moment you are taught not to trust your neighbor because you suspect him of being a secret agent, the moment you stop going to the mosque lest you face the same brutal fate as the Islamists did in the beginning of the 1990s. The interview was over and soon, the story titled "Tunisian Visitor Shares Philosophies, Views of the U.S." was published.

After returning to Tunisia, I felt as if I was no longer the same person, or at least I could not be the same person any more. Then, I created "awadinho.10." This name became my keyword. It became the name of my email, my Facebook account, and most important, my blog. I decided to create my own blog.

Yes, I am a blogger. It takes a particular sentiment to produce something for public consumption—embracing the fact that that my ideas would no longer remain imprisoned within the very limited space of my brain and that "the whole world" would read them.

When you become a new blogger, you think you are the best at what you do. You operate under the impression that you are incredibly unique, that you can see things that nobody else has managed to see and thus have a deeper understanding of even trivial things. You start talking about your blog everywhere you go, to practically everyone you meet. You do not miss the opportunity to insert into conversation a story about how great your blog is. You eagerly anticipate every part of the blogging process: you write, you publish, you convince yourself that "the whole world will read my ideas," and you wait for feedback, for the "whole world" to respond.

Then, when the "whole world" does not respond, you start feeling sorry for the world that is missing out on your genius. You have been blogging for a while and the world is still not yet blessed with your ideas, you, the one-of-a-kind blogger. Yes, it takes you several months to realize that few people care about your ideas, that this "whole world" you conceive of does not exceed ten visitors a day—although this could also be because the "whole world" is being blocked from your blog by the dreaded ERROR 404.

In Tunisia, 404 stood for censorship. Every time one would type the name of a political website or try to search for data forbidden to the general public, the famous "ERROR 404" would appear on the screen, announcing that "big brother" had caught you red-handed. In response, a group of young cyber activists, to whom I did not belong but whom I admired, launched an anti-censorship campaign under the name "Salah 404." Salah is an imaginary character invented to describe censorship. If a Tunisian used the word "Salah," he or she would probably be referring to internet censorship. Their campaign quickly ended, though, as any other anti-government activity usually does, with the same outcome: police troops chasing the activists.

In the weeks that followed this event, I was inspired by the courage of so many active bloggers, and by Salah 404's determination and courage. Cyber activists risking their lives provided a turning point for my own life. It made me realize that activism should not be only cyber- or Internet-based. Work on the field and teamwork were the secret to successful transformative change. The death in 2010 of Khaled Said, a blogger beaten to death in public by two Egyptian police officers while he was in a cyber café, influenced my writings greatly; I became more daring, dire, direct, and sincere. I realized that living in Tunisia and living in Egypt meant the same thing: that being a young man here or there was not that different. It was the same dictatorship, the same struggle for dignity and for FREEDOM.

A couple of months later, my article in the *Minnesota Daily* was published. It was supposed to be a great achievement for me, especially since it was published on the paper's front page. But that was not the case when I lived in a country with such a government and had such a worried and paranoid family. The article became the biggest "sin" my family had ever dealt with. After the article's publication, I realized that I was having difficulty accessing my blog. As the November 2009 elections neared, my blog generated problems. To the visitors, the problems were mainly electronic: receiving viruses, very slow access, unfound pages, and so on. A friend of mine whose father worked at the Ministry of Interior told me that the government had an eye on me. My father's political past also complicated things. It was a hard period for me.

One night when I was looking for my article on Google, I saw my name associated with another article. A new article had been published in the Minnesota Daily, one that mysteriously implied that I was afraid and had asked the editor to remove my name from the initial article. I was upset. This article made me look like a capricious kid, one who does not know what he wants. It looked as if sometimes I wanted to criticize the government and then, other times, I wavered because I was afraid. Who told them that I was afraid or that I wanted them to remove my name from the first article? When I looked up the first article, I found that they dropped my family name and added a new whole introduction that addressed my alleged "concerns":

Editor's note: The last name of the main subject of this story, Ashref, and his family members has been removed from this story since its original publication. The source became concerned of the negative implications that may come from speaking critically of the Tunisian government and its programs upon his return to his home country.

The first thought that jumped into my mind was the reaction of all those who visited my blog. Some of them had even called me a hero (I know I am not, I know that they are exaggerating, but I liked it). I wondered what this mysterious revision would communicate to my blog readers: what kind of "hero" is afraid of having his family name published in an article? I was really afraid this time, not of the government but of my blog visitors. I was afraid of losing my credibility in their eyes.

I was not afraid of the prospect of violence at the hands of government, even though this was very likely. I just did not want to be a disappointment to the Tunisian people who believed in me. I did not want to be that "disappointment" that we in the Arab world had grown so accustomed to expecting in our leaders. Each time we trusted someone or believed in him, he disappointed us. Each time we believed in the opposition's message and promises to us, we soon discovered that they only cared about their own interests. Each time we trusted the so-called intelligentsia we discovered that they pandered to instead of opposed the government. Even in this most recent revolution the opposition disappointed us. The army gave up on us after the revolution, as they did in Egypt. The army became the first enemy of the youth and the Tunisian people, the intellectual elite sided with the regimes, and the artists turned a blind eye to our suffering. I did not want to be the latest disappointment.

The idea of my visitors reading that introduction killed me. It made me disrespect myself to such an extent that I wanted to cut off my own flesh. I wanted to belong to a new body, the body of a real revolutionary. I wished I could be an "idea" hovering in the air and showing up in a body and mind I liked—like the idea of communism starting in Marx's mind and ending in Engels' brain. I wished to be an idea choosing the era I wanted to exist in or the era I wanted to change, an idea moving and growing, like the concept of freedom from Plato to Mill to Rousseau to Mandela. But I was imprisoned forever in this body that disappointed me.

I emailed the newspaper asking them why my name was omitted from the article without my consent. After two days, I was told that the sponsors of my program (meaning the U.S. Department of State) had worried about my safety and asked them to remove my name from the article. I wrote back asking for my right to reply, to tell my people and the visitors of my blog that I did not deceive them as many others had in the past.

The newspaper published my reply, the third article in the series, wherein I explained that I did not regret any of my comments in the original article. And "coincidently," shortly after my reply was published, a "404 ERROR" message appeared on my blog site. I realized what that meant: my blog was officially censored. I was angry, but I could not help suppress a grin. I felt within my soul the hidden satisfaction of being "someone." Censoring of the blog meant that the government was reading my posts, which meant that I had more visitors than I had imagined. It also meant that, somehow, my small blog was bothering the government. The implications were great: if you bothered the government, it meant that you were just and truthful.

But after this short phase of satisfaction, a new phase of paranoia set in. With every cop I saw, I imagined that I would be arrested. Everybody who looked at me I started to believe was a secret agent. I began to feel like all the people in the metro were watching me, following me. I stopped telling jokes about the president over the phone and even attempted to become a "good citizen." A good citizen is one who never opposes the government, never talks about politics, and never reports corruption because it would "harm our economy and the image of our country."

Strongly feeling this palpable fear, I did not blog for a while. (Having a blocked site made it hard to blog as well). Then some fellow bloggers showed me techniques to circumvent the censorship and pass under the government's radar. Just the thought of resuming my blog writing filled me with energy, ideas, and zeal to challenge any threat to my country and its people. However, a stronger feeling prevented me from re-starting. Was it fear? I had experienced fear before, and this was not it.

My appetite for blogging faded away slowly, and I became anxious about what to do next. I spent months pondering and assessing, eventually coming to the conclusion that I loved blogging but wanted to do something more concrete, something on the ground. Blogging and tweeting gave me the impression that I was in an ivory tower, above the common people.

That is when I decided to establish my first association, called Student-To-Student, with the aim of encouraging youth to be more open to volunteerism. Whenever I wanted to express myself, I wrote an article on Facebook, the social media site that had helped us start a revolution.

What the Western world would eventually call "the Arab Spring," and what I call a battle for freedom and dignity, started in my country, Tunisia. It all started with a street vendor setting his body on fire on December 17, 2010. When Bouazizi set fire to his body, I could not help but resume blogging. With each kid who was killed, the will to blog increased. I needed to write something for the people and for my country and for myself.

Most bloggers starting adding another component to their cyber presence. They no longer solely wrote on their blogs. Instead, they went to the internal regions (areas of Tunisia outside the capital city of Tunis) such as Sidi Bouzid and Kasserine to cover the events taking place there. They shot videos, and pictures, interviewed people, and then tweeted their reports onto Twitter or uploaded them on Facebook. They became a reliable source for media outlets. They brought worldwide recognition to the Tunisian revolution and made heads turn to carefully follow what was going on.

Blogging in its traditional form almost vanished during the revolution. It was re-imagined as a medium for sharing videos shot by citizen journalists and as a platform for providing the masses with the latest news. In other words, bloggers became citizen journalists.

Personally, I still believe that Twitter is "elitist" in Tunisia. Only bloggers and activists are on Twitter, so if you tweet, you target a limited though cultivated group of people. The common Tunisian is on Facebook. That is why I preferred using Facebook to share videos, write articles, and inquire about breaking news.

After the revolution, I did not resume blogging. Tunisia after the revolution, in my view, needed people in the field more than behind their laptops. It needed people to leave the screen and the big cities to go to the Tunisian-Libyan border's refugee camps and to internal regions like Sidi Bouzid, Kasserine, Kef, Gbeli, Gafsa, and Jendouba. It needed people to listen to other people's suffering. It needed people to go once again into the streets to deter any endeavor to "steal" the revolution from us, the organizers of the revolution, and drag us into another dictatorship. That is why after the revolution, I created an organization geared towards helping Tunisia and Tunisians. It was an NGO called I WATCH, a watchdog organization working for transparency and transitional justice and fighting against corruption. However, my being active in civil society could not quell my longing to use the Internet again, my nostalgia for being able to talk to the people and pass on positive messages.

I started with videos, encouraging people to donate money, welcome fleeing Libyan refugees and foreign workers from Libya, and volunteer in the camps. The videos also promoted tourism in Tunisia. But my biggest achievement during that period was an event that I started on Facebook.

For most of the world, February 14 is Valentine's Day. But in 2011 for Tunisians, it meant a month since our revolution, a month of freedom, a month without Ben Ali. Thus, I created an event on Facebook asking Tunisians, instead of celebrating Valentine's Day, to celebrate our freedom and show love for our country. The event became very big. About thirty-five thousand people confirmed their attendance on Facebook. The media started contacting me, and the event continued to grow to titanic proportions.

What made the event exceptional for me was a simple idea that I implemented: I bought thirty meters of cloth and thirty permanent markers, and at the event I asked people to write their wishes and expectations for the new Tunisia on that day. Later on, this piece of cloth was called the "Carpet of the Revolution." It now has on it more than fifty thousand signatures. The event venue was Bourguiba Avenue, where the January 14th march had taken place. The number of people who signed the carpet were present, and even more! Every day I look at the carpet and read what the people wrote, what they want to see in their country: it has become my compass.

I have learned that something as simple as a blog can change one's life, especially if one loves and believes in what one does. After the revolution I have witnessed the impact that blogging made at a time when my country needed me the most. I feel really proud when I see bloggers now with the title of "minister" or as Nobel Prize nominees. For all Arab bloggers, I wish you the best of luck. Our way is still very long and the best is yet to come. To Khaled Said and Bouazizi, I say, "God bless you."

*This essay is of course an account of my personal experience. However, allow me to digress a moment to pay tribute to all the Tunisian bloggers: those who refused to bow in front of dictatorship, those who risked their lives to say the truth, those who stood up in the face of tyranny, those who fought for freedom of expression. A salute from Tunisia, the land of martyrs, to all the Arab bloggers and activists, those who survived or those who are still in the arena fighting the specter of dictatorship. To those who earned their freedom and those lying in the basements of*

*Ministries of Interior, to those who eradicated injustice from their lands and those who are still planting the seeds of freedom in their deserts. I honor those who are still fighting, those who died under torture, and those who were raped or saw someone dear to them raped in front of their eyes. I see light at the end of the tunnel. Do not miss the train of history. People like you do not read history, they write it.*

# Yemeni Cartoon
## *by Carlos Latuff*

A Yemeni man and woman bring together a needle and thread to begin to stitch Yemen's tattered flag, which symbolizes the breaking down of Yemen's social fabric and political security following former president Ali Abdullah Saleh's stepping down. Women played a central role in the uprisings in Yemen and across the region, including Tawakul Karman, a journalist, politician and human rights activist who was co-recipient of the 2011 Nobel Peace Prize and also referred to as the "Mother of the Revolution".

# Progress Is Painful, Costly, and Slow

## by Atiaf Alwazir

**ATIAF ZAID ALWAZIR**, is a Yemeni American researcher, blogger, and activist based in Sana'a, Yemen. Since the end of January 2011, she has been chronicling the Yemeni revolution on her blog (http://womanfromyemen.blogspot.com/) with commentaries, videos, and photographs. Atiaf has appeared and spoken on various television and radio outlets, including Democracy Now, BBC, France 24, CNN International, and KPFA radio, about the revolution in Yemen and the pro-democracy movement. Atiaf is also a development professional with over nine years experience in the Middle East and North Africa supporting indigenous civil society organizations to implement programs related to social justice. Her master's thesis was titled "Women in Prison in Yemen: Between Honor and Crime."

The morning of May 11, 2011 seemed just like any other day. I woke up to a phone call about a potential march taking place. The people at the square who had been demonstrating for months had vowed to march that day to the presidential palace in Yemen's capital city, Sana'a. This was not a light decision to make, as many dangers were associated with such a march.

I ate breakfast, watched and read the news, conversed with my husband, and then went by myself to a play rehearsal organized by

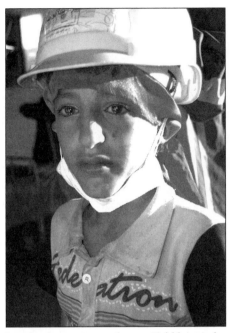

Lost innocence, young boy at Field hospital in Change Square, Sana'a, Yemen

the local youth. The play was about social issues related to unemployment and health care in Yemen. The actors rehearsed some of the scenes, and we as their "audience" gave our feedback. We had a great time at the rehearsal. We laughed a lot, to the point where tears rolled down our faces. After we were done, I met my husband at a café and enjoyed a nice mocha while checking my e-mails. Because electricity cuts are so frequent at our home, there is no guarantee that we will have electricity and Internet there.

As the time for the march approached, I headed to Sahat al-Tagheer, more famously known as "Change Square," the area in front of Sana'a University. This area had been transformed into an arena for a sit-in for the pro-democracy movement. Over time it expanded to cover at least four kilometers. The space was filled with tents, vendors, and protesters who had been present twenty-four hours a day since February 21. As a blogger, I often went to protests to cover these events, take photos, conduct interviews, and sometimes participate in marches. I was planning to document the march to the presidential palace through photographs and video clips.

I arrived at the square at 4:00 p.m. and heard people on the stage calling for a march to the ministry instead of the palace. I was relieved, thinking, "Thank God they didn't go to the palace yet. For that, hundreds of thousands of protesters are needed as protection against potential attacks." The government forces had made it clear that any attempt to march to the palace would be blocked by all means.

I waited at the media committee for a friend, and I saw a couple of people head out to cover the march. Half an hour passed and my friend still hadn't come. I called her and said, "Sorry, but I'm going to head over to the march. Let's try to meet there." As I got up to leave the tent and join the march I heard an array of bullets.

The sound of the bullets was so loud that I assumed the shots were inside the square. People started to look around, wondering where the sound was coming from. Five minutes later, as gunshots continued, someone informed us that they were coming from the blood bank, where thugs and men in security clothes had cornered the protesters.

The blood bank was only ten minutes away from one of the entrances to the square. The protesters hadn't gotten very far from the square and had already been attacked. In front of the blood bank on 26th Street, near the Zira'ah Street entrance to the square, they were attacked from many directions by snipers shooting directly at them. The shooting continued off and on for three straight hours.

I immediately went to the field hospital, expecting the wounded to show up there as they always do. Very critical cases, such as bullet wounds in the head, often went to better-resourced hospitals such as the privately owned Science and Technology Hospital. Others were received at the field hospital inside the square. The field hospital was a former mosque turned into clinic that happened to be inside the square. All the male and female medics and nurses were volunteers who worked twenty-four hours a day. Volunteers were welcome and were given first aid training before joining.

I had visited this field hospital numerous times, and thus most people there knew me. Often citizen security guards stood watch, regulating who went in and out of the hospital. Foreign journalists were usually allowed to enter immediately. To prevent infiltrations by national security and to reduce the number of people in the already overcrowded hospital, Yemenis were asked to present identification cards either as journalists or as a members of one of the committees at

Change Square. Even with these security measures, the field hospital was often overcrowded.

As a blogger, someone not formally regarded as a journalist, I had not been able to obtain a press card. So with no press card yet wanting to document the regime's abuses, I had to get to know the volunteers in the early days of the revolution to secure my entrance into the field hospital. Personal connections in Yemen go far. The volunteers saw me as a regular there, and thus trust was established.

That day, I ran to the field hospital. As usual, I didn't have a press card, and in my rush to get to the hospital I forgot to ask any of the coalitions at the square for a pass. When I arrived, I didn't see anyone I knew at the gate of the hospital. I tried to enter, but the female guard would not let me in. I explained to her that I was a blogger and that I documented information to send it to human rights groups and others. I said, "I'm a regular here, I come everyday!" She looked at me intensely for a few seconds, then turned to her friend and said: "Doesn't she look like the TV presenter on Yemen TV" (the government station)? "Maybe I do, but I'm not her!" I responded in an angry voice. Her insinuation meant that she did not trust me.

Many at the square worry that people from Yemen TV may come to steal footage and "misrepresent it." The propaganda war between government and opposition media had reached its height in Yemen. Both sides had exaggerated information, which led to people becoming extremely distrustful. In Yemen, independent television was non-existent and independent media rare.

"You must be new here. Everyone else knows me!" I informed her. She ignored what I said and told me I wasn't allowed in. I realized this was hopeless, so I went to another entrance. The security man asked me, "Are you a journalist?" I immediately said, "Yes." "Do you have a press card?" he asked. "Let me look for it," I responded. As I rummaged through my belongings slowly, I hoped he would just let me in—after all we were in crisis. Thankfully, he did just that, and said, "Okay, don't worry about the card, welcome in."

As I entered the hospital more bullet sounds erupted. I called my friends at the march, but no one answered. Then I text messaged my husband to tell him not to join me at the square as he had planned earlier. "They are shooting near the entrance of Zira'ah Street where we usually enter the square. Please don't come now. You'll be caught in the middle of it."

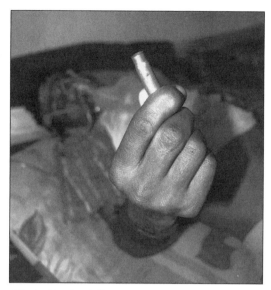

The bullet that kills, Change Square, Sana'a, Yemen

Bullets continued, and one by one, victims arrived, aided by their fellow protesters. I heard a voice calling me "Atiaf!" I turned and saw my friend Mohammed lying on the floor. "OH MY GOD," I screamed, "are you okay?" He was okay, just suffering from tear gas. Volunteers had covered his face with onion and washed his face. Mohammed had been the funniest comedian at the rehearsal just a couple of hours earlier. He had made me cry from laughter; now, just a few hours later, the tears were of sadness.

Minute by minute more wounded were brought to the hospital by heroic men on their motorcycles and by volunteers. Some were shot in the leg, others in the arm. The fact that they still survived after the way they were transported is miraculous.

Every time there was an attack against peaceful protesters the field hospital turned into a big chaotic scene. No matter how hard volunteers and medics tried, it was still a mess. There was a shortage of both equipment and medics. Often too many people were surrounding a victim, and of course the hygiene situation was nothing like a hospital should be. Some of the wounded surely died not from the bullet wounds but due to a simple infection.

I snapped some photos and wrote down relevant information about the wounded. I tried to call my husband and friends, but no one was answering.

Suddenly I saw a young boy standing there wearing a helmet that was bigger than his head. His eyes were full of tears, his body frozen in shock. It seemed that he did not know what to do or where to go. I asked him, "*Habibi*, why are you here? Maybe you should go outside?" He looked at me but couldn't speak. Later I found out that he had helped to bring in his brother, who had been struck by a bullet in the leg.

I snapped more photos and incessantly called people at the march. Most were not answering. Then suddenly I received a text message from my husband that said, "I'm at the blood bank now, but don't worry, gun shots stopped and I'm ok." Irritated, I asked myself, "Does he think we can't hear the gun shots from the square?!!" I tried to call him back, but he didn't answer. Then I tried to contact some journalist friends of mine who were at the march, as they were always risking their lives to cover the events, but again no one picked up the phone. I told myself, this surely means they are hiding. I should stop calling.

I started to really worry but continued to snap photos. Suddenly, my phone began ringing and continued to ring. With every ring I hoped it was someone at the march to tell me they were okay. However, every single time I answered it was someone else wondering if I was at the march and asking about my safety.

A woman I did not know at the hospital came to me and was close to tears. She asked if I knew anything about her brother. She had been trying to call him but got no answer. "Maybe if you call he will answer," she told me. She had seen me at previous marches talking to her brother, and was convinced that he might respond to me, as he did not want to worry his sister. So I called, and miraculously, he did answer. He told me everyone was okay now. Gunshots stopped for a moment. I reassured his sister and went back to snapping photos and interviewing people.

I found a corner where I could sit and watched in awe the number of people going into and out of the field hospital. Every wounded person or martyr had a family who was now looking for them, who was as worried about them as I was for my husband and friends. Volunteers carried some martyrs to the field hospital. Most had been shot in the head. I then went to photograph the dead bodies. The martyrs were usually lined up on the floor, with name tags in order to help human rights advocates to document them, and to enable media to enhance their reporting. Sometimes it took a while to find someone to identify the body, so the body remained nameless. Journalists and photographers often crowded around the bodies. I always found it difficult to take these photos. I felt it was so intrusive to the martyr and the family. But during a revolution, we must document these events for the world to see.

As I approached the bodies I looked at one young man named Abdullah Ali Al-Samry. He was twenty-two-years old, and his brother was by his side stroking his hair. I wondered to myself if Abdullah had had an inclination that today would be his last day. Did he know that photographers would be surrounding his dead body taking photographs of the injuries?

This was not the first time I photographed a dead body. I'd become accustomed to it since the start of the revolution. The first time, I was frozen and couldn't move. But with time, I became desensitized to it—or that is what I thought, until one day I had a breakdown and could not stop crying uncontrollably. I attributed the breakdown to the fact that I had had to sideline my emotions in order to continue documenting the situation. For many months, we had been forced to disconnect from our own bodies and our emotions in this way. Our bodies cooperated with us for some time, but after months of repeated neglect, our bodies decided to take a sudden full stop, and whether we liked it or not, we broke down.

My breakdown occurred in the most commonplace of situations: I was grocery shopping and ran into a friend of my mother's who

Facebook Revolution

I hadn't seen in a long time. She has kind eyes and a tender spirit. In a concerned manner, she asked, "How are you doing, dear?" The question opened a Pandora's box. My eyes started to tear up, and I felt a big lump in my throat. I did not want to cry in the middle of the market, so I quickly excused myself and escaped into the first taxi I saw. Looking out the window, I put my headphones on and listened to music, hoping it would change my mood, but instead uncontrollable tears began to flow. I normally hate to cry in public, but that day, I just closed my eyes and let the tears roll down. It was time to release.

But back to May 11. After I had collected the names of all the martyrs and most of the injured at the field hospital, a man suddenly came up to me and said "Excuse me, do you document violations?" "Well, yes, I'm trying. How can I help?" I answered. He proceeded to tell me that a fourteen-year-old boy had been killed by a gunshot in his abdomen and he was currently at Al-Jomhoriya Hospital. His father was at the square, and he was going to the hospital to identify the body. "Would you come with us to document this?" he asked me. "Sure," I responded in a soft, hesitant voice.

I was introduced to the father, Mohammed Al-Okairi, a man in his early forties. His eyes were in between life and death. I wasn't sure what to say to him, since small talk wasn't exactly appropriate. So I asked, "How old is your son?" He looked at me, his eyes filled with tears, and said, "He's fourteen." Then suddenly he started crying.

I would have liked to take this man in my arms and cry with him. However, given the cultural norms, I couldn't do that. I just stood silently in front of him, and all I could say is "I'm so, so sorry."

The father, two medics, and I entered the ambulance. On the way, one of the medics handed me a blue robe. I looked at it with confusion, and he ordered me, "Put it on. We have to say you are a nurse or else they won't let you in the hospital." I complied and told them that I thought it would be best if I left my large camera in the ambulance and took the small one instead. It was easier to hide. They agreed.

On the way to the hospital we picked up the boy's grandfather. When we arrived, hospital officials directed us to the morgue. It felt like an eternity listening to the hospital staffer rummage through his keys while the father waited patiently to find out whether his own flesh and blood was truly killed. That must have been the longest ten minutes of his life.

As we walked into the morgue the father's hands were shaking. A white sheet covered the teenager's body. The medic slowly pulled the sheet back. The father looked at his son and, after seconds that felt more like hours, he said in a very low voice, "It's Abdul-Rahman." The grandfather yelled *Inna lilah wa inna ilaihi rajioon!* (We all come from God and we will return to him!).

Looking at them, I froze. I physically could not take the photo of the father and the son, nor of the son alone. I had never been in a situation like this one before. I wasn't sure what was appropriate to say or do. Although this would have been the most emotional and expressive photo I had taken to date, I could not take it. I felt I would be taking advantage of their situation if I did.

I was supposed to ask the doctor some questions, but my eyes were fixed on the teenage body. Finally, I remember that I had been brought there for a reason. I collected myself, put my strong face on, turned to the doctor, and asked him some questions regarding the wound, time of death, age of the martyr, and so on. I wrote down the doctor's responses, in my note pad, took some photos of the body, and then left the dark room.

As we stepped out into the waiting room, the father began to cry and the grandfather hugged him. It was the first time I had seen a Yemeni man cry in public. Ironically, both men were hugging and crying underneath a large photo of President Saleh. What an ironic image that was, and what a perfect photo if I had dared to take it, but again, my hands could not take the photo. I wanted to cry with them, I wanted to scream, but I held myself together. I needed to be strong. I needed to show them that, as a woman, I could handle this situation. Most of all, I needed to be professional. I came here for a specific job, and I was going to do it. "I will keep my emotions bottled up, and I will feel that knot in my throat, and then when I go home, I will cry it all out," I reassured myself to get through the moment.

During our trip back to the square in the ambulance we had one extra passenger: Abdul-Rahman, the fourteen-year-old martyr, was lying in front of us. His bullet wounds no longer bled and did not stain the clean white sheets that covered him. The medics were talking together as if nothing had happened.

I felt a chill wondering whether Abdul-Rahman's spirit was with us. Was he looking down at us now? Another ambulance was behind ours and was instructing us to stop. When our driver refused to stop. I asked why. They informed me that security forces on occasion had kidnapped the body to prevent documentation, especially if it was a young martyr. I took down the license plate just in case something did happen, and I text messaged a friend saying, "An ambulance with the license plate "xxx" is following us." Our driver sped up and tried to lose them. He succeeded and we made it back to Change Square, where Abdul-Rahman's body was added to the line of piled dead bodies.

That trip lasted about one hour and a half. When I arrived at Change Square, my husband had not showed up yet. Ten minutes later I saw him in front of me. Despite cultural taboos, I gave him a long hug. Two of my journalist friends were with him. They were all unharmed but deeply shaken, and so was I. My husband proceeded to tell me about the continuous gunshots, the tear gas, and the water cannons used against protesters. To stay safe, he found an iron box used to grill chicken and hid behind it. We stayed at the field hospital for another hour and then decided to go home to upload and send the photos, videos, and information we had collected.

Our only way home was through Zira'ah Street close to the blood bank, where the attack took place. We hesitated, but the gunshots had stopped, so we felt it was possibly safe to leave now. As we left, I noticed a group of protesters heading in a new march towards the blood bank. I instinctively started taking photographs. After the second photo I heard gunshots, but I continued to take photographs. Thankfully, my husband pulled me aside and said, "*Yalla* (C'mon, let's go), we have to go."

Since I was the only woman on Zira'ah Street at that moment, everyone was trying to help me. They formed a circle of protection around my husband and me. As we entered the square, people appeared to be tense, expecting an attack. I covered my face to avoid the tear gas that was coming from the sewage inside the square.

Suddenly we found out that two other entrances to the square had been blocked. There was now only one open entrance. My husband and I went to the middle of the square. We stood staring at each other, wondering if the square would be attacked. It hadn't happened before, and the presence of the many women and children who had now arrived in the square would hopefully prevent an attack as well. Would they really go at us in full force? Not knowing what to do, I turned to my husband and said, "I need a cup of tea." We sipped tea under the sound of gunfire. Others were having dinner, some were reading, while the gun sounds echoed in the air. It felt surreal.

We thought of sleeping there in one of the tents, but I had to upload the photos immediately, and my contact list was in my computer at home. We decided to go out through the only open entrance.

On the way, I prayed that we would have electricity at home so I could upload the photos and videos. Thankfully, we did. Both my husband and I immediately got on our computers and started to send the information via e-mail, Twitter, and Facebook.

By the end of that day, May 11, thirteen people had died. Three hundred had been wounded, fifty of them by gunfire. That night I went to sleep without the energy or ability to comprehend the extent of what I had seen.

Of course not every day during the past nine months has been as dramatic as this one. However, this day was one of the worst for me both physically and mentally. I assumed that what I had seen on that day was the worst violence we would experience.

Unfortunately, the violence escalated four months later. In addition to the usual live ammunition and tear gas, heavy artillery and mortars were used against peaceful protesters, causing heads to be blown off and bodies to shatter to pieces. Throughout this, I kept thinking, how can humanity be so cruel?

The martyrs and the wounded are the heroes of the revolution. There are also many hidden heroes. The men on motorcycles transporting the wounded from dangerous zones to hospitals, the mothers who lost their children, the journalists who risked their lives covering the news, and the nurses who worked endlessly to help the wounded. Many people contributed to this revolution with everything they had. The revolution is for all and by all.

As my mentor explained to me once in an email, "Progress is painful, costly, and slow." Even so, I have no doubt that progress is happening. The determination of a people seeking freedom is an unstoppable force: sooner or later freedom will prevail. The situation will not dramatically change overnight, but the revolution had planted the seed for change to flourish in the years to come. It is the first step of many.

## Battling Bahrain's Crimes of Humanity
### by Matar Ebrahim Matar

**MATAR EBRAHIM MATAR** is a former member of Bahrain's Parliament. While serving in Parliament, Matar represented his country's largest constituency and was a member of the economic and finance committee. In the months immediately following the popular uprising in Bahrain, which took place on February 14, 2011, Matar fought for the basic human rights of those arrested and detained. An active member of Alwefaq Society—Bahrain's largest political opposition society—Matar was one of eighteen MP's who resigned his post after the recent crisis. He holds a master's degree in artificial intelligence and computer science and is married with two children. On May 2, 2011, Matar was taken from his car by armed men in masks. He was arrested, and as he later testified, was tortured while in the custody of Bahrain's government. Eventually, he was coerced under torture to confess to a crime of running over a policeman. Matar believes his arrest was intended to put pressure on his political party.

In January 2011, I was the youngest minister in Bahrain's Parliament representing the Al Wefaq political party, Bahrain's largest political bloc. I was voted to the Parliament with a majority vote of eighty-five percent, but eventually, like many of my fellow members, I was left with no choice but to resign in order to send a message to the government of Bahrain that its violations of human rights were simply unacceptable.

The uprising began on February 14, and I spent the next several months fighting for the basic human rights of those arrested and detained to be granted. But they were not. In fact, after our party resigned on February 27, 2011, in protest of the government's violent crackdown on pro-democracy protesters, things took a turn for the worse.

By the middle of April, just two months into the uprisings, we had officially entered a state of martial law in Bahrain, and I was starting to worry about my personal safety. Since February, the death rate at the hands of the government exceeded three casualties per week. For a country the size of Bahrain, this was an incredibly high rate.

As part of my responsibility towards those who had elected me, I had followed up on the cases of certain detainees to ensure their basic human rights were honored. I was also communicating with many in the international media, including the BBC, Al Jazeera, and Reuters, to pass the facts as I witnessed them. I took this seriously.

Two days before May 2, 2011, when I myself was detained, I gave an interview to Al Jazeera. I told them that here in Bahrain we believe in a secular system and we want to live in a country where everyone is free and can practice his belief without any pressure or any fear. I also said that while we would like to build a strong relationship with the United States, we would like it to be based on respect.

As we entered the summer the government began targeting doctors in order to hide the truth about just how much excessive force was used against Bahrain's citizens by the police and soldiers. To convey just how brutal the government was, nearly all of those who told their stories in a documentary that appeared on *People and Power*,[1] a series produced by Al Jazeera English, were eventually arrested. Even doctors who were simply featured crying in the film were arrested. As news of more arrests came, it became especially difficult for all of us Bahraini activists.

---

1.  http://www.youtube.com/watch?v=IZdyiK-Z5Do

I spoke to the media often. I found myself using on each occasion the same two terms: "crimes against humanity" and "ruling family." I thought that as a member of Parliament, I would have political immunity and would be allowed to exercise it responsibly, but I was wrong. I later realized no one was safe if they publicly used these two terms in the same sentence.

Many of my friends were advising me to change my tone and to keep a low profile. I honestly had never had any direct experience with this type of regime in the context of civil disobedience. I had never been arrested or even interrogated for political issues. Maybe this is why I didn't take their advice seriously. I just kept talking. I kept speaking the truth. A reporter from Reuters wrote about me in the last article he published before the government expelled him from Bahrain. The regime didn't appreciate that this reporter was documenting the crimes that had been ongoing systematically since February.

In his article, the reporter wrote: "One of the last handful still talking was Matar Matar."[2] At the same time, Al Jazeera, who had been generally barred from Bahrain, said, "Member of Parliament Matar Matar was the only source of foreign media to find news of opposition after the imposition of emergency law in the country."[3]

On Thursday, April 28, 2011 Bahrain TV aired "confessions" from protestors whom the authorities claimed had run over two policemen with a car. One of the protestors, Ali Isa Saqer—one of four who died in custody—mentioned my name. He said that I ordered him to run over riot police with his cars on March 17, 2011 when the Lulu (Pearl) Roundabout was attacked by the GCC shield force.[4]

After this aired on local TV, I suspected that I would be arrested or kidnapped at any moment. I was at home preparing to be arrested.

---

2. http://www.reuters.com/article/2011/05/17/us-witness-bahrain-idU
   TRE74G41320110517
3. http://aljazeera.net/Portal/Templates/Postings/PocketPcDetailedPage.aspx?Prin
   tPage=True&GUID=%7B41E0E3D2-3C6B-4EB5-A442-7A5EA8B7C687%7D
4. http://www.youtube.com/watch?v=JW8oUP time: 6:00

I asked my wife to sleep with our children, Ahmed and Sarah, in her father's house. I did not want the children to see me arrested.

I installed cameras that were connected to the Internet, with the aim of recording the moment of my arrest. I thought to do this after finding out what had happened to Abdul-Hadi Al-Kawaja, arguably the country's most prominent activist. He was arrested in 2004 and again in 2007 and was tortured in prison. Then on April 9, 2011, he was severely beaten after police raided his house, dragged him from bed in front of his daughter and wife, and arrested him while he was unconscious.[5] Eventually others in his family were arrested, as was often the case. I was also disturbed by the story of Mahdi Abu-Deeb, president of Teacher Society, whose body was seen falling from the second floor of his house when riot police came to arrest him.[6]

I prepared myself and left what I thought would be my final message to the international community on Al Jazeera English.[7] In this recording, I repeated the message I had sent to U.S. Secretary of State Hillary Clinton, in which I told her that the Bahrainis were looking forward to stronger relations with the United States, and that we wanted to see the presence of the U.S.'s Fifth Fleet in our country not as an obstacle to our quest for reform and change but rather as a sign that the United States was a supportive partner. Apparently my offer was not as desirable as the one the regime was offering. The U.S. State Department still preferred to call the regime a strategic ally, rather than align themselves with the Bahraini people. Meanwhile, we called our own government an authoritarian regime. We wanted our relationship with the United States to positively affect the democracy of our nation, not hinder it.

On Monday, May 2, 2011, at around seven-thirty in the evening, I received a call from an anonymous woman who told me that she

---

5. http://www.bbc.co.uk/news/world-middle-east-13023428
6. http://ei-ie.org/asiapacific/en/newsshow.php?id=5835&theme=rights&country=Bahrain
7. http://www.aljazeera.com/news/middleast/2011/05/201152205239385476.html

had an envelope for me and that I should meet her to collect it. I asked her to deliver it to the headquarters of Al Wefaq, but she insisted on meeting me in person and said she was too scared to go to the headquarters of Al Wefaq. I agreed to meet her near the Alhelli supermarket in my village, Aldaih.

My wife, Amal, insisted on coming with me, since she was suspicious of the woman. When I arrived, masked men dressed in black civilian clothes cornered my car and pointed their guns at my head. Without revealing their identities, they kidnapped me. They were terrifying. They threatened my wife and ordered her not to share any details of this encounter with anyone (though she eventually did). I was immediately handcuffed, blindfolded, and taken to an unknown destination. I worried about my wife. All this was done without anyone showing a warrant of arrest or even any sort of identification.

While I was sitting and waiting in this place, the faces of those who had died in custody before me started to race through my mind. I wondered: Am I going to face the same destiny?

It seems they intentionally kept me blindfolded in order to convince me that I had done something wrong. At the time, I was so shocked with the way I was arrested, I wasn't able to think much further than that. A man asked me, "Do you see anything?" I told him that I didn't. Then he replied. "You will live your entire life without seeing anything."

This statement marked the start of the interrogation. The interrogators did not identify themselves. I asked them which part of the security apparatus they belonged to. They did not answer me. They also did not explain why I was arrested or what I was being charged with.

The interrogation lasted about two hours and focused mainly on the political activity of my party, Al Wefaq. They were interested in learning about the relationship between the political party and other political opposition groups, including the popular February 14 movement. They also asked me about the mass resignations of the Al

Wefaq from the Parliamentary bloc in the Parliament's lower house.

At the time I didn't consider this an interrogation. It seemed more like a political discussion. I was surprised when the interrogator said at the end of the discussion that there were mistakes made on both sides. I respected the fact that he confessed even this much. I certainly didn't expect to to hear such a thing from my so-called interrogator. When they then took me to solitary confinement, I was overwhelmed with uncertain emotions. I was worried about what might happen to me.

On the second day of my arrest, I had barely slept when the guards began a more casual interrogation. They knew I had not slept, but they continued chatting with me at length. I was totally exhausted. Late that night, just as I tried to fall asleep again after many previously failed attempts, I was taken to yet another interrogation that lasted about three hours.

This time the tone was very different. There were two interrogators. I was still blindfolded, but I was able to judge by one interrogator's accent that he was Jordanian. He also insisted on shouting his questions at me. During the interrogation, he kept on interrupting me and even interrupting himself in an attempt to present himself as the smart one, capable of discovering any mistakes or loopholes in my story.

"You may be classified as uncooperative, and based on that we would have to deal with you in a totally different way," he said to me. So I spoke in detail and told him my personal beliefs and opinions and those of Al Wefaq in an attempt to get myself out of this situation.

I was asked if I had given an order to Ali Saqer to run over policemen. I said no. Then he asked me, "Do you mean we tortured him in order to get him to say this about you?" I replied, "I will not elaborate."

I have a bad habit of not being able to control my anger and then end up talking very loudly. I was trying to tell them that the regime failed to deal with the crisis properly, but I was so exhausted that I could barely formulate the sentences. The interrogator then said resolutely, "You are now classified as uncooperative," and he then told the guards to take me. It was midnight on May 4, one day after my birthday. I'll never forget.

After this day, they handled me completely differently. They would place me, handcuffed and blindfolded, between two metal desks. Then they would begin hitting those desks as loudly as they could, being careful to miss me. With each shockingly loud noise, I was worried that I would be hit next.

As they took me back to solitary confinement, one of the guards told me the man in the next cell had died. They had been beating this man harshly, but I was sure he had not actually died. Instead, I took this as their way of reminding me that they had been given the green light to kill people. Even so, the comment was enough to destroy my outlook and well-being.

It was midnight now, the third night that I spent barely closing my eyes and sleeping at all. I was beyond debilitated. It was bad enough being prevented from sleeping, but they also refused to let me sit down. They forced me to stand the entire time with my hands up, while persistent loud knocking echoed from my cell door. The threat of physical torture in the event that I sat down was constant. This continued throughout the night until the next day at noon. Then I was transferred, with others, to an unknown destination. They took us to get a brief health check-up and then finally a small lunch.

But I wasn't able to eat. I felt as though my entire body would reject anything I put in my mouth. One of the guards came over to force me to eat. I told him I could not eat. He said to me, "It is not your choice, you must eat." I insisted on not eating. "I will teach you how to obey orders," he said. "I will request responsibility for handling you from here on out."

Then he took me to the basement of a building that I would later find out was the National Intelligence Authority Building in Al-Qala'a, Manama. I was put in a room that measured three meters by three meters and left there until the next morning, May 6, 2011.

During the night a man entered my cell and said to me, "You can be treated in two ways, either as a human or as an animal." He told me the choice lay with me and gave me a pen and paper. He asked me to write a confession to the charges. "Write it all down," he said.

On that day, I was kept blindfolded and interrogated again about the former activity of Al Wefaq and its relationship with other political associations and the diplomatic service. I would eventually be forced by them to sign my name to validate the entire interrogation despite being unsure what was said, written, or even discussed.

On May 18, I was taken without any notice to a military destination that I would later learn was the Qurain military prison. Upon arrival I was verbally abused and made to stay under the heat of the sun for hours on end. The guards there harassed me further, forcing me to stand whenever I heard the national anthem, which was playing repeatedly on a CD containing other national songs. Later, the guard asked all of the detainees to sit down except me. He said he wanted me to stand the whole time. At this point, I was so exhausted and was struggling to breathe as my face had been covered with a canvas bag the entire time. I was slowly losing my strength, both physically and mentally. I started running out of air. I was choking and began to panic. I asked the guard for help, but he responded, "I don't care if you die."

I felt that I might simply die, right there. To survive, I disobeyed their orders and tried to remove the cover from my face, willing to deal with whatever the consequence might be. The guards then started to form a circle around me. They prevented me from removing the cover. In fact, I was forbidden to see any of their faces. An Indian guard helped me and offered me a little bit of water—thank God.

Once again, I was brought into the interrogation room and the investigation began without any lawyers present. They kept asking me one question: about the charge of having given orders to overrun the policemen. Each time I denied the charge, they would only ask me again.

The guards began insulting me again. They swore and cursed repeatedly until midnight. I was threatened by one of the guards, and after I tried to complain to his supervisor, the threats persisted. He was angry at me for having complained about him. Then I was then taken to the same military destination that I had been to several weeks prior.

When I arrived, I was dragged from the car, beaten with batons, and kicked repeatedly in what seemed like each of my organs. All the while the guards were swearing and cursing the most vulgar insults at me. A man they called "Al-Sheikh" was there. He began to curse and insult me with abusive words as he beat me severely on the face, ears, and head with his hands and the baton he carried. He threatened to use electric shocks, and then he pointed a gun at my head. He said he didn't want to stain his hands with blood so he would postpone killing me until his next visit. Later, they dragged me to the car to take me to the national security building.

On June 12, 2011, I was taken to the military court without having been told where I was going. I only found out where I was when I arrived in court. I was not given the opportunity to contact my lawyer or to request his presence. I also was not informed by any legal process of the date of the hearing. The hearing's record proves this matter, as I did not even receive our case papers until after the hearing. I was unprepared to defend myself.

Despite many lawyers and families asking about me since I was detained in early May, I was not allowed to contact my family for twenty-seven days. The nature of the charges against me were not even discovered or presented to my lawyers until forty days after my arrest.

I was not provided a fair trial. I was in solitary confinement during most of the trial, blindfolded. Simple requests from our lawyers were ignored. I was ready to prove my innocence, but the military court never gave me the opportunity to make my own case.

While I was in solitary confinement, I felt the sympathy of a few of the guards. This encouraged me to talk with them occasionally, which did at least help pass the time. We learned some anecdotes about each other. While that helped, I reached a conclusion: In order to survive, I would have to force myself to sleep even if I wasn't sleepy and to leave the bed immediately the moment I woke up, because lying there with your mind racing and unable to sleep is the most effective way to damage your patience. I needed to avoid evaluating what was happening to me. I also promised myself I would try as hard as I could to refrain from placing any blame on myself for winding up here until I was released.

My case was to be decided on July 5, 2011. After spending forty-five days in solitary confinement, I was transferred to military jail, where I was no longer isolated. I joined Mahdi Abu Deab, the head of the Teacher Society, Mohammed AlTajir, the primary lawyer for most political cases in Bahrain, and my colleague in Parliament Jawaf Fayrooz, who saved Mohammed Ali Al Alawi, a clerk. It was a big relief for me.

Before my arrest I had been busy reporting the ongoing human rights crimes. But it wasn't until I was in military jail that I realized the extent of the torture used. I was shocked at the stories I heard. Apparently there had been more, much more torture use than what I had been reporting to the international NGO's, media, researchers, and diplomats.

While I was in jail, I began recording the violations again. My family called me on several occasions, and they told me that the Bahrain Independent Commissioner Inquiry (BICI), which was ordered by the King, would be visiting us in the jails. In the meantime, I decided to document the cases of fellow inmates.

One of the most shocking cases I came across was that of Yousid Al Jazeeri. He was driving his car when he was targeted and shot by thugs and riot police who had attacked his village in Sitra. Yousid decided to stop the car and lie on the ground. By this time, the riot police were running towards him. He does not remember any more of what happened, but later, when he woke up at the hospital, he found himself injured in his leg by a bullet. He realized that he had been shot from a range of less than one meter, when the police had reached him and found him on the ground. Meanwhile, when he woke up at the scene of the crime, the riot police began torturing him by prodding at his wound.

While these sorts of violations were documented by Al Jazeera English and the Australian TV station SBS,[8] they were not included in the BICI, which I believe raises a lot of questions.

As I write this essay, Yousid remains in detention, like hundreds of others, and is still to do this day charged with attacking security forces.

My story is just one of many that depicts the systemic violations of basic human rights in Bahrain. I have one question I would pose to the U.S. State Department: Knowing my story, and that dozens of others have similar stories, is it still worth calling the Bahraini regime a "strategic ally and friend"?

I spent about three months in custody. I went through four jails during my detention. Sometimes I would get some sort of indication that my suffering might be coming to an end, but then it would continue and my hope would collapse. My family, especially my wife, was living with the same feelings at the time. They would be promised that my release was imminent and then be told the opposite. This fluctuation of hope and disappointment made it seem that I was jailed for years.

On August 7, 2011, one of the commanders came to tell Jawad Fayrooz and I that we had five minutes to prepare our bags to move. I noticed that for some reason, this commander seemed to have difficulty telling us that we would be released. Somehow or other, perhaps he was lonely too; it almost seemed as though he was going to miss us. That fleeting moment is tough for me to describe. I was surprised by the potential of people when I noticed his hesitation to let us out. It was sincere, not sinister.

When I was released, I realized just how much the Bahraini people appreciated those of us who had been speaking out at a difficult moment in our history. I also felt a big obligation to those who remained in custody and refused to surrender despite their circumstances. At the same time, I knew it would be best to maintain a low profile for

8.  http://www.youtube.com/watch?v=00HUTfKLris

a period of time and study the situation before taking a position I might later regret.

I kept my phone off for one week, and I did not answer calls for a second week after that. But I could not take a break for more than two weeks, given the situation that was unfolding. Sayed Hadi Almouswi, the head of the Human Rights Department of Al Wefaq, was overloaded with the documentation of tens of thousands of violations that had to be forward to the Bahrain Independent Commissioner Inquiry (BICI).

I began working on one of Al Wefaq's biggest projects ever. More than five hundred volunteers interviewed the victims and filled in forms to record their testimonies. We entered all this information into a database, wanting to be sure, at the very least, that the victims' stories were documented.

A team analyzed the data, and eventually we gave the BICI more than eight thousand pages of gathered findings. I was responsible for passing these findings to members of the media, NGOs, and other researchers.

Some of these findings were used by the Bahrain Human Rights Center to publish their Shadow Rreport. Al Wefaq decided not to publish its findings separately in order to avoid any hint of discrediting the BICI work so that it could be utilized for reconciliation. This was not an easy decision, because there were many indications that the report did not tell the entire story. Even so, it rose above my expectations in documenting some serious violations by the government and in being truthful. It reported systematic violations, and trials and detentions violating the freedom of expression.

Looking back, I think the United States did well in encouraging Bahrain to establish the BICI and to accept it. On November 23, 2011, U.S. Secretary of State Hillary Clinton said, "The Government of Bahrain has committed to establish a follow-up committee to implement the report's recommendations, and we urge full and expeditious implementation of these recommendations."[9]

But as is often the case in the Arab world, this was all promised but the facts on the ground were different. The report wasn't accepted totally by the Bahraini regime. The regime refused the conclusion about the role of Iran, or the lack thereof. It also refused to take accountability for high officials who gave directives to torture, and instead repeatedly declared that these were mistakes made by individuals.

Despite the regime's clear obligation to implement all recommendations, the government chose to accept and implement certain parts, wrongly interpret other parts, and ignore others. Meanwhile, the statements by politicians and by NGOs in the United States were nearly opposite. The State Department repeatedly declared that Bahrain's regime did accept the report, while Joe Stork, Deputy Middle East Director at Human Rights Watch, commented: "The report is very credible … but it seems that they have learned nothing."

Still, I find solace in knowing at least that in Bahrain, and maybe in much of the Arab world, our fields have been plowed and now we are just waiting for the rains to fall.

---

9. http://www.state.gov/secretary/rm/2011/11/177735.htm

# Not Your Prisoner
## by Arabian Knightz ft. Shadia Mansour
(translation of Arabic lyrics by Adel Iskandar)

During what has been described as a murderous political regime, the youth of Egypt adopted hip-hop as their voice of resistance. Emerging in this space was **ARABIAN KNIGHTZ**, an Egyptian hip-hop group that established themselves as lyricists using the sharpest swords in the land: words and music. They also created the most consistently original sound of any group to pick up the mic: a voice for rebellion, strength, and hope for the youth of the Middle East. Arabian Knightz came together in 2006. Its members, Rush, Sphinx, and E-Money, soon surpassed their peers in bringing an authentic Arab perspective to a hip-hop culture otherwise dominated by Western voices. Their mixing of English and Arabic raps exemplifies their versatility and universality. The group recently launched their debut album, *Uknighted State of Arabia*, featuring instrumentals dominated by traditional percussion instruments and players. Co-produced by West Coast producer Fredwreck (Farid Nassar), it is the first album of its kind.

## Ehab Emoney

In a tongue they believe lacks art, I will speak of:
Every dream drawn, from their anger it was buried,
Divided, wrapped in pain, thoughts in this audible period
And the solutions that only salvage the marginal subheaders
Terrorist, in eyes guarded by opportunism
After world wars, protected, hidden
Forgotten, discarded on displeased shoulders
Out of sight, leaving Arab lands dependent
With visible passivity, opportunism
Behind Islamic flags showing their intentions
Fraudulent, stubborn, psychopathic
Secretive, selfish, strategic, against humanity
And after pleading, still monitoring from viewing halls
To every humiliated Arab awaiting help:
"It is finished, they have broken the word 'solidarity' between us,
From our minds, they have taken the game-winning cards."

## Hook:

I want a country free from injustice!
Want a country free from defeat!
Want a country free from humiliation!
I want my land and the land of the Arabs, Arabs, Arabs!
Second Arabic Verse (Shadia Mansour)
We are walking, with dignity and self-confidence
*Your laws, with steadfastness of blood*
*You wouldn't be talking from behind the pistol*
*We will relieve*
Tell me who is sleeping at night, for real!
As you build barriers, we are raising our children,
Where ever we are, our numbers grow
We are the reason you cannot dare shut an eye
There is a big difference between resistance and decision-making.

## Karim Rush

Destructive Destruction Destroying my District..
Anti Christ Running in spreading evil wisdom..
I'm Destroying my Oppressors in Arabic settlements
known for blowing up beats and loving it!
my peeps die in the streets while yall close your eyes. . .
2 of y'all are kidnapped you call it a terrorist crime
the media is backing up murderous propaganda..
while we fight eternally like immortal high landers. . .
Al Durrah Sheikh Yassin, The Pains Unseen. . .
forging your own stories for the Blind to see. . .
want to draw your own opinions 'bout the bombs we face?
what's your opinion if you're slaved and your mom is raped
it's too easy to speak when you're far from the heat
to the white house i creep and yes i'm armed to the teeth
with a mic and a pen and a pad here is your evidence
weapons of mass destruction Mr President!

## Sphinx

They're dropping bombs over Baghdad Lebanon Afghan
Palestinians, belad Saddam listen Islam is all about the
peace man but wars up in these streets man got me losin
sleep damn mr politician I got a little question how come
you are eating and all your people "isn't" I am on a mission
to break up out of this prison if you're with me share my
vision let's start by saving the children.

# Muslim, Christian –One Hand!
## by Adel Iskandar

**ADEL ISKANDAR** is a scholar, author, and activist whose research focuses on media and communication in the Arab world, as well as the intersections of media, identity, and politics. He is the author/editor of several works, including *Al-Jazeera: The Story of the Network that is Rattling Governments and Redefining Modern Journalism* (Basic Books, 2003) and *Edward Said: A Legacy of Emancipation and Representation* (University of California Press, 2010). He teaches in the Communication, Culture, and Technology Program (CCT) as well as the Center for Contemporary Arab Studies (CCAS) at Georgetown University in Washington, D.C. Adel has lectured in over twenty countries and is a frequent commentator on Arab media. He is currently working on two books on dissidence in the Arab world.

The megaphone was passed to her not because she was a leader or a professional chanter. Sure, she was a recurring face at many of the Tahrir protests, but Heba was far from being an organizer. She was given the megaphone because all the other sloganeers had lost their voices in the last two hours of shouting as they marched out of Al-Azhar mosque towards Tahrir Square—the epicenter of the Egyptian revolution. Heba tightened her veil by tugging on the fabric until it reached her hairline, folded the corners in front of her ears, and brought the megaphone up to her mouth. She took a deep breath and, with fresh vocal cords, she let out a screeching cry: *Yasqut, Yasqut Hokm el 'Askar!* (Down, down with military rule!)

I had been advised not to venture out that day, but I hadn't listened. Protests were now deemed extremely dangerous, and everyone knew in a moment's time things could get ugly. Just a few days prior, on October 9, 2011, I was sitting in front of the television transfixed by live coverage of a tragedy unfolding. Thirty-one protesters had been killed at a rally. It seemed the powers that be were trying to scare us out of civil disobedience. But today, knowing a protest was taking place, I couldn't stay indoors. The agony of solitary commiseration was unbearable. I needed to know I wasn't alone in my mourning, my anger, and my outrage. So without informing anyone, I left the house and made my way through the surprisingly empty roads of downtown Cairo to the one place that every Egyptian can call home—Tahrir Square.

I am not certain what I was looking for or expecting. But upon arrival, I found nothing. Tahrir was unusually empty. Very few vendors or carts were around. Business was non-existent, and visitors to the iconic square had dwindled to none. A visceral feeling of melancholy came onto me. It was just eight months ago when Egyptians overcame fear, protested in the millions in this very square, and toppled their stubborn pharaoh. But today, in the face of another tragedy, it was barren and lifeless. In my head, I cursed those who had instilled fear in the hearts of Egyptians once again. For consolation, I convinced myself that while most Egyptians were in their homes and chose not to take to the streets to mourn their fallen brethren, they were all unanimously supportive of their cause. They all lived in a virtual Tahrir. They all sympathized with the families of the martyrs. But there was no evidence of this. I could not prove my hopes.

I wandered around looking for anyone to speak to, any conversation to seek consolation from. I found a group of five men standing next to a sidewalk littered with the day's newspapers. They were discussing, in a very quiet tone, the incident, making my attempt at eavesdropping extremely difficult. It was a sensitive time. Everyone was fearful and paranoid. One of the men saw me. He inched closer to his friends, alerted them to my presence. "Even the walls have ears," he said while giving me a suspicious stare. They fell silent, moved a few meters away, and huddled closer.

Since when did people in Tahrir watch over their shoulders and censor themselves? This square, the birthplace of Egyptian freedom, had been overtaken by fear, suspicion, and paranoia. The extreme violence of recent days had left Egypt's revolutionaries weary, fearful, disenchanted, and reluctant to continue demonstrating. This wasn't the home of bustling democratic expression, where every Egyptian came to speak his mind. It seemed the revolution had come to an end. An eerie silence hung over Tahrir. I sat down on the edge of the sidewalk and stared at the empty square with a somber lament.

*Yasqut Yasqut hokm al-'Askar!*

*Yasqut Yasqut hokm al-'Askar!*

The sound of fury tore through the silence. Heba's voice on the megaphone erupted from the farthest end of the square: *Yasqut Yasqut hokm al-'Askar!!* (Down, down with military rule!). I leapt to my feet and cautiously approached the source of the sound. As if breathing new life into the square, the chants brought people out from neighboring streets to get a closer look. As the march approached Tahrir Square, Heba's voice grew louder and more urgent, "The people demand the fall of the field marshal!" (leader of the military).

*Yasqut Yasqut hokm al-'Askar!*

*Yasqut Yasqut hokm al-'Askar!*

A feeling of relief and contentment came upon me as I heard the voices of the protesters reverberate in the afternoon air. The revolution had not succumbed.

Heba had come out this particular afternoon to register her fury at the violence, the injustice, and the incitement. The chant against the military had become standardized in the months that followed the fall of the Mubarak government, as the ruling Supreme Council for the Armed Forces (SCAF) slowly demoralized the youth revolutionaries, committed atrocities against them, and locked them out of political deal-making. But the chant had a particular resonance that day. Just a few days earlier, on October 9, 2011, and only a couple of kilometers from Tahrir, the blood of Coptic (Egyptian Orthodox Christians) protesters was spilled at the doorsteps of the Egyptian radio and television building known as Maspero.

The October 9 marchers had come out en masse to challenge the military's conduct of the post-Mubarak transition period. There had been an unusual spike in sectarian violence against Copts and their places of worship. While all Christians around the country were pained by the uncharacteristic violence, most of us found the incidents to be suspicious. In just eight months, Egypt had witnessed more attacks against Christians than any period in recent memory, and virtually all of these seemed unprovoked and not in line with popular public sentiments. It seemed like someone was trying to sow seeds of hate between Egyptians.

As the months went on, with no one brought to justice on any of these counts and with the ruling military junta doing little to resolve suspicion, Copts began turning their frustration towards SCAF. They had failed to protect or secure Christian communities, and they did little to assuage their fears. So when a church was attacked in Aswan and the governor of the southern governorate claimed the building was not a licensed place of worship, Christian protesters and Muslim sympathizers staged a march to Maspero. Many of those marching in this procession had begun pointing fingers not at their Muslim brethren but at the SCAF, whom they suspected were benefiting from a climate of sectarian tension, which would derail the revolution.

*Yasqut Yasqut hokm al-'Askar!*

"Down, down with military rule," shouted the unusually courageous crowd who paraded out of the densely populated and cosmopolitan area of Shubra (within walking distance from downtown Cairo) holding candles and carrying crosses. Many had come out with their families. Mothers and fathers brought their children to exercise a right never before afforded to them during the Mubarak era. Empowered by a new Egypt and propelled by calls for justice, they demanded that the military step down in the face of a wave of sectarian violence that the SCAF was at best unable to deal with and at worst was implicitly stoking. But it seemed the military was in no mood to be challenged. Minutes later, these protesters were brutally attacked by those charged with protecting them.

The perpetrators of the attack, unimaginably, were Egypt's own military. In an absurdly ironic David versus Goliath scenario, the state's most powerful institution and the country's weakest minority collided, leaving thirty-one Christian demonstrators dead and hundreds injured. Many of those killed had either been mowed down by armored vehicles or shot by live ammunition.

As the sounds of screams and wails tore through the nighttime sky, in a studio whose windows looks onto the carnage a news anchor powdered her nose before the "On Air" light came on. When it flashed, she was in tens of millions of Egyptian homes simultaneously. When she opened her mouth to report what was happening just meters away to horrified audiences across the country, she declared: "Violent Coptic protesters attacked the military, killing three soldiers and injuring many!" It did not stop there. She called on the "honorable people of Egypt" to come out and defend their armed forces. Few answered the call, but those who did went on a witch-hunt looking for Christians who, they were led to believe, had perpetrated alleged crimes against Egypt's heroes in uniform.

Mobs armed with swords, knives, clubs, and makeshift weapons wandered around Maspero inspecting everyone's wrists for tattoos of crosses, which are common markings among Copts. During the eighteen days of protests that toppled Mubarak, Christians stood hand-in-hand around their Muslim brethren to protect them during their prayers from the attacks of pro-Mubarak mobs. They would raise their hands to reveal their cross tattoos. It was a sign of interfaith solidarity. But on October 9, these same tattoos turned into targets of reprisal. Egypt after Mubarak, it seemed, had descended to a new low.

The incident was so disturbing that it paralyzed Egyptians. People sat in their homes, watching divergent coverage of the events. State television absolved the military and accused the predominantly Christian protesters. Some private networks showed the reality of the horror, filming from the morgues and hospitals where bodies were strewn across the floor. Many had been mutilated, contorted and flattened beyond recognition under the weight of armored vehicles. At no point in the Mubarak era had anything this vile and grotesque occurred, not even when the regime was fighting for its last breaths. The delicate balance of Egypt's religious diversity had been disrupted. No one knew what this meant or what could be done to rectify the situation. The whole country seemed to have frozen in time.

But not Heba. With the trauma of that day still fresh and palpable, her eyes scanned Tahrir. There were more onlookers and voyeurs in the square than participants and only a handful echoed her chants. People still seemed puzzled, unsure, and afraid. Who had committed crimes against whom? Who was the victim and who was the perpetrator? Should they believe Heba's criticism of the military or the state television anchor from a few days earlier?

Heba was becoming infuriated by the blank stares all around her. "How could they not be outraged?" she thought. Her voice cracked. She was overcome with misery and sorrow. It was then that she broke from the typical chants and improvised an off-key slogan, "The Copts have a righteous cause!" At a time when everyone seemed a fence-sitter, Heba took a side. The small protesting crowd that came with her repeated:

"The Copts have a righteous cause!"

"The Copts have a righteous cause!"

The couple of hundred protestors marched around Tahrir in hope of picking up more supporters and veered onto a side street en route to the Cathedral in Abbaseya, a few miles away. It was their plan to lead the procession from Al-Azhar, the most respected seat of Islamic higher learning in the world, to the main Coptic Cathedral to mourn and salute their Christian brethren. This was supposed to be a time of sectarian tension, but Heba and her cadre of loyal protesters were intent on disrupting that.

It was all too surreal and moving. As I watched the Muslim Heba lead protesters to a church to mourn the death of Christians a few days prior, I was overtaken by an amalgam of pride and hope. Tears welled up in my eyes. I stood immobilized as if enchanted by the sight. In my emotional daze, I felt a sudden and strong thrust to my back as I was tossed off the road and onto the nearby sidewalk.

"Be careful, *ya basha*," shouted a voice behind me. As I caught myself from falling, I turned around to see that a middle-aged man who wore his beard and white garb in the manner often associated with Salafis had pushed me out of the path of an incoming vehicle. I was surprised and grateful. Throughout this march, he voluntarily guarded the protesters by helping the flow of traffic around them, keeping them off the road, and making sure they were not attacked by thugs and hostile groups. I thanked him profusely. He nodded and dutifully returned to his navigational responsibilities. With one arm enveloping the marchers and his other fist in the air, he shouted "Muslim, Christian! One hand!"

As the procession crawled along, it came to a bottleneck leading into Abbaseya, a densely populated area that is home to the Ministry of Defense, and where recent flare-ups had occurred between protesters and supporters of SCAF. As we passed under a bridge, people emerged from the side streets, first out of curiosity and later in solidarity. The sound of the chant "Muslim, Christian, one hand!"

amplified as it echoed off the buildings and the bridge overhead. Our feet became more confident and the stomping shook the ground.

Intent to document what was a unique procession, I raced ahead to its front. I needed to show friends and family that this country had not splintered. I needed evidence to illustrate that its social fabric had not been torn and that its unity was preserved, even after the regime's attempt to sow discord between Egyptians. I took tens of photographs. But what caught my attention the most was a young woman who stood out in the crowd. She was the only person who was completely silent. She did not chant or shout. She spoke to no one. She wore nothing but black. And while everyone's sorrow and anger was palpable, her face radiated peace and tranquility. She wore a pendant with a hologram engraved in the form of a young man's face. His long shaggy hair was tucked behind his ears. In this picture, he was smiling broadly from cheek to cheek. As I stared at her, someone noticed my fixated gaze, leaned over my shoulder and whispered into my ear, "That's Mary, Mina Danial's sister."

In the lifetime of a nation like Egypt, whose seven-thousand-year lineage spans civilizations, dynasties, and empires, there are many landmark occasions to celebrate and mourn. While two dates, January 25 and February 11, both etched their mark in the Egyptian calendar in 2011—the first for the first eruption of the revolution and the second for the toppling of Mubarak—that was also a year of near daily sacrifice and bloodshed. And October 9 of that year, some eight months after Mubarak's fall, has become another unforgettable day in modern Egyptian history. On that day, the political fault lines in Egypt were redrawn, and the revolution was re-ignited.

Egypt's Christians, the majority being of of the indigenous Coptic Orthodox denomination, had spent the preceding thirty years in relative hibernation. They had retracted themselves from public life, grown increasingly insular, and lost trust in any state institution. They had delegated all social, cultural, religious, and political duties on their behalf to the Church. Their contribution to Egypt's history was gradually being omitted from the national curriculum, and the state rendered everything related to them an issue of national security. Using a combination of blackmail and fear-mongering, the ruling National Democratic Party (NDP) had effectively silenced them and ensured their full compliance. The government guaranteed Christian loyalty by waving the Muslim brotherhood opposition as a boogeyman to scare them. In response, like all institutions in Egypt during Mubarak's era, including all ministries and Al-Azhar, the Church actively disengaged its clergy and congregation from politics.

So although the Copts were facing the same predicaments as all Egyptians, as a minority with "special status," they had been indoctrinated to believe that being a spectator to events guarantees self-preservation. But some broke from that mold. History had shown that Copts suffer the most when they are disengaged from public life, not the opposite. As a Copt myself, I had committed myself to Egypt's protest movement many years ago, albeit from a distance since I resided in the United States. Sadly, it was always just a handful of Christians at protests, and I had effectively given up trying to compel other Copts to participate. Although I understood their fears and concerns, I was convinced that the emancipation of Egypt's minorities would come only in the context of an intertwined, multidenominational, unified, collective movement against autocracy and corruption that disempowered Egyptians of all stripes.

When the revolution first erupted, the Coptic Church, like Al-Azhar, discouraged its adherents from joining the protest movement. Many disobeyed this call to stay home. On the first Friday of the revolution, January 28, 2011, the now infamous Day of Rage, Christian protesters had surrounded worshippers hand-in-hand, guarding their Muslim brethren in Tahrir Square in the face of attacks from security forces and Mubarak's gangs. They did so for every prayer. When Mubarak was finally toppled, the country rejoiced as one—Muslim and Christian.

But it wasn't long before things got complicated. A revival of empowerment and feelings of heightened dignity reverberated across the country. Everyone demanded a better life as the revolution spread to every corner of the nation and trickled into every institution. The remnants of the old regime, which remained steadfast in retaining power, were being challenged, as attempts to dislodge it grew bolder. The state, now under military rule, tried to counter this by describing all further demands as "factional" protests, arguing they were divisive rather than being in the whole nation's best interests. Factory strikes were "factional." Teacher's protests were "factional." Sit-ins demanding media freedom were "factional." Any protest by the Nubians of Upper Egypt, the Bedouins of Sinai or the Western desert, or the Copts was painted as "factional," "sectarian," "divisive" and "opportunistic." So when the largely Christian protest marched towards the state television building on October 9, 2011 to protest attacks against Coptic places of worship in various parts of the country and the government's failure to protect them, the SCAF was not in a mood to tolerate what it saw as insolent, dissident behavior from a feeble "factional" minority.

Among the peaceful procession of the young and old, rich and poor, was a shaggy-haired twenty-five-year-old man with a childlike smile. Despite the somber mood of the march, with many holding candles, this young man's face radiated with energy and optimism. His was a known face. He had been at most protests from the early days of the revolution to marches against the military's rule during the transition period. Many of those who met him in Tahrir didn't know this young man was Christian. It did not matter. During a crescendo in the revolution, when Mubarak supporters armed with knives, swords, and batons galloped through Tahrir on horses and camels to punish the revolutionaries, this young man joined his brethren in protecting the square and earned his battle wounds. In one photo from February 2, 2011, a medic can be seen removing a bullet from his leg. The young man is laughing off his wounds. If he could smile back then, he could smile now, for he had seen worse days in the fight to remove Mubarak.

As the thousands-strong procession approached Maspero, something strange was in the air. Despite the melancholic and controlled tone of the protest, the atmosphere was unusually tense. The television building they were heading towards was heavily fortified by armored vehicles and military personnel. Everything was about to change. The sound of gunshots rang in the air, and panic spread in the crowd. The soldier that had stood idle in front of the building now lifted his shield off the ground, adjusted his helmet, and raised his baton in the air. In an unexpected turn of events, hundreds of soldiers charged the crowd of protesters and attacked them senselessly as if herding animals. Screams filled the air as people tried to rescue their friends and family from the hands of the men in uniform.

Out of the blue, an armored personnel carrier came racing through the crowd, swerving from side to side as people scurried out of its way. Once it reached the end of the road, it turned around and accelerated back, scraping the sides of parked cars. It was headed straight for the clusters of protesters. It veered onto and off the sidewalk in an attempt to plough into as many people as possible. Screams turned into wails as the blood of bodies mowed down by the army vehicle flowed onto the street. Crushed torsos, flattened skulls, and body parts were scattered on the ground as people tried to help the injured and identify the victims in the dark night, while watching their backs for further attacks.

I watched this massacre unfold on the screen in utter disbelief. This unspeakable horror was wholly unexplainable. My body felt numb. I was left speechless for hours, and a A sense of helplessness fell on me. The great Egyptian revolution that the world had rejoiced in, that inspired similar movements in the region and beyond, that world leaders had raced to commemorate, had died before my eyes. I was subconsciously mourning not only the lives of those lost in this carnage but also the innocence of a once-utopian revolution.

Some seven hours later, when the bloodbath came to an end, the Maspero massacre had claimed thirty-one lives. The young man with the bushy hair had been involved in another attack on the people by the tyrannical state. Once again he inspired those around him. Once again, despite the horror, his smile radiated stubbornly as if taunting fate. Once again he was a victim. But this time, fate had called his name. His lifeless body lay on the cold hospital floor with two bullet holes. One had pierced through his chest. The other entered the back of his head. His name was Mina Danial.

The ruling military junta had set a historic precedent and killed its own people in cold blood. They counted on the Muslim majority to overlook the massacre and support the military by condemning their Christian countrymen and women. But they had miscalculated. Their foolish barbarism had stripped Mubarak's military of its camouflage, added to the ranks of the revolution's martyrs, and turned that young Christian man, Mina Danial, into the new Khaled Said.[1]

For months and years to come, the chant *Iqtil Khaled, Iqtil Mina, kul rosasa betkaweena* (Kill Khaled. Kill Mina. Every bullet strengthens us!) would be a rallying cry for unity between Muslims and Christians against tyranny. Today Mina Danial is immortalized on an Egyptian flag named after him that has become a symbol of the continuing revolution. The flag bears the symbols of the crescent and cross interlinked alongside the word hurriya (freedom). Below it is a red fabric sheet with a stenciled image of his likeness. Two young revolutionaries, Tarek Al-Tayeb, a Muslim, and Michael Karara, a Christian, withstood tear gas, beatings, and rubber bullets for many days as they alternated waving this flag on the frontlines of the battles between protesters and the security forces.

When Egypt's military rulers inherited power from Mubarak, many hoped they would be the benevolent force that would shepherd the country towards democracy. But SCAF has dashed these

---

1. Khaled Said is the twenty-eight-year-old businessman from Alexandria whose brutal beating and murder at the hands of two police officers in the summer of 2010 kick-started a wave of demonstrations and activity in the social media that led up to the January 25 protests and the toppling of Mubarak.

hopes. Instead, they have taken pages out of Mubarak's playbook and used religion to drive a wedge between Muslims and Christians in the country. And in instances like the Maspero massacre, they have surpassed their predecessor in both brutality and impunity. As Egyptians called for justice, the military responded with arrogance and disregard. Despite the photographic and videographic evidence that incriminates the military police for the atrocities on October 9, the military has instead blamed the victims, accused the protesters of incitement, and washed its hands of any wrongdoing. They still hope to erase any memory of this crime and come out unscathed.

Egyptians often say that the worst criminal is "he who kills someone and walks in their funeral." On the first Coptic Christmas after the Maspero massacre, SCAF did just this. General Hamdi Badeen, the man who oversaw the conduct of the military police on that bloody night, sat in the front row of the mass and, smiling, shook hands with Coptic Pope Shenouda to congratulate Egypt's Christians. Many in the audience watched with disgust. And when the Pope thanked SCAF for their "wise management" of the country, a few outraged youth interrupted the speech with screams of "Down, down with military rule!"

*Yasqut Yasqut hokm el 'Askar!!*

*Yasqut Yasqut hokm el 'Askar!!*

The army generals have tried to appease the Christians since the Maspero massacre. Appearing to be the only supporters of Christian political representation, they appointed five Copts to Egypt's first post-Mubarak parliament, expecting silent consent from Egypt's Christians in response.

Yet they have misjudged the new generation of Egyptians, of which I count myself as one. We are proud, unrelenting, and indefatigable. Egypt is full of Hebas who will speak truth to power against all odds and in the face of the gravest danger. The SCAF has underestimated the humble yet confident power of a sister's quiet agony. Although they are soldiers, they have lost sight of how to defend our honor and dignity. When they killed us at Maspero, and in subsequent incidents at Mohammed Mahmoud Street, at the Cabinet sit-in, at the Port Said soccer massacre, and elsewhere, they repeated Mubarak's mistakes. By killing us in the name of stabilizing the country, they have broken the delicate social contract with us, the people. Now we, those with the least power and greatest conviction, are the only source of legitimacy. The specters of those gone are greater than when they were living. Their as yet unwritten stories will break through the silence to unite a country, in defiance of all odds.

We might be an overly romantic, irrational, and unrealistic generation, but we are the future. And when we finally prevail in *our* Egypt, there will be, as Caribbean poet Aimé Césaire put it, "room for everyone at the rendezvous of victory."

# After Years of Silence
## by Baraa Shaiban

**BARAA SHAIBAN**, an interior decorator, was born in Yemen. His life course has led him to participating in politics, social action, and revolution because of his belief in diversity and the freedom of speech. Baraa was a contributor to Yemen's Youth Movement in early 2011, serving on the movement's media team. His decision to join the movement came after he witnessed the violent crackdown on protesters in the early days of the uprising. He is the founder of Life Makers Foundation and blogs at commentmideast.com and bloggerswithoutborders.com, a newly established non-profit organization helping connect bloggers to one another, and helping them to assist others in need. In addition, Baraa edits a Facebook page dedicated to sharing news about his country in English: facebook.com/EngYemenNews.

On June 11, 2011 around 10:00 pm, my cousin and I had dinner together. Afterwards, we split up on one of the busiest streets of the city, each going our own way.

Unexpectedly the street was empty at the time. It was so quiet and dark, even the street lamps were off. I waited for a few minutes for a taxi to come, but a voice inside me told me to keep moving. This voice became louder especially after I heard a stranger shouting at me to stop. I ignored the stranger and kept moving until I reached a checkpoint of the government's Central Security Forces. I realized that I had nowhere to go. A group of armed civilians came from behind me and pulled me to a car. They tied me up very quickly and then masked me as soon as they pulled me inside the car. They put me on my stomach, with my face down, and started beating me with the backs of their weapons. I felt like time had stopped. All of the moments of the revolution during the preceding months past flashed through my mind. After about an hour I finally realized: I have been abducted. And the first question that came to mind was, "What is going to happen to me when they are done?"

Fear filled my heart. I realized I had to focus on what was happening around me. The people in the car barely spoke. The only thing I remember hearing clearly was a man saying, "Is this the guy who has been sending stuff on the Internet?" Eventually the car stopped. One man grabbed my arm and twisted in behind my back, and continued to twist until I felt as though my bones were about to break apart in his hands. The car started slowly moving again—but I still couldn't see anything. I could feel that we were in a hilly area, and then the car stopped again.

The same guy came again and twisted my arm in the same way; the pain was unbearable. I did not know if I would ever be freed from the pain. That would be the sequence throughout the night; intermittently stopping and twisting my arm. It was torturous. If they wanted me dead, though, they would have surely killed me already.

I thought of my mom and my fiancée and told myself if I wanted to see either of them again, I should be strong enough to surpass this. These people wanted to break me down, but I would not regret the revolutionary work I had been doing. If I was not on the right path, none of this would be happening. The car kept on stopping and moving and the guy continued to torture me for about seven hours. The last two times, I was able to hold myself tight and conceal the fact that

I was in so much pain. I became angry enough to resist fear and told myself: what can be worse than what was happening already?

Finally at dawn, they tossed me out in the exact place they had abducted me from, right in front of the Central Security checkpoint. When I stood on my feet, I took the first taxi I found and went home. My family took me to the hospital to get the necessary treatment. Early in the morning my friends rushed to the hospital to see me. It was my most horrific experience during the many months of the revolution.

I was born in a middle-class, educated family in Yemen, and I can say that religion—a word misunderstood by many nowadays—had a big impact on my life. My father received his engineering degree in Britain, and my mother received a Ph.D. from the University of Cardiff. My parents tried their best to invest in their children's education so they registered me in one of the best schools in the country.

My interest in politics started at an early age. In 1997, when I was twelve years old, the country had its second parliamentary election, and I followed the results of those elections very closely.

Although I was still young, I could see how the situation in the country was getting worse on a daily basis. The people were not able to secure their basic rights, including the right to education, the right of employment, and equal citizen rights. President Ali Abdallah Saleh spoke of the government's supposed accomplishments when he addressed the nation on TV, while, in reality, things were headed in the opposite direction. Most of the officials in the country must have obtained a certificate in corruption before being appointed to their positions.

In 2003, the country held its third parliamentary elections, but my interest in politics had taken another approach. I, along with my friends, decided that we would support the opposition representative (Islah Party) for the district. We were fed up with Parliament members, who only made themselves publicly visible a few days before the election to obtain voters. They would offer empty promises and spend some money on the poor families in the area, only to abandon us later. The number of people in our district was about six thousand. Almost half of them were registered voters.

Since my friends and I were well known for our social activities in the neighborhood, securing voters for our candidate wasn't that difficult. We were soon contacted by Islah members from our district to help us organize our activities. When the election day came, our candidate won with an overwhelming majority. Still, I didn't join the Islah party because I wanted to remain the same person the people knew before the campaign—an independent youth.

In 2004, I was influenced by the TV show *Life Makers*, at the time the most viewed TV show in the Arab world . Amr Khaled—a well-known Egyptian reformer in the Middle East—spoke about how the Muslim youth should take a role in the development of their countries. Apparently, I would later find out that I wasn't the only one influenced by *Life Makers*. Activists started to gather from all over Yemen to launch a youth organization in order to mobilize the *Life Makers* projects. In March 2005, Life Makers Foundation was officially announced. It quickly became one of the biggest youth organizations in the country, with almost ten thousand members in the ten main cities in Yemen.

Life Makers Foundation was a new and different experiment. It gathered youth from across different sectors of society for one cause: Yemen. Regardless of which political party you belonged to or what Islamic school you followed, your role was always welcomed in Life Makers. The TV show and the organization itself taught me how to communicate with others, how to reach the public, and most important, how to connect with people regardless of their background.

The period between 2005 and 2010 was a very important one in Yemen's history. The regime launched six wars against the people of Sa'ada, accusing those who follow Houthi—a religious leader in the northern part of the country—that they were trying to bring about a return to the kingdom that ruled Yemen before 1962. In 2007 the people in the South took to the streets. They started demanding basic rights such as reforming the wages system, but the regime met them with excessive violence. The southerners' demands then escalated, leading to a call for a split from the northern part of the country. The people were angry about the theft of public wealth, such as granting hectares of lands to army generals while, elsewhere, ten civilians had to share the same substandard flat.

The regime quickly started to claim that some southern cities sheltered Al-Qaeda members. Unfortunately the international community, in particular the United States, bought this reasoning. They began tailoring their foreign policy towards Yemen to reflect the security concern that Yemen could become a flourishing hub for a militant organization affiliated with al-Qaeda, AQAP (Al-Qaeda Arabian Peninsula). Because of this potential threat, they reasoned that they should assist the Yemeni regime by all means. All kinds of intelligence flowed into the country during this period under many different titles: journalists, researchers, academics, and so on. Most reports coming out of Yemen argued that Yemen was heading towards complete disaster. There were three possible predictions of what was to come: a civil war like Lebanon, anarchy like Somalia, or an Islamic state like Afghanistan.

During a seminar at the University of Amsterdam in 2007, I told the audience that Yemen was witnessing a wake-up call among its youth, and I explicitly described the youth as the saviors of Yemen. After all, Life Makers was a clear example of just that. I was confident that the country's youth, though inexperienced, could prevent Yemen from any impending disaster.

As time passed I grew more convinced that things in the country would not change while the General People's Congress, headed by Ali Abdullah Saleh,was in power. The regime kept launching one war after another on the people of Sa'ada, facing the Southern Movement brutally, blocking the possibility of the opposition parties (the Joint

Meeting Parties, or JMP) reaching a political resolution, and playing the Al-Qaeda card to the international community.

International support for Ali Saleh's regime increased despite the regime's reputation and evidence of its corruptness. In 2009, the United States announced that it intended to fund anti-terrorism activities in Yemen with 300 million U.S. dollars. It also trained and equipped the Republican Guards and the Special Forces headed by Ali Saleh's son, Ahmed Ali, under the name of anti-terrorism forces. We weren't surprised to later learn that Ali Saleh authorized American airstrikes on Yemeni soil and that women and children were among the victims.

By 2009, political life in the country was reaching a dead end. The JMP announced that they would boycott the 2009 elections if the GPC didn't announce actual reforms to the electoral system and if it continued to run the High Committee for Elections on its own. They refused to join the elections with the current electoral registry and demanded that a new one be formed. The JMP also demanded several reforms in the electoral system.[1]

The parliamentary elections that were scheduled for 2009 were delayed for two years. By the time 2011 arrived, nothing had really changed.

In an interesting turn of events, the GPC announced that it intended to run the elections alone if the JMP decided not to take part. It also announced several amendments to the constitution. The main amendment would be to revise the presidential terms, allowing Ali Saleh to run for presidency in 2013, which according to the original constitution would have been the end of his presidency. In response, in early January 2011, JMP parliament members held a strike in front of the Parliament, insisting that the president should end his term by 2013 and that no constitutional amendments should take place.

---

1. For example, JMP demanded that the electoral system turn to a quantitative method instead of the district representative method.

## The Revolution

When the revolution started in Tunisia in late December 2010, I watched it on TV with great interest, but I didn't imagine that the "Arab Spring" would reach our country so quickly. When Ben Ali, Tunisia's former president, fled Tunis, marking the first victorious Arab revolution in recent history, a group of university students and political activists in Yemen instinctively mobilized in front of Sana'a University, declaring their solidarity with the Tunisians and chanting slogans against the current regime in Yemen and its policies. The connection had instantly been made, though the security forces quickly stopped them from demonstrating.

Then when the revolution started in Egypt, everyone in Yemen watched the events closely. Egypt is a focal point in the region, and any change there would likely affect the situation in Yemen. Less than a week after the start of the Egyptian revolution, the opposition parties in Yemen, along with the civil society organizations, called for a mass demonstration to be held on February 3, 2011. When I saw the crowd that day, I said to myself: "This is it. Our time has come, and we can make it too." The demonstrators demanded that the regime be overthrown, and asked for the quick resignation of Ali Abdullah Saleh.

On February 11, 2011, the night Mubarak stepped down, a group of youth in the city of Taiz, inspired by the ousting of Mubarak, went out into the streets, announcing the beginning of the Yemeni revolution.

In one of the many protests held near Sana'a University, the security forces along with thugs tried to crush the young people gathered in the squares. The scenes of brutality moved me viscerally, and deeply enough to inspire me to participate in the Yemeni revolution. My friend Hamza, one of the founders of Life Makers, gave me the final push when he asked me: "Where are you? Come to the square, it's time to do something."

Since I could speak English, I offered my writing and translating services to the media team in Change Square in Sana'a. I hoped to amplify the voice of the Yemeni revolution to reach the outside world, just like the Tunisian and Egyptian revolutions did.

It was extraordinary to see the gatherings in the square grow with each passing day. We were careful to maintain as much order as possible while protesting in a civilized manner. Weapons were prohibited in the square and everyone who entered was searched carefully. The youths' spirits were high. We were all convinced that this revolution would succeed. Protesters were finally criticizing Saleh and his family explicitly in public for the first time. Every day, new details about the corruption of this regime were revealed and more people joined the uprising.

The regime quickly sent thugs and security forces to break down the youth in the square. But we youth were resilient. Sometimes we would find ourselves trapped on all sides, with regime followers shooting bullets and throwing stones at us. But like rocks, we did not waver; we knew our cause would prevail. Victory was present in the eyes of everyone in the square.

The revolution had some magical element that attracted everyone to it. Perhaps it was hope. Whoever arrived at the square couldn't leave, and whoever had been quiet finally broke their silence. The sound of the youths' chants were so loud that they rocked the whole country. No matter how hard people tried to close their ears, invariably the sound would reach them. "The people want to overthrow the regime." The youth showed a solidarity never before seen in Yemen, and it caught the attention of all those watching at home in the country and perhaps in the world.

For decades, we had been frustrated with our aging leaders, who resigned only by dying—and then left their positions to their sons inherit their positions. The economic situation of the country was a frequent subject discussed in the square. People were now asking questions and demanding answers. As every day saw more people join the revolution, by the end of February 2011 we were able to claim that the president no longer had constitutional legitimacy and that the only legitimacy was the legitimacy of the revolution.

However, two weeks after the beginning of the revolution, divisions within the revolution started to appear. People began chanting for different things. We struggled to find common ground with those around us. We knew we had to have unified demands, and everyone entering the square had to know exactly what had brought them there.

A well-known activist and a friend of mine, Gobool Al-Mutwakel, held the first meeting with the aim of bringing the youth in the square together so that they could get to know one another and prepare for the future. People came from different groups and sectors, with different backgrounds and views, belonging to different tribes; yet we managed to unite towards one goal: a better future for the country and new leadership. Every group nominated one person to attend the meeting, and we formed a committee to finalize our points. Throughout the revolution we continued to meet at each critical and challenging juncture.

I travelled to Taiz in hopes of finding revolutionaries elsewhere in the country to connect with. Freedom Square in Taiz was amazing; the number of people in the square was greater than the number in Sana'a's Change Square. I contacted the media center for Taiz's Freedom Square and offered my services. I was warmly welcomed by the team, which was composed of media professionals including journalists, photographers, cameramen, and editors. They seemed pleased to have my assistance. The director, Wadhah Alyemen, was like a brother to everyone on the team, and quickly we became good friends. I discovered that the media center served largely as a connection point among most of the youth in Freedom Square.

On Friday, March 18, I prayed in Freedom Square. After prayers, I met with the media team and had lunch. Al Jazeera was broadcasting live from Change Square in Sana'a at the time. Images rolled of snipers shooting at people leaving the mosque after they finished their Jummah (Friday) prayers. As time went on, the number of victims was increasing. We quickly rushed to Freedom Square in case similar levels of violence reached our area.

Just a few days later, several officials from the government announced their resignations, the most significant being Ali Mohsen Al-Ahmar (the president's close kinsman and the commander of the First Armored Division, the pro-revolution branch of the army). His resignation led to more resignations within the army and the government. The revolution was at its most powerful moment, and many thought that it would be the end of Ali Abdullah Saleh's regime.

When I returned to Sana'a, the first thing I did was visit what is now known as the Martyrs' Roundabout, where so many youth were slain on March 18. Their souls could still be felt. It was as though their blood was still freshly wetting the ground.

I contacted my good friend Hajer Al-Nahari (who was a revolutionary well before the revolution even started) to collaborate on organizing a silent march from the Change Square stage to the Martyrs' Roundabout. The march would end with transforming the area into a monument with flowers and candles, so visitors would be reminded of those who died, and hopefully also reminded of the necessity for revolution. We will never forget that day. That was the day we became completely determined to topple the regime once and for all.

While I was in Taiz, a friend of mine, Mohammed Al-Shami (one of the founders of Life Makers) had been attending the youth group meetings in Sana'a on behalf of my friends and me. When I returned to Sana'a, the youth had almost completed writing down the goals and demands of the revolution. We officially announced that we were going to hold a press conference to share the demands of the youth and the revolution's goals. Our group became known as the Watheeqah Coalition, which means the "Demands Document Coalition."

Connecting with coalitions and being present in the square was the key to reaching more people. You must talk to people's hearts in order to reach their minds. People want to see people on the ground, not just behind TV screens. They love those who understand their suffering and carry their hopes.

We were able to get in contact with most of the youth coalitions and groups in Change Square in order to unify our demands and then prepare to travel to other cities to spread the demands to the youth in the other squares across the country. Since I already had contacts with the youth in Taiz, and Mohammed Al-Shami had contacts with youth in Aden, we proposed to visit those two cities. Before travelling to Taiz, we came in contact with the Freedom and Change Forum, a group of businessmen active in the square. Mr. Abdullah Al-Mutareb, the forum general secretary—was keen to sponsor the youth activities and interested in forming a youth council that would be an umbrella for all the youth coalitions in the square. We agreed that we would work together, especially since unification of demands is the right platform for creating a youth council, and having a youth council is the first practical step to move the revolution forward. This became doubly important after Ali Saleh refused the American Embassy's proposal that he should step down from his position, along with Ali Mohsen, and leave the country.

I traveled to Taiz and saw that, despite their limited resources, including having only one meal a day sometimes, the youth there had been doing an incredible job. The team had a newspaper for Freedom Square that was published regularly. The images coming out of Taiz, which were broadcast on Al Jazeera and other TV channels, were largely distributed by the media team.

I again used the media center as my starting point and tried to visit every single coalition and group in Freedom Square in order to share the Demands of the Youth document. Then Mohammed Al-Shami asked me to come to Sana'a to organize a trip to Aden and prepare for a workshop we were holding for the youth coalitions in Aden. Before I left Taiz, I met with Wadhah and the media center directors, and we agreed to continue our work and keep in touch to meet either in Sana'a or maybe again in Taiz. I took the first plane to Sana'a. Two days later, on April 19, Mohammed and I flew to Aden.

The situation in Aden was very different from that in both Sana'a and Taiz. Due to the divisions among the people, the city had seven squares. It appeared almost impossible to find a way of uniting the diverse protests taking place in Aden.

Mohammed and I were already convinced that the way to bring the different groups together was to meet each group individually and win them over to the idea of workshop to discuss the collective demands of the youth of Aden. The idea was to list the points everyone agreed on and propose ways we could work together to accomplish them. At the same time, each group could carry on with its own activities individually.

On April 21, just three days after arriving, we held our workshop. On the 23rd, each group nominated two people to attend a closed meeting to write a final version of the demands of the youth of Aden. This led to the first Unified Youth Coalition in Aden. The groups who at first refused to join eventually contacted us, hoping to start working with us on unified activities.

This experience only reinforced my belief that you cannot unify all people under one party, but you can find common ground and coordinate activities towards broader shared goals. It's also important to create initiatives and projects, not wait until all the people agree on a certain idea. This gave me an idea on how to approach the youth in the squares, especially before announcing a youth revolutionary council in Taiz. I travelled to Taiz and back to Aden, and ran several meetings in both cities. We were fueled with will, and nothing seemed impossible to us. We were certain that we would achieve our goals, no matter how difficult and steep the path might be.

Aden has a much higher presence of security forces and checkpoints than Taiz and Sana'a. The day before I left Aden, government forces attacked the youth in Mansoorah, a neighborhood in Aden. We had no weapons to fight back except our cameras documenting the attacks in order to spread the word to the press. The people faced the security forces with bare chests, while the soldiers were equipped with heavy machine guns.

With my own eyes I could now see why the people in the South had felt oppressed; they had to face incessant brutality for so many years, with no one to tell their story. This revolution was necessary to unite the people in the South and the North. This experience in Aden compelled me to invest more in fighting for the rights of the southern people. I was convinced they should be given a priority by the youth of the revolution all over the country, including in the North.

In May 2011, activists from all over the country arrived in Sana'a in order to discuss the coming scenarios for the revolution. During the four months that had passed, we were able to create a network of activists capable of escalating the revolution. We discussed the fact that we might not have this opportunity again and started to work day and night until finally we announced a Media Revolutionary Council on May 10.

The Media Revolutionary Council's main task was to to plan how to escalate the protests. The youth were able to extend the sit-in by 550 meters in one day, reaching the Old University Building, only 300 meters away from Zubairy Street (the heart of Sana'a). The plan was to extend the sit-in and the march one block each day in the direction of the presidential palace, to trap Ali Saleh and his associates, leaving them with no choice but to flee quickly. Political forces quickly tried to stop this unexpected move through their members in the square. They realized that escalating any further would jeopardize the political resolution they had been working on since March. We tried very hard during the month of May to complete the last page of the revolution, but there were more voices cautioning us to stop in order to prevent further bloodshed at the expense of freedom.

On May 22, Ali Saleh announced the beginning of a new violent chapter when he officially refused to sign the Gulf Cooperation Council Initiative (the resolution the political parties had been working on since March). According to the initiative, Saleh would hand power over to his deputy, Abd-Rabbu Mansour Hadi, in return for immunity from prosecution, which many of us protesters still rejected at the time.

Ali Saleh tried to drive the country into a civil war by attacking the Al-Ahmar family, the head of Hashed Tribes Confederation (the biggest in the country) on the 24th of May. Not long after, that he repeatedly attacked the First Armored Division. The revolution had reached a decisive moment. Those who remained at home during the revolution, away from the streets, began to blame the youth for driving the country into instability. After that, the regime blocked fuel and power from reaching the people, and everyday living conditions became very difficult for the average Yemeni. Explosions and heavy fire could be heard all night, every night. But the revolutionary youth decided not to abandon their sit-ins and demonstrations. Fear heightened, and the situation became even graver.

Ali Saleh was clearly running out of options, so he decided to try to resolve the situation militarily. On May 29, security forces in Taiz launched a full-scale attack on the youth who had been demonstrating for almost four months in Freedom Square. At least twenty were killed, and hundreds more were injured. The forces even looted the field hospital in the square and burned the tents. Any youth attempting to resist was killed.

I decided it was time to spread the word to the globe, so I contacted Faizah Al-Sulaimany, an activist who had been documenting the violations by the security forces. My contacts and friends in the media center in Taiz made it possible for me to quickly learn what happened on May 29. Only two days after the attack, Faizah and I were able to get the names of eighteen of the martyrs and many of those injured, and we also got in contact with the medical doctors present during the death of those youths. We immediately began preparing a report on the incident, including photos and videos .

We continued to update the report and have it reach as many people as possible. We wanted to let the international community, especially human rights activists, know the truth about what was happening our country.

A few organizations in Switzerland contacted us and explained that they were interested in continuously receiving the information we were providing. Faizah received an anonymous call warning her not to proceed—ironically, this was the sign that we were on the right path.

It was at this point that I was abducted. A few weeks later, Faizah contacted me after having been abducted in a very similar scenario. I wondered then just how important and critical the information we were gathering and publishing was. Faizah and I were lucky, but many others disappeared and have yet to reappear.

Regardless of the difficulty that Yemen is experiencing, we will never be able to return to how things were before February 2011. Knowing this gives me solace. We may have to struggle for some time, but the people's will is stronger than any tyrant. The people of Yemen have woken up, and nothing can stop them now. The price we are paying in this moment is the cost of years of silence. Being free is the right of every human being, regardless of race, creed, nationality, or tribe. The Yemeni people have touched the soul of freedom, and they cannot, and will not, go back.

# Escaping Politics: When It Runs in Your Blood, It Ain't Easy

*by Dina Duella*

**DINA DUELLA** is a Libyan American freelance media professional and adjunct professor in the Department of Communication at Chapman University in Orange, California. She received her master's degree in Communication, Culture, and Technology from Georgetown University, where her research focused on images and representation of Arabs and Muslims in film and television. Dina has a background in politics and international relations, having worked for the U.S. Congress, the United Nations Information Centre, and most recently with the National Transitional Council of Libya. She hopes to continue her work on diversity and representation in film and television, and she plans to use her experience to develop and contribute to a media industry in a free Libya.

M y mother told me recently, "You can't help yourself, can you? *It* runs in your veins." The *it* she was referring to was politics.

I'll never forget the stories I heard growing up: a relative shot point-blank by a Gadhafi thug in front of the Vatican, my aunt's husband tortured in Abu Salim prison for thirteen years, my uncle forcibly drafted into the army and tortured repeatedly when trying to escape. Every Libyan family has countless stories of Gadhafi's atrocities. My fiancé can tell you one of the most famous cases of brutality.

His uncle Sadiq Shwehdi, as a student, was hanged in a basketball stadium full of people in Benghazi in 1984. Gadhafi televised the hanging as a warning to anyone who dared to defy him.

Hearing those stories as a young child growing up in Canada drew me into the world of politics. From participating in Model UN and student government in high school to majoring in political science in college and later working as a field representative at a local congresswoman's district office and then on Capitol Hill, it seemed my whole life has revolved around politics from an early age.

My political activism became focused on Libya, my parents' homeland, in the summer of August 2010. This was half a year before the February 17 *thawra* (revolution) when the uprisings of the Arab world started, and just a few months before Bouazizi's inspiring moment in Sidi Bouzid. Having just finished graduate school, I decided I wanted to spend some time in the Middle East. A friend of mine had been living in Libya since the beginning of the summer and encouraged me to attend a youth conference put on by the Libyan government. I decided to attend and take advantage of the free airfare courtesy of the Libyan government so I could visit my family and see all the new developments in Libya that I had heard so much about.

Needless to say, not much had changed since my visit five years prior. Sure there were now a few nice hotels, but health care, education, and the basic infrastructure were still suffering. At the conference I met the founders of *Vice* magazine, who were shooting a documentary on youth culture. I worked with them as a fixer for a few days, translating and assisting them around town. It was difficult to interview people, since citizens were paranoid and too careful to talk honestly about current affairs. The *Vice* team left disappointed and produced a segment for their MTV show, *The Vice Guide to Everything*, that amusingly bashed Gadhafi, ensuring they would never be allowed into Libya again.

I was eager to experience Ramadan in the Middle East, so I stayed in Libya and spent time with my family. I made friends: some expats, some born and raised in Libya, and some from the diaspora who had returned to work. I quickly learned that some of the friends I had made were not "approved" by the Libyan intelligence.

In September 2011 I went to Cairo for a week with my cousin, and upon my return to the Tripoli airport, it became evident which friends were not approved. As I stepped off the plane, two men in civilian clothing approached me. They informed me that there was a problem with the exit stamp on my passport. They assured me it was fine, but I would have to go downtown to resolve the issue. My aunt insisted that she drive me, and they agreed, so long as we did not stop anywhere. Once inside the car, my aunt guessed that this had nothing to do with a stamp and everything to do with my American friends from the embassy. Her hunch turned out to be correct.

For the next three days, I was stuck in a conference room in a dilapidated nondescript building downtown. At any given time in this room, there were about seven men chain smoking and writing notes on carbon paper. It was like something out of a bad KGB movie from the 80s—think *Black Eagle* with Van Damme (set in Malta, so close!) My uncle begged them to let him in so he could translate for me, but since they had been following me, they knew that my Arabic was just fine.

The interrogation was terrifying, comical, and frustrating all at once. Because I had some American friends, I was immediately dubbed a spy. The line of questioning was absolutely insane and revolved around trips I took to Yefren (in the Nafusa Mountains) and Leptis Magna. They questioned me about my family history and concluded that since my maternal grandfather was from Jadu, a town close to Yefren, I was automatically aiding the Americans in creating an uprising of the Berber (Amazigh) people of the Nafusa Mountains. It didn't matter that I couldn't speak the Amazigh language (nor could anyone in my family); I had to be guilty. The levels of paranoia among the intelligence were astounding. There were times when I couldn't believe it was real.

The second allegation was that I was assisting a Canadian archaeology professor (who according to them was also CIA) in spying on a British Petroleum oil contract outside of Leptis Magna (one of the oldest Roman ruins in the world located eighty miles east of Tripoli). The presumption was that we were spies trying to thwart BP's contract in order to secure it for an American oil company. Yes, I know what you're thinking; this Hollywood movie-esque scene makes Black Eagle look good, especially because my martial arts skills are nowhere near Van Damme's.

The politics of this situation were ostensible. The paranoia rested on a political reality. In August of 2009, convicted Pan Am Flight 103 bomber Abdel Baset al-Megrahi had been released by a panel of three Scottish judges on compassionate grounds. Many international observers were skeptical of this action, and in the summer of 2010, American lawmakers set up hearings to investigate suggested links between al-Megrahi's release and oil deals. As a result, the Libyans tried anything to deflect from this, including creating improbable storylines similar to that of awful '80s spy cinema.

After three days of detention, they decided to release me. This came after they confiscated my passports (both Libyan and American), laptop, camera, and business cards. One of the men actually showed a bit of remorse and said that it wasn't my fault. He explained that the Americans had just used me, and that I was in the wrong place at the wrong time. Another man told me that I was confused. I wasn't a real American, and I should come back home and live in Libya and marry a nice Libyan. He even offered to help me a find a job (perhaps with the intelligence?). The story hit the international press, but because I was still Libyan at the end of the day, they withheld my details and only mentioned the archaeologist. For example, one headline read, "Ottawa querying Libya on Canadian held as US Spy."[1]

---

1. http://www.google.com/hostednews/afp/article/ALeqM5hQXvbF9iJg9sY7bM-SCQ_SyEldXQg

Understandably, my family thought it would be a good idea for me to leave Libya, and so I departed a week later, the first week of October 2010, not knowing when or if I would be able to come back. Then, just a couple of months later, in December, a young man in Tunisia displayed a level of courage that no one else could have even imagined.

With Tunisia's proximity to Libya, both culturally and geographically, I became fixated on the events that were transpiring there. There was so little written about Tunisia in English. Seeing all the information disseminated on Twitter, directly from Tunisia, I became hooked. On Twitter, you can follow people you do not know and learn about them. Twitter broke down barriers and became a genuine information-sharing portal. Especially during the Tunisian revolution, Arabs, academics, and journalists were saying they had "Twitter in one ear, and Al Jazeera in the other." Suddenly, tweets were very important.

When Ben Ali fled, Gadhafi, a long-time friend of the Tunisian dictator, reacted immediately. He patronized Tunisians, telling them that *Tunis el khadra walit Tunis el soda,* meaning that "Green Tunis," revered in the Middle East as a fertile and lush land, had turned black and barren. Immediately protests broke out in the eastern city of Al Baida in Libya, with people frustrated over inadequate housing. The government attempted to quell protestors by offering housing for all and issuing a few checks to protestors.

The Egyptian revolution came about, bringing Al Jazeera English to the forefront in the West and motivating other major networks to focus on the region in order to compete. Now that media attention had shifted from Tunisia to Egypt, Libya was the meat of the sandwich and all eyes were on us.

As soon as the January 25th events commenced in Egypt, there was talk of a revolution in Libya. At that moment I started to follow the protests very closely. I called friends and family in Libya constantly, trying to draw out any information I could. But they were much too worried to talk freely, and rightfully so. I immediately changed my

Twitter handle to make myself anonymous (for fear that my family in Libya would be affected), and started tweeting about the February 17 revolution in Libya, which early on was called the Mukhtar revolution after Libyan hero Omar al Mukhtar.

Websites opposing Gadhafi started multiplying. The Enough Gadhafi website, created by children of the exiled opposition, had been around for a while, and more were created, most notably, libyafeb17.com and feb17.info. The Libyan diaspora became glued to these sites for any information they offered and immediately started protesting in solidarity. Libyans around the world were preparing for what could be the worst scenes of the revolutions.

I was in the United States at this time. I found myself halting my job search and the consulting work I was doing for a media company. I decided to instead jump full force into the revolution.

I quickly became obsessed with finding ways to combat the media blackout. I had contacts in the media and harassed every single person I knew. Through both conventional and unconventional methods, people were soon contacting me. A producer from Anderson Cooper's show contacted me via Twitter, and from there I was helping *AC360* produce segments on Libya for the show for months.

The Libyan community in Southern California organized a task force to deal with various issues. We created committees that focused on lobbying, media, humanitarian aid, and outreach. Soon, similar groups were formed across the U.S., Canada, and Europe. Having previously worked for Congress, I wanted to see how I could help the efforts of the Libyan community in D.C. We organized a press conference in D.C. with people who spoke out about how Gadhafi's terrorism had affected them as Americans. Days later, the no fly zone was implemented, and, feeling a sense of accomplishment, I returned to Los Angeles to continue work on the humanitarian effort.

Shortly after, I received a phone call from a friend informing me about a new TV channel that was going to be launched in Doha, Qatar for the Libyan opposition. The channel was headed by Mahmud Shammam, a Libyan opposition member with a strong background in media. Shammam was currently the editor-in-chief of *Foreign Policy* in Arabic and had previously worked for Newsweek and Al Jazeera. When I heard about this, I knew that this would be the best way I could contribute to the revolution. I flew out to Qatar immediately.

Mr. Shammam wanted me to host a show called *'Ayn 'ala 'Assima*, or Eye on the Capital, a show that was aimed at reaching out to besieged Tripoli. I knew this was not possible; not only were my language skills not up to par, but appearing on air would endanger my family in Tripoli, especially after my stint in detention. I convinced him that I would be helpful behind the scenes, given my experience, and stayed on to produce. In the period leading up to the launch of the channel we had very few staff and very massive tasks to accomplish. To say these weeks were hectic, stressful, and impossible would be an understatement. Somehow in six days, we were able to launch with three television hours. The rest of the airtime was filled with promotional clips and repeats. Ask anyone in television to give you an estimate of how many people it takes to produce one television hour. We had roughly half of that for the entire production.

With the formation of the National Transitional Council (NTC) and the appointment of Mahmud Shammam as the Minister of Information, we knew that the channel would morph from being the voice of the opposition to the voice of the NTC, and that it did. My job at the channel was producer of the political talk show *Fi Siyaasa* (In Politics). Soon I found myself in the thick of the politicking. Mr. Shammam had asked me to go to D.C. with Dr. Mahmud Gibril, the head of the Executive Committee of the NTC. I met with the Prime Minister in Doha and then was off to D.C. for a week that could make or break the Libyan cause. After meetings with Washington's elite to establish a case for the recognition of the NTC, we returned to Doha with hope.

The bottom line was: Libya needed money. I had listened to Minister Ali Tarhouni (responsible for Finance and Oil) explain this perhaps a thousand times to everyone from the former director of the CIA Leon Panetta to the U.S. Treasury: we needed our money, and we needed it now. The problem was: we couldn't get it until we were seen as the legitimate representatives of the Libyan people. All the Washington power players told us this was not going to happen. As soon as I returned to Doha, I went back to work producing the show and trying to find new ways to reach the Libyan people. Pro-Gadaffi pundits were launching a very effective propaganda campaign, and we knew we needed to combat them more aggressively.

A couple weeks later, Mr. Shammam approached me about moving to Benghazi. There had been talk of moving the entire channel to Benghazi since that Libyan city had been liberated for quite some time. But since we were being financially supported by Qatar, we were still facing obstacles in doing so. Shammam wanted me to set up his office for the NTC and become his Director of Communications. I was more than happy to embark on this new challenge.

Being in Benghazi was like an out-of-body experience in some ways. It was my first time there, as my family was from Tripoli and I had only visited the Western part of Libya. It was surreal to see expressive graffiti all over the streets and the independence flag waving on every corner. It was even more surreal because I knew this was Libya, but it didn't really feel like Libya. Not because it was finally free, but because it felt just a tad bit foreign. I didn't know anyone, had never been there, and even the dialect was slightly different.

Before I departed for Benghazi, my Libyan friends in Doha who were from the east warned me that I had to be careful. They said, "Don't think Benghazi is like Tripoli. It's very conservative, and, well, you're blonde." Translation: your blonde hair is not covered. Needless to say, I was a bit nervous, but once I got there and adjusted, I realized all that "advice" was useless. The people there could not have been more welcoming. It's true, most women wear hijab, although I did spot a few without it. And no one ever made me feel uncomfortable.

My colleague Nina and I were very interested in the role of women in the revolution and tried to interview as many women as possible. One night as we were filming an episode, we decided to go to the main stage in Maydan al Hurriya (Freedom Square), where the rule was men-only after sundown. Much to the chagrin of our male colleague, we headed over and interviewed young men, old men, and even some very young girls who were there with their fathers. We asked people why they gathered there every night and what the revolution meant to them. We even asked why the area was segregated after sundown. They explained it was for women's protection because it could get very crowded, and also because in addition to speakers there were prayers every night.

Since neither Nina nor myself were claustrophobic, we decided to go back again the next night, and this time we went on stage with our boss, Mr. Shammam, while he addressed the crowd. This was significant because we had gotten to know the people in the square, and now they recognized us for the work we were doing as women for the revolution, not just as silly girls asking questions. From that point on, we noticed more women speaking on the main stage and becoming more active.

My main role was working with NGOs, international journalists, and media teams who were operating out of Benghazi. My goal was to assess their needs and see how we could coordinate with them to make their jobs easier. Safety was also a major concern, as journalists were threatened and targeted in war zones regularly. For example, the Al Jazeera van was the only victim of the Tibesti hotel bombing. Thankfully there were no casualties other than the poor van, but it was quite a scare for all the people staying in the hotel (myself included).

After a few weeks, I went back to Doha to check on things. The effects of the stalemate had reached our staff, who were very few and overworked. Our staff came from all over the world, including Libyans of the diaspora and Libyans from Libya. A few of our anchors had formerly been on State TV, their only option if they wanted a career in media in Libya at that time. Only a small percentage of the staff had any media experience. The rest were from various career paths, but they learned quickly and worked very hard. One of our anchors had been a computer engineer prior to joining the team, and she proved to be very successful because of her passion and dedication. While in Doha, I continued to assist Prime Minister Gibril's office in managing communication efforts, and soon I was asked to be his press secretary.

I found myself on the road with Gibril and the delegation again, this time to Spain, where we met with the Foreign Minister after they had recognized the NTC. Around this time a flood of recognitions for the NTC came in. With the growing international support, however, the situation in Libya itself was growing more critical.

Following these diplomatic visits, I returned to Benghazi, where I witnessed the growing seriousness of the situation first-hand. The rebels coming back from the frontlines looked on edge. Lots of the media had rotated out, many of them moving to different parts of Libya as they saw Benghazi slowly returning to normalcy with less potential for breaking news. I spent much of my time acquainting myself with the new local media: radio, newspapers, magazines, and TV channels. At that point we established offices for the executive committee members. Things seemed to be progressing in some ways and stagnant in others. I met with many people from the Nafusa Mountains who came to the rebel capital of Benghazi to seek assistance for their towns. Ramadan was right around the corner, and people were devastated by the effects of war. The NTC had a new initiative called the Temporary Financial Mechanism that aimed to distribute some of its unfrozen assets directly to families in the liberated areas. They started with the Nafusa Mountains, which had seen some of the most intense destruction.

All appeared to be calm until one day there was a large protest in front of the Tibesti Hotel against the NTC. That evening we worked late, with meetings until around 2 a.m. The next day General Abdel Fattah Younis, a defector who was commander of the rebel forces, was killed. The chaos that ensued in Benghazi that day was intense to say the least. General Younis was from the eastern part of the country, and his family wanted answers and an investigation into his death. Controversy still surrounds his death until this day, while the NTC has supplied the public with very few explanations of the tragedy.

Back in Doha, we were in the process of adding new programs for Ramadan. Viewership in and out of Libya skyrocketed, and we decided to build on that momentum. At one point Libyans were watching Libya TV more than Al Jazeera, which was exciting and also daunting. We knew we had to continue to fight the media war against Gadhafi's talking heads. The beginning of Ramadan helped us, as people in Libya discovered a renewed sense of hope and the revolutionaries were pushing harder on the front lines. It seemed as though the stalemate was lifting. There was a sense among everyone that victory was very near. Members of the NTC traveled to Tunisia in preparation for a move into Tripoli.

Fast forward a couple weeks—Tripoli was liberated. The Tripoli coverage by our channel was a disaster. Tension among the staff was palpable leading up to this moment, but after the liberation of the capital, many of us could no longer be silent. It felt like the event that we had been preparing for had been usurped from us. Libyans in Libya and in the diaspora had serious complaints and concerns about our coverage, and rightfully so. While Al Jazeera and Al Arabiya were producing amazing images and up-to-the-minute headlines, our presenters hosted a series of talk shows around the clock. Yes, our coverage was a twenty-four-hour line-up of *The View*, sometimes even with the same horrible comedic jabs. It was both inappropriate and embarrassing. Unfortunately, it was a result of the management's complete monopoly on the entire process. Suddenly, the production team, the creative team, even the anchors and presenters had no say in what was going on air. It was a nightmare, and the staff decided that enough was enough. If the Libyan people could stand up to Gadhafi, then we reckoned that we could stand up to a manager who was asserting power in a Gadhafi-esque manner.

We listed our grievances professionally and thoughtfully to Mr. Shammam, who understandably was much too busy with the NTC in Tripoli to hear our problems in Doha. We had passed the point of no return with the management. Unfortunately, the outcome was not in our favor, and Mr. Shammam decided to keep the manager on after an investigation into our concerns. More than twenty people signed the petition with the intent to resign if the situation was not resolved. This group of people, myself included, were the core staff that built up the TV channel from zero. Because the channel's founder was also a member of the NTC, my work with the council came to an end at that point as well.

I returned home to Los Angeles and tried to resume a normal life, but after experiencing the intensity of the Libyan revolution, I found this to be nearly impossible. I decided that I still needed to be involved. It was true that most of the country was liberated, but a colleague of mine reminded me that this was when the real work began. And it's true. Tunisia and Egypt, who had gone before us, were still struggling in the months after their much shorter revolutions.

I decided I wanted to get away from politics—a vow I had also made years earlier, after I'd grown disillusioned while working for Congress. My mind went back to my master's thesis, which had been rejected by Georgetown University because there wasn't a professor who "knew enough about Libya" to advise me. I wanted to look at the absence of a popular culture industry in Libya, specifically, at how and why Gadhafi stifled cultural production. I had witnessed first-hand in Benghazi the vacuum of cultural production being filled after the revolution. From street artists to poets, filmmakers to musicians, people across Libya, young and old, were participating in the creation of a national identity.

Perhaps alongside the politics running in my veins was a bit of vengeance. I had enough fuel for this fire from the three days I was held in detention, which is nothing in comparison to what many others have endured. That experience had made me part of something I was passionate about, the land of my ancestors, my country, *biladi*. I had witnessed and was a part of history. I never guessed that the discussions in Dr. Laurie King's class on youth culture in the Arab world in the fall of 2009 would be discussions in which the whole world would engage a little over a year later.

In Libya, it was the youth who brought about change. The arrest of a young lawyer named Fathi Terbil in February of 2011 had sparked the youth to come out in protest against injustice. And as many journalists noted, the rebel army was comprised mostly of teenage boys and young adults in baseball caps and jeans. It's these young men, like my cousins who went to university and worked hard but still could not afford an apartment, who were out there on the front lines with nothing to lose. Young women fought too, secretly calling news agencies with information, sewing independence flags and hanging them in the middle of the night, and recording anonymous videos with messages of allegiance to the revolution.

The New Libya is going to need a lot of help. Although we are rid of a tyrant, there is still a long road to freedom, democracy, and all the other rights young people fought for that they might not understand just yet. Libya has had a history of long and bloody battles, and the February 17 revolution was no exception.

Because of this legacy, it is my hope that Libyans living around the globe will return to their country to help rebuild it. Living in exile as our parents' generation did was no picnic, but at least it afforded our generation the luxuries of education and diverse experiences. It is precisely these experiences that can help foster the ideals of freedom and democracy and see them to fruition. I have many friends who have already made the commitment and moved back. One friend argued that each person should go back to their city and help rebuild it, as opposed to going to the capital out of convenience. And they have already accomplished much, as it was the youth who enabled this change in the first place. It is the youth who must take this duty on, so that the blood of their brothers, friends, and companions was not shed in vain.

In less than a year's time, I went from the uncertainty of not knowing if I could return to Libya after my arrest to feeling joy at a Gadhafi-free Libya, something I did not think I would ever experience. I would never have guessed when I was interviewing people on the streets of Tripoli in August of 2010, that it would be my last time receiving fearful and stifled responses. There were moments where I stared in disbelief at the graffiti-laced walls in Benghazi, wondering how this came to be, remembering the billboards of Gadhafi's face in Tripoli I had seen just a few months earlier.

The resilience of the Libyan people truly proved that anything is possible. It is my hope that in the next forty years, instead of being known for a dictator's outlandish costumes, Libya will be known as a leader in innovation, science, medicine, and the arts. Investing in the youth will be the key to achieving this. After all, they are the ones who brought us *thawrat 'febrayir*, the February 17 revolution. Who knows, maybe the next Steve Jobs or Oprah Winfrey is in Libya, waiting to share his or her brilliance with the world!

## Inspired by Revolution to Educate My Generation
### by Jalal Abu-Khater

**JALAL ABU-AHATER** is a seventeen-year-old Palestinian blogger and activist living in Jerusalem who recently graduated from high school. An aspiring journalist, politics enthusiast, and dedicated blogger, and a founding member and secretary of Palestine Model UN (PalMUN), Jalal writes for ElectronicIntifada.net and for various online magazines and local newspapers. He is passionate about what it means to be Palestinian in Jerusalem, and how to achieve peace with justice. In 2012, Jalal participated in the ninth Annual Model UN Conference, organized by students, which has inspired him to hold a similar event in Palestine.

### Tuesday, January 25, 2011

I came home after high school and immediately turned on Al Jazeera, as I had been doing for weeks since the uprisings began in Tunisia and then Egypt. I watched footage of large clashes on the streets of Cairo between protesters and police. *Wala'at!* I thought, which is a common word in Arabic to convey "It's really caught on fire!"

Judging by the passion on the faces and in the voices of the protesters, it was clear to me that this was the beginning of something new in Egypt. It made me hope that more Arabs would actively overthrow their leaders through demands for dignity. My father, however, was more skeptical, insisting that Egyptians might riot and rebel for a while, but their enthusiasm would likely fade and they'd give up. He did concede that these types of protests were becoming more common in Egypt, but he was also quick to point out that they had yet to lead to any serious shift or outcome despite worsening conditions.

Then on January 14, the Tunisians made "ousting an Arab dictator" a reality. At that moment I knew deep down that I was right: this was something new! Egypt would be next!

Even though I had to be up at 6:30 a.m. the next morning for school, I couldn't resist staying up until 4 a.m. to follow the news on Twitter and watch online video streaming from activists in Cairo. There I was, sitting in my little room in Palestine, watching a revolution unfold before my eyes in Egypt, or as it is often called in the Arab world, *Misr, Umm al-Dunya* (Egypt, Mother of the World). I couldn't turn away because I felt that as long as I was watching, somehow, the uprising would continue.

I slept for a little while, and within seconds of opening my eyes, I reached for my computer. Then, at school, in any free moment I could find, I would escape to the computer lab. My friends and teachers didn't believe that Egypt, and the entire region, would be shaken by this movement. But I didn't give up hope.

## Friday, January 28

I woke up that Friday morning and sluggishly pulled out my chemistry textbook to study for a test. Of course, Al Jazeera was on in the background, as it had been for weeks since clashes had broken out in Tunisia. I started to notice as crowds of Egyptians filled the streets, marching against police brutality in different cities in Egypt. When the news anchor read "Thousands are marching in Suez, Alexandria, and other cities," my heart was filled with joy. I knew it! Change was destined to come.

Indeed, change did come, or at the least the promise of change had arrived. Although I was addicted to watching the news on TV at the time, I managed somehow to miss the moment Omar Suliman announced that Mubarak was stepping down. I was on Facebook and happened to read a chat message by a friend who said: "He is gone!!" I jumped off my seat and immediately turned on the TV.

Al Jazeera was rolling live footage from Tahrir Square without any commentary, just the sounds of hundreds of thousands of ecstatic Egyptians jumping with joy. I will never forget that moment. The situation felt surreal. I stood up. I was completely numb in front of the TV. I couldn't move or say anything. Even recalling the feeling causes my eyes to swell with tears. I rushed into my room, updated my Twitter account, contacted a few friends, and got dressed up to go celebrate in the streets with my Palestinian neighbors in Ramallah. Hundreds of us flooded the streets to celebrate Mubarak's downfall, cars beeping and the euphoria growing throughout the night.

The next morning at school, everyone was still overcome with emotion and the hallways were buzzing. When we arrived to homeroom, our teacher smiled at us and said, *sabah al-thawra*, which was "Good revolution!" rather than "Good morning!"

It is difficult to properly express just how inspired I was by what I had watched unfold just a few hundred miles away as first Tunisians and now Egyptians had demanded their right to live with dignity.

I couldn't help but think, perhaps selfishly, that I wanted this change too. We in Palestine needed change more than ever. I did not want to watch my children grow up as my parents had to watch me grow up, with little hope of justice and dignity. The Egyptian revolution, as it was being called here, had affected me in such a fundamental way that it is difficult to specify with words. What was happening in Egypt, and would eventually take form in nearly every Arab country to various degrees, inspired us Palestinians; it reminded us that nothing is impossible and no one is invincible. For over sixty years we had been protesting, through both non-violence and armed struggle, in an attempt to change our circumstances, without any significant gains—just more losses. Any struggle requires determination in order to succeed, but determination requires education and awareness first.

Though I was only seventeen, I was old enough to know that if I wanted to bring the change that our people yearned for, I should start with my own community. And so I did.

When the uprisings in Tunisia and Egypt unfolded, there were many attempts by us, the youth of Palestine, to mobilize people to spill into the streets to fight occupation and injustice en masse. But most of these actions had failed to create a critical mass due to a lack of confidence and a malaise after sixty years of struggle. Many of us lacked the faith that we could succeed. Sometimes even I was tempted to see things this way.

I began racking my brain, trying to come up with an action plan. What could I do as a teenager inspired by the Arab spring/summer/winter—whatever you want to call it? I was convinced that educating my own people should be the first step so that when revolution came, we would have the awareness and preparedness to govern ourselves. That is when it occurred to me: I would do it through MUN.

At my school, the Friends School in Ramallah, we participate in the Model United Nations (MUN) worldwide program. Each year the MUN club sends students abroad to participate in various conferences modeled around the U.N. General Assembly. The idea is to gain experience that can then be shared with your own community. Model UN gives us an opportunity as students to discuss global affairs and international relations in a mature and comprehensive manner.

Back in March 2010, I had participated in the National High School Model United Nations conference that takes place annually in New York City. I was the youngest in a delegation of six high school students who participated. In that conference I represented Lebanon in the General Assembly's Legal committee. I wasn't one of the strongest delegates, but the experience I gained there, debating with other students, challenging each others' perspectives, and working together to find solutions, inspired me. Spending those three days trying to articulate my ideas while listening and considering the ideas of others gave me a certain confidence and spirit.

Later that year, in November 2010, I took part in the ninth Annual Model UN conference at the Amman Baccalaureate School in Jordan. This conference was completely organized by high school students with previous Model UN experience and proved to be one of the most challenging and astounding conferences I had ever attended.

After the revolutions in early 2011, it occurred to me that the time was right to do a Model UN event in Palestine. It would be the first-ever such conference held in Palestine for Palestinian students.

I was convinced that without a focus on education Palestinians would remain powerless, unable to guarantee their basic human right to live freely without the oppression we endure from Israel and without our own divisions, which are perpetuated by our leaders.

I was chosen to be the secretary of our school's Model United Nations club. I sat with the board members, Areen Bahour, Dalal Awwad, Ali Al-Ahmad, and Mona Yasin, and started planning how we would organize this unprecedented event. We collectively believed that this would be an opportunity to reach a young generation of Palestinians with a wide variety of interests, experiences, and knowledge—and that would surely be a first step in bringing about an end to our struggle.

If I could not succeed at this, than how could I imagine eventually succeeding at influencing a massive grassroots movement large enough to bring change to the current situation in Palestine? My plan was to work on educating my generation and myself first.

Certainly there were already many platforms and methods for reaching the young generation, but I was sure Model United Nations could be one of them, if for no other reason than to instill knowledge and hope in the youth. Every one of us has his or her role in the community, and I had found mine as a high school student.

We could call for more marches, boycotts, and other forms of non-violent popular resistance. But how do you rally a generation that doesn't fully understand all the issues and demands? In order to succeed at revolution, the youth needed at least to understand their history and the prospects of their future better.

My best friend, Ali, who was the fundraising co-chair on our MUN club's board, said to me, "Organizing such a conference is not just any act, it is a patriotic act. The most essential goal of our project is to reach out to the minds of Palestine's youth, who are like us, to develop their understanding of the world they live in and of what the world is like outside of Palestine."

Of course, we faced many setbacks. We disappointed each other many times and reached levels of frustration when we all almost gave up on this idea, but something told us to keep working at it.

A conference of such a scale required funding, a team of students dedicated to making the conference happen, and of course participants from every school we could reach. Our first step in gathering funds for the conference was holding a fundraising dinner event in Ramallah. We invited the families of students. It was quite successful. We gave a short presentation on what motivated us to hold this conference, and the attendees, many of whom were generations older than us, seemed impressed. With the amount of money we made, we were able to start some of the conference preparations. We had four months until the conference commenced.

In the summer of 2011, we held a miniature Model UN conference aimed at preparing young students in our school for the real Model UN experience. That miniature conference included teaching sessions during which five of us each taught a class of seven or more students about international protocols and all the other procedures and preparations.

As the new school year began on September 1, we worked tirelessly, contacting schools to invite them to the conference, which was now less than a month away, on September 23. That date was coincidentally the date when President Mahmoud Abbas was scheduled to speak at the United Nations about Palestine's bid for statehood.

As Palestinians, the United Nations has played an important role in shaping our formative lives. We joke that most Palestinians can recite UN Resolution 194 before they can even count that high.[1]

Understanding the role the U.N. plays in the conflict and occupation that controls our lives is one reason why students at the Ramallah Friends School formed Palestine's first and only Model UN club. Hundreds of U.N. resolutions had passed under the pretense of upholding Palestinians' rights, condemning Israel for raids on Gaza, for building in Jerusalem, for not complying with the U.N., for attacks in the West Bank, for continuing to build illegal settlements, for failing to observe U.N. orders, and for deporting Palestinians and arresting children. However we had yet to see one that would bring us more freedom or meaningful change.

Unfortunately, and perhaps expectedly, we were forced to postpone the conference by two weeks because the situation in the West Bank had grown tense and serious due to increased settler violence against Palestinians. A lot of students who attend the Friends School and many of the conference participants live in Jerusalem and West Bank cities like Bethlehem and Nablus.

Those who live in Bethlehem and Nablus were not able to come to school that weekend because the road between Ramallah and those cities was dangerous. Settlers were blocking roads, demonstrating, and often attacking traffic with rocks and sticks. Many of my classmates described the horror they felt when their parents' cars were stuck in traffic and settlers were throwing rocks, beating their cars with sticks, and screaming at them. The Israeli police and army were responsible for those roads, but of course they didn't act quickly or efficiently, turning a blind eye instead.

---

1. The term "General Assembly Resolution 194" refers to the UN decision from December 1948 calling for an establishment of a Conciliation Commission to facilitate peace between Israel and Arab states. The significance of this decision is the proposed solution to the refugee problem, which was interpreted by the Arab side as permitting the "right of return of the Palestinian refugees."

Sadly, we have lived with settler violence our entire lives. Given the settlers' impunity, we came to the collective decision that postponing the conference was wiser than risking the safety of any of our participants. We were frustrated and not sure if we would be able to get all the participants to and back from the venue safely. But we decided not to cancel the conference. Although none of us were pleased with the postponement, we chose to look at the bright side and took advantage of the two-week delay to contact even more schools.

So, as members of the real U.N. Security Council began a series of closed-door meetings to bury the Palestinian Authority's U.N. membership bid, we students participated in a more productive meeting of a better-modeled U.N. Student delegations came from schools in Ramallah, Jerusalem, Bethlehem, Nablus, Haifa, and Nazareth. We contacted a school in Gaza via email, because physical participation meant they would have to try to leave Gaza through Rafah and then travel by plane to Jordan and hope that Israeli authorities would allow them into the West Bank. We didn't want to burden them with this unnecessary hardship.

More than eight schools had confirmed they would attend. These schools made up of Palestinian students who deserved to learn from the experience and to increase their own awareness of the environment around them politically, socially, financially, environmentally, and even technologically.

We assigned three committees in the PalMUN conference: General Assembly, Economical & Social Council, and Arab League. I was set to be the president of the Arab League committee, which isn't included in all Model UN conferences, but we thought it would be an enlightening experience for the participating students to get to know the Arab League more. We felt that the students should understand how the Arab League operates, even if it has largely proved to be ineffective at bringing about any noticeable changes for the Palestinians. The Arab League did prove relevant amid these Arab uprisings when it suspended Syrian membership and imposed sanctions for Assad's refusing to respond to a peace plan that would require Damascus to end the bloodshed, free prisoners, and start dialogue with the opposition.

Twenty-one students represented the Arab League. With open doors, various issues were put on the table for discussion. During our conference, the future state of Palestine was discussed and was eventually recognized by the conference's General Assembly. Not surprisingly, not all of us agreed on the U.N. bid. It was a heated debate, with a wide range of positions on the best and most practical ways forward. In the Arab League, topics about foreign military interventions in Arab affairs and the Somali famine and civil war were discussed, but unlike the real Arab League, we were able to come up with strong resolutions aiming to solve the problems.

I set two discussion and debate topics. One was: "Providing secure methods for delivering relief and aid to the famine-stricken people of Somalia." The other was: "The question of foreign armed intervention in Arab affairs, and the possibility of coming up with an Arab alternative." I was hoping these topics would help us address our ultimate aim: to understand how we, as aspiring future leaders, could build a more just international system and ensure that the U.N. lives up to its potential as the force for change it was created it to be.

The day of the conference, Friday, October 7, finally arrived. I managed to sleep only four full hours that night. I woke up early that morning and headed to school to help my colleagues finalize everything and welcome the student delegations.

I was worried the entire first day of the conference. I was waiting for something to go wrong, or someone to cause a problem, but no such thing happened. The opening ceremonies were inspiring as the speakers all emphasized the fact that this event was organized by students alone.

Our school's principal, Mahmoud Amra, made a comment to the press who came to cover the event's first day: "This is the time a new wave of Palestinian youth opens their eyes to various world issues other than the Palestinian struggle. The way to success is through knowing the world you live in and learning from other people's experience. Raising awareness and enriching young minds with knowledge is what this conference is really about, and I am proud that students of the Friends School are organizing this all by themselves."

The conference went ahead as planned. The delegations' supervisors kept commending and praising the Model UN board for our efforts to make this happen. Teachers who arrived with delegations from participating schools expressed their amazement and admiration that the conference was organized entirely by a group of seventeen-year-old students.

Ms. Nidal Barham, supervisor of the delegation from the Talitha-kumi School of Bethlehem, told us before she and her students returned to Bethlehem, "I was not hopeful for the young generation. All I saw was young kids messing around on Facebook and not caring for the world they live in, but you guys have changed my perspective. You proved me wrong. Thank you." I will never forget her words.

One hundred and thirty students participated in this first-of-its-kind conference, and I am sure all of them left with knowledge and experience that hopefully will benefit their lives. Sure, the conference was nothing like thousands and thousands of youths joined together in a square. Yet within a larger revolution, sometimes you have to have smaller revolutions in which you can take initiative. And that is what we did. If we are going to overthrow the region's dictators, we must also prepare the next generation to understand its history and plan its future. Education will end the cycle of corruption in which we have been living. I am convinced that the students who participated will be messengers in their respective communities, spreading the insights they gained to other youths around them.

I consider organizing this conference one of the biggest achievements of my life. Yet it was nothing but a first step in my quest to serve the people of Palestine with whatever I can. I could feel the pain of every Palestinian suffering injustice; that was what motivated me. I believe that we, the young generation, are responsible for healing our people's psychological wounds, for fixing the course of our struggle, and for getting everyone back on their feet again. It is up to us to instill hope in the generations to come to continue to fight for the right to live with dignity and enjoy justice and equality. The Arab revolutions proved that nothing is impossible, including justice in Palestine.

I still cannot believe that, as high school students, we accomplished so much. While it seemed inevitable that the PA's membership bid would soon be made obsolete, we weren't going to lose sight of the resolution we had made. Palestinian youth deserve better from this world. Occupation and continuous conflict have demoralized our people, but we'll never give up. Witnessing the sustained popular movements across the Arab world made us aware of the plight of others. By comparison, the conference was hardly as critical a moment in history, yet it was a step in the right direction, envisioning and modeling the U.N. as it was meant to be.

# Faceless Brutality
# in Egypt's Revolution
*by Sarrah Abdelrahman*

**SARRAH ABDELRAHMAN** describes herself as an activist, video blogger, and actress. In 2011 she was awarded the prestigious Edberg Award for her use of social media during Egypt's revolution. In the Sweden-based Edberg Foundation's words: "Sarrah Abdelrahman is awarded for her courageous use of social media, giving young people a voice in support of democracy causes that are universal to all people regardless of age, gender and cultural affiliation."

Sarrah recently graduated from the American University in Cairo with a bachelor's degree and a double major in journalism and theater. Before the historic events of January 2011, the aspiring actress considered herself a student activist but still apolitical. Now, she proudly claims her place in Egypt's youth revolutionary political movement.

I've always wondered what it was that gave them the license to be so brutal. I couldn't tell if it was the uniform, the batons, the boots, or brainwashing. It seemed that the Egyptian police had found comfort in maintaining their power through stomping on us, both physically and spiritually.

In June 2011, I had just graduated from university. I should have had all the time in the world for fun, which was long overdue, as I had been struggling to finish my studies amidst a violent revolution that had begun on January 25, 2011. But for several months, I had been becoming increasingly depressed, watching the revolution, which had captured my imagination and which I truly believed in, be hijacked by a military dictatorship.

It had been six months since I had attended my first protest. On January 25, I was twenty-three, and I will always remember it as the day my life fundamentally changed. I owe so much to this day. It gave me life, it gave me a sense of ownership over the physical and figurative space my body occupies. I learned that day the importance of three principles: freedom, bread, and social justice.

On February 11 we all felt victorious when former President Hosni Mubarak stepped down and the army took our side, pledging to protect the people. "The military and the people, hand in hand," we had chanted. But then, only two weeks later, watching those same revolutionaries who had managed to oust a military man (and dictator) from power were getting attacked, arrested and tortured, I was depressed.

For months as the revolution continued, I felt a creative block, which for me is very unusual. Ever since the brutality began against protesters I struggled to write and to create the video commentaries about the revolution that I had been uploading to YouTube, some of which had garnered hundreds of thousands of views.

To distract myself, I attended social gatherings for "fun." Sometimes I would flash a forced smile for the sake of a stranger in an attempt to simply remember what it felt like to really smile.

I would meet friends at a lecture or at the movie theater to pass the time, but my heart was hardly ever there. My fake smiles were masking anger at what I was witnessing happening in my country, as the military chose to protect their power over the people. One question both overwhelmed and consumed me: "How will we dismantle and restructure this body of rotten, power-hungry monsters?"

The emotional rollercoaster I experienced as I watched friends get arrested and taken away, and the constant disappointments throughout our revolution, had been exhausting. I grew worn out with disappointment, not only with the military itself but also with the fact that we, the people, had believed in them. It is that kind of disappointment that kills your ambition.

Those fake smiles that had stained themselves on my face were never a true reflection of how I felt. They simply helped to pass the time while creativity eluded me.

For me, creativity is my fuel. It is what makes me wake up in the morning. I've always loved the arts and, specifically, the art of performing. I have been on stage since I was seven years old. I love to act, not just on stage, but to really live, actively. Everything is always exaggerated in my head. Throughout the revolution, aside from attending protests and helping to document evidence of police brutality, I began creating videos and uploading them to my YouTube channel. I used an in-your-face kind of commentary, editing together rants and drawing from our culture to help provoke a much-needed discussion about the direction of the revolution and the future of Egypt. I wouldn't consider this my profession, but I am an artist by nature, as art is the source of my happiness and most of my income.

On June 28 there was an evening tweet-up at a downtown rooftop café. A tweet-up is basically when people set a time and date for a social gathering in public to discuss a topic or simply to meet. The avatars on Twitter who we had all come to know throughout the revolution turned into faces, and trolling turned into a proper real-life debate.

The lighting was low, with lots of chairs and fake grass carpeting shining underneath Cairo's moon. Of course, like most tweet-ups, I wouldn't have missed this one for anything. I had never seen so many people at a tweet-up; you couldn't even hear the person talking to you. The revolution, I thought to myself, was very much still alive.

Just as the space became almost too full, my friend Gigi, holding her open laptop, came to show us a video of the families of the martyrs murdered by the military in Tahrir Square and elsewhere across the country. It seemed the families of the martyrs had been tricked into leaving their ongoing sit-in against police and military brutality at the State Media Building.

The videos Gigi showed us were of police officers using electric tasers and batons to beat the families. She also told us that many had decided to go protest at the Ministry of Interior to send a clear message to the military leaders that they would not tolerate this kind of brutality. She also told us about clashes between rock-throwing protesters and the armed soldiers.

Surprisingly, only Gigi, another friend, Effat, and I went to the Ministry of Interior to join the protest. Yes, we were in a room full of "digital activists," but no one else came with us.

We took a cab, but because of Cairo's notorious traffic we eventually hopped out of the car and began running towards the Ministry. When we arrived at the battlefield, rocks were strewn on the ground and many there looked confused. It seemed that they, like us, had no idea what was really going on.

We could see a cordon of Egypt's Central Security Forces, a paramilitary force responsible for assisting the police. Fear could be felt in the square; anxiety was palpable. I saw many familiar faces arriving. Whenever something serious happened, the same faces would descend on the scene to investigate, understand, and quickly join in. These were the faces of Egypt's revolutionaries.

These revolutionaries had become my family because we shared a bond that was more important than our backgrounds. This bond was a common dream. Our shared dreams are the streams of blood that makes us a family. And that moment, when I arrived at the latest clash with police, seeing those familiar and familial faces made me feel safer and stronger, even in the most dangerous of situations.

My thoughts were interrupted by a loud "Haaah!" sound that came from the CSF as they broke their horizontal line protecting the Ministry and began to run towards Tahrir Square.

The square was only three blocks away, but they took off in a gallop. We assumed they were retreating, so we ran after them, cursing them out and clapping our hands in victory. We always felt most victorious when we could get police officers, particularly an entire group of them, to leave the premises. We felt as though we had reclaimed our country, or at least a part of it.

My friends continued running after them, but I stayed in the square to speak to the people and find out more about what was happening. The square was clearing up quickly, but then I spotted a high-ranking police officer walking from the Ministry of Interior towards Mohamed Mahmoud Street. He and two other policemen were marching towards the tiny street that leads to Tahrir. Men in normal clothes, but holding large swords, surrounded the officers.

Being as naïve as I was, I tried to run after them to find out what was happening, but one of the "guards" with a sword scared me away. This is not a proper police force, I thought to myself. This is a mob. Worried for my safety, I decided to back off.

At that moment, my friend Mohannad phoned me:

> M: Are you okay? Where are you?
>
> S: I'm at Mohamed Mahmoud Street, man. All is fine, police retreated too, but you won't believe what I just saw.
>
> M: What? Where are you?
>
> S: By the ministry.
>
> M: I thought you were at Tahrir!
>
> S: No, is something happening there?
>
> M: Are you kidding? People are dying at the square!!
>
> S: I'm coming right...
>
> M: Make sure you go through Talaat Harb Street! Right now, you're on the wrong side of the battle!

Mohannad was right. I was on the same side of the square as the police, and they were attacking people from Mohamed Mahmoud

Street with their backs to me. I tried to turn around to get to Tahrir Square from Mansour Street and then Tahrir Street. Then I reached the edge of the square, and there it was. I saw it, a full crack down: tear gas, batons, rubber bullets. What happened? The CSF was trying to take over the empty square to prove that they were back. This had started with the families of the martyrs over by the Ministry of Interior. Why were they ordered to take over the square?

They would always crack down....

But something was different this time. I wasn't as brave as I usually was. I was terrified.

For roughly an hour, I was on the edge of the square and Tahrir Street that leads to it, safe but scared. I saw friends coming in, saying hello, passing me by, and I was still there, scared. I tried to tell my friends to hold my hand and take me to battle, but perhaps they didn't understand eye language.

The sky was raining tear gas, and dozens of injured were being carried out of the battle, leaving trails of blood behind them. Seeing them was giving the protestors more energy to defend the square.

Suddenly I saw Noor, one of my best friends, going into battle. Noor was there at my first protest, and he always knew what to do. He always knew when to run and when to leave. I didn't feel awkward asking him to take me further into the square. But a few meters before the real battle, I told Noor to continue without me. I was still scared.

I was alone in the midst of thousands who were running from all over the capital to protect the square, and then I started mastering my fear. Two steps forward, a tear gas bomb hit. I ran a hundred steps back, and the same thing happened again and again for about an hour. Somehow with every extra step, I felt lighter.

It's as if with every fear barrier broken, a layer of that creative block went away, a layer of depression was peeled away, and I could feel the desire to live again. Despite the tear gas, which was more intense than any of the old tear gas, and the amount of running we all had to do, I was just so happy for the rest of the night. Or for a while, anyway.

During these battles in the square, friends carried the injured to safety while others followed to make sure they were okay. This particular night, this scene played out frequently. Kids on Vespas assisted in making sure the wounded and those tending to them were safe.

Suddenly I saw familiar faces running after an injured guy who was being carried out of the square. I tried to catch up but could not get closer, though I could hear people saying that it was my friend Noor. What? I thought. Noor? How? He always knew where to run. How could he have been hit?

I ran, making my way to the ambulance, and pushed someone who was about to get in with Noor out of the way so that I could go with him to the hospital. Noor was conscious. It is impossible to describe how I felt. There was a big cut in the skin on his forehead, flesh was coming out, and I could see his skull. As the nurse tried to clean the injury, a tear gas bomb landed right outside the ambulance doors, which were open. We couldn't breathe. This was our reality; when we took to the streets, we never knew what to expect, only that it would be chaotic.

The nurse made a half-assed attempt at taking care of Noor's wound and quickly pushed him out of the ambulance.

I spent the next hour trying to convince Noor to go to the hospital, but he did not want to leave. In pain and badly needing God-knows-how-many stitches, he wanted to continue the fight. He eventually did go to the hospital, and I stayed. I had to stay in the battle.

And that was when I decided to go to the front lines.

Rocks, rubber bullets, tear gas; the battle was happening on a dark street. You couldn't see anything; the only thing that was clear was which side you were on. I ran into so many familiar faces amidst those flying past me in the crowds. One of them was my friend Lobna. We left together and tried to find something that we could use as a barricade, but we failed and returned to the battle.

The fighting stopped around 4:30 a.m. My friends and I decided to go home. In my friend's car, we passed by the Ministry of Interior, where we saw hundreds of CSF soldiers littering the ground as they surrendered and the sun began to rise.

Noor eventually had to go through a serious surgery. He now has a prominent scar on his forehead. Like many others, he will forever be reminded of the revolution every time he looks in the mirror. For me, that very same night, my creative block somehow disappeared. I slowly became able to start smiling again. I am not sure why; perhaps it was what I had witnessed that jolted me and my creative juices so that they were flowing once more.

What has yet to change is the judiciary and security systems in place. Power corrupts, especially if you're given a uniform, a weapon, sunglasses, and boots. With this bizarre gift of the license to kill, nothing seems to stop the soldiers from abusing their power and their own people. I don't really know what goes through the heads of every individual working in the failed security systems of Egypt, but I know for a fact that we as Egyptians will not accept their boots on our faces. We will not accept them stomping on us.

Although more than a year has passed since the revolution began, and we have held elections, I still feel as though my voice has not been heard. I still feel that the voices of the millions who have taken to the streets have not been heard. How can we have peace, when we don't even have basic justice?

On February 2, 2011, just over one week after the initial protests on January 25, the army stood by while Tahrir Square was being attacked by thugs. It only came to my realization on February 25, almost a month later, that the Supreme Council of Armed Forces is everything but the protector of the revolution. They have ignored the will of the people and instead stormed forward with their oppressive tactics, and in doing so they have proven themselves to be just as brutal, if not worse, than Mubarak, the dictator.

I can only be proud of the patience of my fellow Egyptians. The time will come when the Egyptian people will take a stoic stand, and when they do, it will be strong and invincible. If we have been able to sustain ourselves without a government or any real security systems, let alone justice, we will succeed and achieve our goals. There is no doubt in my mind that as we rebuild Egypt, we will serve as an example to the rest of the world.

# It's about Dignity
## *by Omar Radi*

(translated from French to
English by Nada Ayad)

**OMAR RADI** is a freelance journalist living between Casablanca
and Rabat on the western coast of Morocco. He studied finance and
political sociology in Casablanca. As a youth, Omar joined the anti-globalization movement through the network ATTAC Morocco,
striking for social and cultural rights with his comrades in the Moroccan Association of Human Rights. In 2011, Omar co-founded
the #Feb20 Movement, the leading street opposition to the Moroccan political regime. He received many death threats as a result of
his activism.

Omar is also the co-founder of the news website www.lakome.
com. He has written for the Moroccan magazine *Telquel* and has
also worked for *Le Journal Hebdomadaire*, a critical weekly magazine that was closed by authorities in January 2010. Omar is a member of the network www.Mamfakinch.com (which means "We'll
never give up"), a group of journalists/activists/bloggers/hackers
that gives updates on social movements in Morocco.

One morning in March 2011, I found out that a group of public teachers were rallying in front of their ministry. Authorities
were not pleased by the rally and were thus ready to intervene. With a

still camera and a small video camera in my bag, I ran to the ministry, which was already being guarded by the police.

Some teachers were lying on the ground, while others were bringing them necessary care. The most serious cases were transported to the emergency room by their colleagues in private cars, since the ambulance, following the order of the authorities, refused to take them. There were also some firemen present, but no fire. Actually, this is not true; because beatings were the authority's only response, some of the teachers, at the peak of their humiliation, decided to self-immolate. That's when the firemen intervened. The scene lasted all day. Fire, water, baton, fire, water, baton—a morbid scene. That's what was happening right in the center of Rabat, the capital of Morocco, two hundred meters from the royal palace.

March 2011 was one month after protests broke out in most of Morocco's villages and cities. Young people took to the streets, the only place where they could protest their marginalization, discrimination, humiliation, repression, and years of being neglected. Slogans and chants were heard everywhere. For decades, Moroccans had internalized their hate, responding only with fear and indifference towards what had happened to them and their compatriots. Ben Ali's stepping down, Mubarak's demission, and other peoples' uprisings quickly transformed their indifference. Moroccans were eager to learn this "new" lesson: nothing can impede a people's will. Many believed this—from young people like me, to marginalized inhabitants of small forgotten villages, to silver miners from the South, to students and women.

The weeks before February 20, 2011 were especially charged—charged with action and mobilization, but equally charged with hope, and with waiting. We didn't know what would happen. February 19, the day before "the big day," fear was mixed with courage and hope. We had enough adrenaline to start selling it! We were prepared for all possibilities: repression, severe restrictions, everything and anything. With a closely guarded Plan A and Plan B, we took our courage in our hands and headed for for Bab El Had square in Rabat, the place designated as the start of the protest. In Casablanca, Tangiers, Fez, Marrakech, and more than fifty villages and cities, we started our coordinated protests.

The international press came to cover the beginning of what they called "Arab Spring" Moroccan style. The slogans were new. The protests attracted many young people, which had never been the case before. Many among the youth were girls, also something never seen before. On our posters we chose to print photos of people in powerful positions in Morocco: the generals of the army who had committed serious human rights violations against the previous generation and figures from the royal family, "the real shadow government," who stifle political progress for their own economic benefit. These were symbols of real economic predators who had transformed our country into a mafia headquarters where mechanisms of democracy and of justice never function.

"Majidi, Get lost!" was one of the chants. Mohamed Mounir Majidi, the king's private secretary, was involved in suppressing the independent press. This was the first time that this person who made the economic world tremble was named in public, without fear, without shame. The people wanted his departure. They wanted an investigation of his fortunes—his and those of other childhood friends of the king who were still in business. Another target was Fouad Ali El Himma, who was the real minister of the interior during the decades of Mohammed VI before he withdrew from the government to create the Authenticity and Modernity Party (PAM) and the "Friends of the King Party," which became the biggest party of Morocco, and an extension of royal control of the political realm.

These "great masters" of the country had not anticipated that the mobilization would be so big. Before the February 20 Movement, no political force had been able to mobilize and protest on the same day, at the same time, in fifty different locations. The state was in a panic. We could feel it. We could see it in the faces of the heads of security.

We could see it in the media treatment of the February 20 Movement. The day before the protests, radios and televisions announced—over and over—the cancelation of the protests. But it was too late; the machine had already started

The days that followed February 20 were particularly violent. The police force, which up to that point had not yet intervened, began to beat the activists ruthlessly. In Rabat, on February 22, we decided to assemble in front of the Libyan cultural center to protest Gadhafi's regime against his people. The security turnout was impressive. All the activists were clubbed, many were arrested. A lot of the young people among us, the fifteen- and sixteen-year-old high school students, had never experienced this much violence. And they were likely to experience it again.

## Political Supply and Demand

The birth of the movement and its actions multiplied while we waited for our next national meeting on Sunday, March 20. At the beginning of March, the public media had invited the members of the movement for an open discussion, prompting a semblance of hope. Sadly, this disappeared on March 9. That day, the king of Morocco gave a speech and announced that they were going to start working on constitutional reforms, without giving more details than that. The next day, a commission for the revision of the constitution was created. The movement was then invited to make its propositions.

Our response came quickly: we will not participate in this commission. The reasons were numerous: First, it was a counseling commission, that is to say, it had no other purpose than to serve the king's interests. Second, the members were assigned by the king, and the country's biggest experts in the constitution were not invited to give their opinion, primarily because they completely rejected the 1996 constitution, which the king had upheld. Third, this was a "revision," not a rewriting, of the constitution, which meant that they intended to only make minor changes to the existing one.

Four days later, on March 13, the activists of #Feb20 in Rabat were savagely attacked in front of the headquarters of the Unified Socialist Party, a leftist organization that supported the movement. Young and old were atrociously beaten, and many sustained fractures. The images from these scenes uploaded on YouTube gave one goose bumps. Rather than suppressing the activists, however, this action by the government had the opposite effect: it radicalized the activists. A force surged through them: they would not be satisfied with either silence or waiting..

The March 20 march was more massive and its demands stronger: "You may make promises but we know you are lying," the protest said. The movement wanted a real constitution with a real separation of powers. We also asked that the figureheads of corruption, those who still sat at the top, be tried. We demanded that they give back the money and the wealth they had stolen. We also demanded an investigation of our natural resources and who benefited from them.

Our only voice from then on was in the street: yelling, screaming, and shouting our anger against what the king offered us, and insisting that it was not the solution. And the monarchy continued on, full speed ahead. Many intellectuals were alarmed by this. Only if we had headed quickly in the direction of serious reform would the streets have calmed down a little bit. However, the government acted as if we were not worth listening to; their only response was to send in uniformed police carrying batons.

April 24 was the biggest day of mobilization in all of Morocco's history. People in more than 114 cities and villages went out to the streets—as before, all at the same time. The regime was shaken. How could it be that after a speech from the king the population would continue to protest? The media conspiracy broke out again. In the eyes of the state, the movement was a bunch of extremists, homosexuals, nihilists, people with self-destructive tendencies who were being manipulated by outside forces. Simultaneously, new forces of oppression made their appearance: the bullies, the fascist brigade—people rounded up for a hundred dirhams each (about $12 US), having no clue what they were being thrust into. They attacked the activists of #Feb20 with knives, sticks, and stones. But nothing changed; the people stayed in the street.

We decided then to change our tactics. We were certainly fighting for a real democracy, but it was necessary to modify our demands. We decided to organize a picnic in the forest near a secret detention center, run by the secret service, that Salafist detainees passed through before being transferred to prison. They would be tortured in this center for several weeks in the hopes of coercing them into confessing.

On May 15, we met up in downtown Rabat, A lot of activists from other cities joined us. With musical instruments, food, and drink in our backpacks, we headed towards the detention center. The first group to arrive was surprised by the presence of the "anti-terrorist units"—horrible masked, hefty agents. The agents targeted all of us. The chase began. We were tracked down every street, and a lot of us were arrested. Even the journalists were viciously beaten and prevented from doing their work. That night, Al Jazeera, who was banned in Morocco and who had broadcast the amateur videos we had made with our cell phones, invited the governor, Khalid Naciri, to speak. He insisted: In this center, there's only one administration.

During May, the repression continued and intensified. May 22 will be remembered as a day of extreme violence in all of Morocco's big cities. Journalists were prevented from doing their work while the police zealously continued doing theirs. An order was given out to use all forms of force, even the most excessive. We only had our legs to get away, but we came out in great numbers. "Capture Omar and Hassan and break their legs," we heard while running, terrorized.

That day, in Safi, a city known for its phosphates, the activist Kamal Aamari was severely beaten, and he succumbed to his wounds a few days later. The 28th and the 29th of May were equally violent. In Casablanca, twenty thousand policemen were stationed, waiting to intervene in all the small rallies. The images of police violence against peaceful protestors drew attention to our cause, but it did not help us on the ground. Terrorized by these scenes of repression, people deserted the protests. They were afraid; four months of revolt and freedom of expression could not erase fifty years of terror and atrocities. They could not erase the fear and the individualism ingrained in normal Moroccan culture.

Despite all this, we kept going, but the physical and mental oppression weighed heavily on us. Our numbers dwindled, and during the national protests that followed, only 40 of the 114 cities and villages were mobilized. Throughout the summer we kept up the pressure in the street, trying to convince people to go outside. It was the period of the constitutional referendums, about which there was no debate: the constitution confirmed the king's power, affirming his position as the head cop, the head judge, the head imam, the only one to decide matters of foreign policy and national security, the guarantor of liberties—the list goes on. The king was not to be questioned. There was no measure of accountability regarding him or his entourage. Despite all this, the regime made the people vote on the new constitution: the king invited the people to vote yes. Their yes was a "yes for the king," not for the constitution. We might have pushed the people to boycott this referendum, but the king would have won all the same. Then the regime revealed its next step: elections.

## The Fight Will Be Long but Worth It!

As summer led to fall and schools were back in session, people were re-energized. The constitution was adopted, so the people—the unemployed, the union activists, the miners—returned to the streets, and a lot more uprisings took place. In the countryside, a permanent sit-in was organized in the village of Imzouren, where the villagers fired the local leaders and closed the administration. There was a general strike in Beni Bouayach, where the residents prevented the political parties from making their electoral campaigns. In the South, the miners of Imider mine, the seventh-largest producer of silver in the world, conducted a sit-in for five months, turning off the water supply for the mine and camping on the mountain to make sure the water stays off.

In October 2011, the electoral campaign began. Several parties from the left as well as #Feb20 decided to boycott this step of the electoral process. An anti-democratic process that marginalizes, discriminates, and oppresses all without giving the people any confidence will not lead to democracy. The political parties campaigned like they did in the era of Hassan II, King Mohammed VI's predecessor: there was corruption, with troops being rounded up for the campaign, criminals and drug barons representing themselves as candidates, and few young candidates being represented.

The old guard was back with its powerful force. The campaign was lackluster and didn't hold people's attention. During the elections, only 45 percent of registered people went to the polls. This represented 22.5 percent of people of voting age. And 20 percent of the votes were nullified. The results of the elections were predictable: the Islamists of the Justice and Development Party (PJD) took power. This party appropriated the slogans and the demands of #Feb20: "down with despotism" and "an end to corruption." In the eyes of the people who voted, this party embodied integrity because it used Islam as its reference. "These are pious people, they will certainly take the management of the public's affairs seriously," people said. They were also people who had never had power. Moreover, the rest of the political landscape represented corruption, theft and looting, and obedience to the central the government and its broken promises. The game and how it would turn out had been known in advance.

The spotlight was on the February 20 Movement. What did the activists think about this? What would they do?

After their victory, the PJD addressed the February 20 Movement. They acknowleged that they had come to power with the help of the activists. But what power? This was the trap we fell into, and we realized it a little too late.

Al Adl wal Ihassane, the other Islamic component of the opposition, active in the February 20 Movement, decided not to go out in the street and support the PJD. From then on, #Feb20 was composed only of progressive forces, a little less powerful than Al Adl Wal Ihassane. The PJD promised to respond to the #Feb20 claims. However, our claims could not be satisfied within the existing institutions.

This "reprieve" imposed on us by the PJD and its victory gave us time to reflect. We realized that this party would be powerless against the powerful corruption of the state and those in the king's sphere. The current constitution allowed Al Adl wal Ihassane to react only to the structural problems pertaining to the political regimes. The PJD only represented a makeshift structure to curb the dynamic protests in the street. We demanded a radical restructuring of the regime and the end of its impunity.

If the PJD lacks the courage to carry out its promises and fails its mission, the streets will erupt again. This time the anger will be different because an economic crisis is taking over the country, people's morale is at its lowest, and everyone feels hopeless about their future. Concerning the PJD's victory, the Moroccan political regime is playing with time, waiting to find a solution to Morocco's financial and economic crisis, waiting for the passion of the angry people to calm.

Except that the problem does not lie where the regime thinks it is. The problem lies in the nature of the regime itself, which always creates this kind of situation, seeking a way to curb the people's fire. If these tensions accumulate, resulting in a serious crisis, with more uprisings, civil disobedience, massive protests, the people will realize that #Feb20 has been right. It just might be too late to do anything about it without bringing about still greater damage.

# By the People, For the People
## by Hummingbird

**HUMMINGBIRD** is a Syrian translator, writer, and citizen journalist. She was born in Saudi Arabia but moved to Syria with her family when she was twelve to continue her education. Hummingbird graduated from Damascus University with a degree in English Literature and worked as a freelance translator. Two years ago, due to the economic and political situation, she left Syria and settled elsewhere in the Middle East, where she currently works for a multinational company. Hummingbird admires bohemian art, mainly Klimt's paintings; sometimes she draws her own sketches. Her hobbies are reading poetry, history, and existential philosophy, writing short stories, and swimming. She contributes to World Pulse (www.worldpulse.com), a global communication network for women.

(EDITORS NOTE: Hummingbird is a pseudonym this contributor is using in order to protect her loved ones, who remain in Syria.)

"We prefer to die under shelling, but not to be slaughtered," my sister told me in July 2012, just before my family fled the area they were living in. A horrible massacre took place there; more than 70 innocent civilians were savagely executed. We lost many neighbors and friends that day.

It is a habit for Syrians to wait. Waiting for news about whether one of our loved ones has been killed, hurt, or worse: arrested and suffering unimaginable torture. Waiting to hear news about whether our houses have been destroyed, looted, or burnt. Waiting for death and hope. We wait for the end of tears. A life of a Syrian has become a game of waiting for signs of logic swirling in the vicious circle of the Assad regime's killing frenzy.

For the last couple of years, while living in Syria, I would constantly ask myself: How on earth do people still go on living here? The Assad regime turned us into slaves seeking its loyalty. We would fight each other for the crumbs the regime threw at us.

Life in Syria contradicts basic human values and challenges stamina. We were told that Syria was in a state of war with Israel, the United States, imperialism, and colonialism, and all the –isms. Therefore, we had to endure our status quo of poverty and degradation. Our country's resources and dignity were hoarded and kept for this mysterious "greater cause" of fighting the "isms." The law was a matter of mood by an official, an army officer or even a trivial undercover intelligence officer. Syria lived under emergency law for forty years, civil groups were totally banned even if it was a book club, any social exchange was forbidden, and citizenship turned into appeasement to the ruling family.

I never thought that Syria would ever rise. But it seems that the course of history and humanity cannot contain such an entity as the Syrian regime inside it anymore. I never thought that Syrians had this epic courage, one that I only read about in Homer's poems. For, who could confront a death machine with flesh? The Syrian revolution is a loud outcry against decades of lies and humiliation, against the elimination of humane conditions and the mutilation of peoples' souls.

Fear is the main factor upon which governing mafias like the Assad regime rest their "legitimacy" to rule. Whether it meant learning my ancestral language of Kurdish to expressing my views online (even under an alias!), I was constantly gripped with fear. Fear of torture haunted us even in the virtual world. Despite the fact that I was using an alias name, I was terrified. Cases of cyber Syrian activists brutally attacked by security forces were not uncommon. Even when I tried learning Kurdish, which is banned in Syria, it was met with my teacher's hesitation and concern, as the simple act of learning the language could mean being charged with treason, or worse, a death sentence.

As a Syrian Kurd, I lived in limbo. To be safe, I could either do one of two things: say that I was once a Kurd, but now no more, or remain silent about my ethnic background. To the Syrian regime I was an inferior citizen, an unpatriotic traitor that must be kept away from the rest of society. I had to deal with this stereotypical image of Kurds all of my life. I was one of the lucky ones to have citizenship. One could say that I was not discriminated against to the same degree as my fellow Kurds because I could be considered an Arab and because I didn't know my mother tongue, but my life was certainly not easy.

Many of my family members were denied citizenship under the regime's political strategy of marginalizing the Kurds. We were in double jeopardy: first as Syrians, and second as Kurds. There is no exact number of the Kurds in Syria, but Kurds are estimated as ten percent of the population and are concentrated in the Northeast areas of Syria. Any hint of Kurdish culture was erased from history, like denying the great historic leader Saladin's Kurdish background. Some of the regime's other actions against Kurds, besides banning the use of the Kurdish language (and even Kurdish names) and excluding us from history, included: execution without trial, mass murder, exploitation of our resources, stripping citizenship, and forbidding a newborn from being registered. Because of these measures, my people were severely restricted from accessing education, working, traveling, obtaining health care—and yet, ironically, Kurdish men were still obliged to do military service.

When the revolution started on March 15, 2012, we noticed that the regime started attempting to appease all minorities, including

Kurds. The Syrian government offered to give citizenship to all Kurds and to recognize their cultural rights. In an effort to win our loyalty, the government went so far as to send a delegate from the government to Kurdish areas to participate in the celebrations of Newroz, a Kurdish holiday (which never happened before, and it did not happen this year, nor ever again). Still, we have not yet heard any call to investigate or indict those responsible for the 2004 massacre in the Kurdish areas, or receive explanations for the killing of many Kurdish youths during their military service.

Many Kurds did not take the bite. This was clearly a move to create strife between Syrian Kurds and their fellow compatriots. Many Kurdish youth organized coordination committees to communicate with their brothers and sisters in other Syrian cities. Before many cities in Syria revolted, the Kurds were already on the streets protesting. I wanted to start an organization but my hands were tied, as the country I am currently in will not tolerate this.

Everyday I recall the image of the sweet face for a young man who used to work as a taxi driver in Daraa, one of the first Syrians who lost their lives when the protests exploded in Daraa. It was all for the sake of their children.

Affected by the media coverage of revolutions in other Arab countries, a group of playful children wrote on their school's blackboard: *the people want to topple the regime*. The following day, security forces stormed their school and pulled these children out of their classes. The people in Daraa only wanted their children back; they knew their beloved children were being tortured savagely in prison. I was not astonished by the actions of the security forces. I just wanted to know who ratted these children out! A teacher, a cleaner, another student's parent? People who are suppose to protect the children. This is a parcel of the destruction of human personality and society the Assad family practiced for many years. Every time I hear of the torture of children in my country it feels like a horror story, almost unreal, but it is real. I wrote two articles to express my unbearable pain and devastation, hoping to awaken Western audiences to these children's silenced voices. Back then I felt a void; all I imagined was a lullaby sung by death and rattles covered in blood. Once I had a nightmare of a playground full of graves of children and the chilling wind moving empty swings. This playground became their final place to rest and find peace.

Once upon a time, a sweet, chubby thirteen-year-old boy with rosy cheeks named Hamza disappeared when he was carrying milk and biscuits to children like him in the besieged city of Daraa. The Syrian regime's forces prevented food from entering the city as a mass punishment was inflicted on its people for rising up. Days after, his family received Hamza's mutilated body back from the regime. This was not new, it happened all the time since this regime came to power, but it was never covered by the media. At first, I thought that these were individual cases. But after the torture of the schoolchildren in Daraa and the murder of Hamza, it appears that killing children was done systematically and by Assad's troops and with intent, as the tragic massacres yet to come in Karm Al Zaitoun, Houla and Qubair also revealed.

With each crime committed by the so-called "government" my insides were boiling. All I wanted to do was to open the door and run, madly screaming about the thwarting of our innocence and perception of goodness in this world.

As the children of Syria were a constitutive factor for igniting the revolution, they became a target for Assad forces. The mass punishment policy of the Syrian regime did not exclude Syrian children. Like their parents, these children faced arrest, torture, sexual molestation, and brutal death under shelling or roaming genocides committed by Assad's *shabiha* (government hired thugs/mercenaries) and death squads. Syrian forces violated international and humanitarian laws concerning the protection of children. On July 25, 2012, the Local Coordination Committees, in collaboration with the Centre for Documentation of Violations, was able to document 1,612 children who were shot by regime forces and by the army's heavy weaponry. So far, the child martyrs include 1,160 males and 452 females. 120 were executed and 33 were tortured to death by various security branches. The deaths of these children opened the adults' eyes to their collective bleak future.

## Reaching out to Syria

As part of Voices of the Future program for empowering women to speak and work for their communities, I contacted Syrian activists inside and outside of Syria, especially women. I interviewed the famous Syrian author Samar Yazbik and I talked to activists in Homs during the shelling of Baba Amr. Nothing was enough, I felt that my actions were so small and insignificant compared to the grave violations of the sanctity of a human being. I believed in the media and its ability to support human rights and urge people from all around the world to support the Syrian people's right to be liberated.

While violence in Syria intensified, many people fled their homes and went to neighboring countries. I couldn't take the indifference of many organizations and states to the Syrian refugees. I decided to make a report about the sufferings and needs of the refugees. I packed my camera and took a plane to Amman, Jordan in March 2012. There I met with a group of Syrian activists living in Jordan. Some came with their families after the massacre of Hama, and some fled the current oppression. These activists were kind and courageous. They wanted me to relay their voice to the international community. No faces were shown in the videos I took, only recorded in my memory.

I met with a family who fled from Homs. When I went to their rented house I felt as if I was visiting a neighbor that I had not seen in a long time. We had a morning coffee and started talking about what they witnessed. The father was caught on a barricade by the regime's forces and tortured barbarically. He showed me his arms, which the forces had twisted backward at the elbow, and pictures of his bruised face after the torture. The family told me that no organizations were helping them, and when I asked why they didn't seek the help of the

United Nations High Commission for Refugees (UNHCR), they told me that they didn't trust the organization because they believed that they prevented refugees from moving freely. (I wondered myself: who could trust the UN anymore after the observers they sent to document and mitigate the killing frenzy in Syria proved too indifferent and scared to actually help us with our problems?) Finally, the father told me that he was ready to go back into Syria and take pictures for me and the media. He told me that he was ready to fight.

I went to meet a young man in his early twenties who was paralyzed after being struck by a bullet. However, it was not the bullet to his back that put him in the wheelchair, it was the wrong operation. He had such a lovely face. He told me that he was shot during a peaceful protest. He saw his friends die beside him. His family took him to a hospital where amateur doctors attempted to operate on his wounds—an operation that went horribly awry. I saw his tears falling from his cheeks. I was deeply shaken because both of us felt like toys, like rags. He did not cry when he recounted how he was shot. He cried because he felt like he was not worth anything to the amateur doctors. I asked him what he intended to do when he was released from the hospital. He replied that he would return to Syria and join a peaceful protest, for he wanted freedom.

In the Mafraq area in North Jordan, I sat with an old man. He was shot, arrested, and tortured inside the hospital. He was responsible for protecting the rebels and supplying them. He was smiling and optimistic, his grey beard surrounded his deep wrinkles. His age did not stop him from being an active and vital contributor to the revolution. We had some tea and talked of what happened to him. He was shot in the leg, arrested, and taken to the hospital. In the hospital he was tied to the bed and savagely tortured. He was only released after a powerful figure within the government pulled some strings. Then he fled to Jordan to treat his swollen and rotten leg. He was lucky to be able to keep his limb. Finally he told me that when he could walk again, he would go back and join the fight.

At the end of that day, I went to a house that sat on a top of a hill near Mafraq. There I met with a conservative family. They welcomed me in their house and we sat on the mattresses that lined the floor. I met a grandmother, her daughters, daughters-in-law, and her grandchildren. They had left their houses in Daraa. The grandmother did not know where her sons were. When incidences of rape and violence increased in their area, she decided to flee with her daughters and daughters-in-law, and head for Jordan, where some of her relatives took them in. All she wanted, she told me, was to know where her sons were and all she dreamed of the day that they would be re-united back home.

When I went out, a friend was accompanying me in my journey, called me to stand with her up the hill, as I walked up, more green plains revealed in front of me garnished with white and red flowers scattered here and there. She said: look, this is Syria, the plains of Hauran. I was fighting a temptation to run through the fields, they looked so lovely and peaceful, they looked like the future we all seek.

I had to go, the night was falling and I had a flight in two hours. On my way back, I hugged my camera and I dreamt that all these people would find serenity one day, would find relief and peace one day . . . and the same for me too.

It is time for the people to talk about what they want.

In the beginning of the 80s, a huge genocide occurred in Hama city, the number of people killed at that horrific time is between 20,000 and 40,000. No one knows why the world remained silent at that time, and no one knows why, when the world knew about it, it did not call for any investigation about the massacre.

Today, the world is still watching, but no one can deny what is going on. We are tweeting endlessly, posting on Facebook about what is going on, translating news and videos from Arabic into English and other languages as activists and volunteers. In the beginning, there was a lot of debate on what to call the Syrian troops and the situation in Syria. I used "Assad battalions" or "army forces loyal to Assad."

Activists did not agree, they were still considering that the Syrian army was loyal to the people and in some way or another would act exactly like the Egyptian army. Activists also did not explicitly call for toppling the regime; they wanted more freedoms and reforms in the country, while I called it a revolution, and I knew that if the Assad family did not leave the government by stepping down willingly, then nothing would change in Syria. This family always treated Syria as a piece of personal property like a ranch, the way it was handed over from the father to the son. But I can't say that there wasn't hope in my heart that some reforms and further freedoms would be made for the people by Bashar Assad. He and his wife made a show of supporting civil societies and the youth, and promoted themselves as reformers. Yet in reality the country was sinking into more corruption and oppression under their rule.

Local Coordination committees were formed, in each governorate, city, village, and even neighborhoods. The Coordinations were the first civil groups to establish themselves firmly in Syria, but of course they had to remain undercover. These new entities were the first to surge as movers for more democratic political life in Syria. They worked as civil journalists and they tried to raise awareness about peaceful revolutions and the power of civil disobedience and strikes. One youth many Syrians called the Syrian Gandhi was Ghiath Matar. He had a dream of joining hands with his country's national army and that no Syrian would shed the blood of another fellow Syrian. He took water and roses to give Assad soldiers on the barricades of his small town near Damascus. Ghiath was a staunch peaceful fighter for freedom, and he always preached about civil movements. But one day, the soldiers to whom he once gave roses arrested him. After a while he was returned back to his family as a lifeless body full of marks of severe torture. We were shocked at what happened to Ghiath. It was a clear message to all activists, bloggers, and civil movements that this is what they will get if they dare to raise their voice. Many activists inside and outside Syria kept their identities secret and used alias names so they would be able to carry on their activism. If an activist lived abroad, there was a risk that one of his/her family members would be killed by the regime.

The Coordinations spread horizontally because a hierarchical structure is subject to breach by Syrian regime, no one can be fully trusted, either because a member could be an informant, or an arrested member might break down and talk about their work and individuals working with them. There was also the problem of communications between different groups because everything was monitored. The horizontal structure of the Coordinations made them all equal. This is healthy for diversity in Syria in the future. Youtube and Facebook were and still are the main tools for the Coordinations.

The Assad regime immediately prevented any independent media from getting inside. Only loyal journalists and publications were allowed in, while the distrusted journalists were always accompanied by Syrian intelligence forces and taken to areas where Bashar Assad loyalties prepared preset performances to show their support and love to their leader. Assad's media program focused on sending multiple messages to each group. A machine started working to distort any facts of the revolution while sending contradictory messages to the world to confuse everyone and prevent any action to be taken. Many battles were fought, and are being fought, on many media outlets to correct the false images and information promoted by the army employed by Assad diplomats around the world. Russian, Chinese, and Iranian media were also participating in the distorting campaign and delivering the same stories promoted by Syrian state media. Assad media also tried to steal the slogans and songs of the revolution. During the besiege of Daraa, many Syrians tried to take aid to those in need inside the city, but they usually were chased and sometimes shot dead by Assad forces. One leaked video shows how Assad forces brutally shot a number of Syrians trying to smuggle food into Daraa during the embargo. The soldiers were mocking and disrespecting the dead bodies of their own citizens, and mocking the bags of canned tuna and cookie boxes they were carrying. Assad soldiers were placing guns and bullets beside these innocent civilians, so Assad state media would come and shoot these people to claim that they were militants who wanted to kill the residents of Daraa.

Leaked emails and documents from the Syrian government showed that some foreign media also helped the Syrian regime in weaving its web of lies. Leaked emails showed that an American journalist went to the Baba Amr neighborhood in Homs pretending that he wanted to cover the clashes between the rebels and Assad battalions, but he had communications with Syrian security forces and people from Assad office. The communications showed that this reporter gave information of what he knew about the rebels to the Syrian regime. Other documents obtained by activists show the Syrian regime hiring journalists from India to write to the Indian public what the regime wants.

## The revolution evolves

After months of facing mortars and tank missiles with flesh, after months of losing loved ones and seeing their children slaughtered before the eyes of the entire world, many Syrians couldn't take it anymore. Some started to hold light personal guns to protect the peaceful protests from being attacked by Assad soldiers and Shabiha. An armed movement named the Free Syria Army was started by an officer defected from Assad army, Hussein Harmoush. Like the Coordinations, the Free Syrian Army was not able to be built in a hierarchal order because of the security breaches and lack of communications. And as the Coordinations were made by Syrian activists as a reflection of the people's will, the Free Syrian Army also came as a genuine reflection of this will. These FSA rebels are the children of Syrians, which is why they have financial and emotional support from many people.

As the popularity and strength of Syrian Free Army started to grow, the Syrian regime started to use its air force firepower. This came after the international diplomacy failed in its mission to bring peace to Syria, and failed to elevate above its greedy interests and power display over the corpses of Syrian children. Most Syrians now only hope and trust the FSA. But the work of the Free Syrian Army is not just fighting with the regime. They carry out other duties such as: protecting field hospitals, doing rescue missions, helping and protecting Syrian refugees to flee to safer areas, securing a safe path for the defectors from the Syrian regime, and taking food and medicines to those in need. One example took place in Mount Zawiya area in north Syria when members from the FSA fixed and operated bakeries to supply people with bread. The FSA also gathers information about the movements of the Assad army, Shabiha, and locations of snipers from a wide network created by Syrian citizens in each and every area that work as eyewitnesses. The FSA as part of the Syrian people is nurtured and incubated. Many volunteers said that they did not chose to carry a weapon but they had to, and they would like to end this war so they would return back to their farms, schools, jobs and houses. Recently the FSA issued a code of conduct to respect human rights and spread awareness among the rebels on the forbidden practices.

## What is wrong with the world?

Arming the people was not a choice that Syrians took willingly. They remained peaceful for months while all kinds of weapons were used on them. We are all aware of the negative effect of the spread of arms, but this was an action of self-defense. On the other hand, tons of weapons were delivered regularly to the Assad regime and no one did anything to stop the flow of these lethal supplies. To this day (August 2012), we did not hear anyone speaking of taking Assad and his allies to International Criminal Court nor any member of his regime. Until now, the world insists on calling the demands of the Syrian people a "crisis" or a "civil war."

Our revolution is not composed of a certain religious group or ethnicity, it is a comprehensive revolution that Syrians from different backgrounds and beliefs have participated in. A couple of months before the revolution started, Bashar al-Assad stated in a media interview that Syrians "are not ready for democracy." Assad treated his people as politically uneducated, but he forgot that freedom and dignity are innate in humans. But it seems that the world buys what he was selling. To call the revolution in Syria a mere "crisis" is a forgery of people's demands for their basic human rights. To call what Syrians are facing anything other than a legitimate struggle for rights will allow the international community to dodge the responsibility of protecting civilians, and in some way— unintentionally—such definition is giving an excuse to Assad to erase his opponents, who are thousands of Syrians. Describing the situation in Syria by a fight between the regime and groups of armed opposition is a dwarfing of the aspirations for freedom by many Syrians, it is an exit for international community from its humanitarian responsibility to protect human beings, and it is an inferior look at the right of Syrians to achieve their long awaited democracy.

On June 14, 2012, Amnesty International issued a report providing evidence of crimes against humanity and war crimes that are widespread and systematic which were part of Syrian government policy "to exact revenge against communities suspected of supporting the opposition and to intimidate people into submission." Amnesty International adds that a decisive act must be taken by the international community. Just a few days ago, FAO stated that about 3 million Syrians need food. Official numbers state that more than 20,000 Syrians have been killed, about 200,000 arrested, more than 100,000 are refugees, more than one million Syrians are displaced inside Syria and thousands have disappeared, and still these numbers are growing.

There is need for action in any way possible. The proxy battles between regional and international forces must end. Our souls are not a matter of bargains and betting.

At this moment, I am sitting at home incessantly praying that I shall not be the one to receive "the call" (like millions of Syrians). Right now our history is being shelled and bombarded. Right now another child is raped inside Assad prisons. Right now Assad troops are killing livestock and setting fire to someone's crops in order to starve people. Right now Assad troops are burning the beautiful forests in north Syria to prevent refugees and rebels from hiding under an oak tree. Right now, the Syrian central bank and treasury is empty because all the money is used to purchase death machines. Right now the future of Syria is being dismantled by Assad's crimes and the world's silence and apathy.

And yet, we are waiting for the dawn.

# Change in Saudi Arabia Is Inevitable
## by Ahmed Al Omran

**AHMED AL OMRAN** is a Saudi blogger and multimedia journalist. Born and raised in Hofuf, in eastern Saudi Arabia, he received his bachelor's in pharmacy from King Saud University in Riyadh. He later earned a master's degree from the Graduate School of Journalism at Columbia University ,and he currently works as a production assistant for the social media desk at National Public Radio.

Ahmed was an early contributor to Global Voices, an international community of bloggers, and is the man behind "Saudi Jeans," one of the most well-known and longest standing blogs in the Middle East. Ahmed started writing the blog in May 2004 as an experiment to improve his command of English. Quickly, he began generating a lot of traffic. The blog aims to provide news, commentary, and personal views on political and social issues in Saudi Arabia, with a special focus on freedom of expression, human rights, and women's rights.

At the age of twenty-seven, Al Omran is at the forefront of a generational movement seeking to challenge Saudi Arabia's entrenched elite. Ahmed was nicknamed "the Saudi blogfather" for his essential role in the creation of Saudi Arabia's nascent blogosphere.

When I finished high school in 2004, my father asked me what I planned to study in college. When I said "journalism," he paused for a moment, looked me in the eye and said: "Listen son, I know you like journalism, and you can probably be good at it. But you are a Shi'a. They would never let you make it in this country's media."

Saudi Arabia is a predominantly Sunni Muslim country. Shi'a are a minority, comprising 10–15 percent of its population, and they suffer from discrimination in many aspects of public life, including opportunities for employment and business prospects. The situation for Saudi Arabia's Shi'a has slowly been improving since King Abdullah ascended to the throne in 2005, but there is still a very long road ahead towards equality. Officials always claim that laws in the country do not discriminate between citizens based on their religious background, but evidence on the ground proves that discriminatory practices are alive and well, even if they may not be legislated.

Being a member of a religious minority is tough, especially in a country like Saudi Arabia. It fills your life with glass walls and ceilings. My father, for example, came of age during the 1980s, when anti-Shi'a sentiments were intense, to say the least. He was content to simply be able to make a living and support a family, even as he was being deprived of most of his other rights.

Growing up in the predominantly Shi'a town of Hofuf in the Eastern Province of the country, I came to learn of such discrimination and how to cope with it, but I remained determined not let it rob me of my dreams.

I was young. I did not know much about life, and I thought maybe my father would know better. He suggested I study pharmacy, a major that seemed consistent with my high grades and offered good prospects of a well-paying job in Saudi Arabia. Becoming a pharmacist was not what I really wanted to do, but like any good Saudi son, I listened to my father. Soon, I moved to Riyadh, where I enrolled in the required courses to pursue a degree in pharmacy at King Saud University.

But I struggled from the beginning. I was not enjoying my studies, and I was spending way too much time online—which where

I discovered blogging. I started reading seminal bloggers like Dave Winer and Jason Kottke. Then I began to find Arab bloggers who were writing in English, like Mahmood al-Yousef from Bahrain and Zaydound from Kuwait. At the time, most of the Arab blogs I was reading were written in English because blogging platforms and software like Google's Blogger and MoveableType did not support Arabic.

Reading these blogs inspired me to start a blog, as I thought it might help me improve my English. But I had no idea what to blog about. So I plunged in without thinking much about it. "I'm doing this just for fun," I told myself. I'm a moody person and I get bored very easily, and so I thought in three weeks I would get sick of the blog and move on.

I called my blog "Saudi Jeans." In the very first blog post, dated May 10, 2004, I tried to explain the name:

> The fact is, there's nothing called "Saudi Jeans" but this blog. There is no Saudi Jeans. I made up this name because I'm Saudi and I do like jeans. I think that "jeans" is a symbol of a lot of different things and ideas here in Saudi Arabia. Things and ideas that a lot of people say are bad and have nothing to do with our culture and traditions, but in the same time everybody uses them and believes in them. It highlights a dichotomy that I find inherently relevant and interesting to me.

At the beginning, my blog was more like a diary. I wrote about different things, but most posts were about personal matters and links to stuff I considered interesting or funny. Yet this blog, which I was sure would cease to exist just weeks after I started it, attracted more attention than I had ever expected. I was receiving many questions and comments about Saudi Arabia from other bloggers, so I started to focus my posts more on the political and social issues in my country. It just sort of happened that way.

At this point I was really enjoying blogging—perhaps too much, since I neglected my school work, which I hardly found interesting. Just as I was beginning to consider changing my major, my father suddenly passed away. His abrupt departure left me both devastated and confused. On the one hand, he was no longer here to stop me from changing course. On the other hand, I was hesitant to decide on a new major while I was still upset about my father's death.

After months of confusion and indecision I reached a compromise: I would get the pharmacy degree in memory of my father, and then I would pursue my master's in journalism. All the while, I was continuously updating the blog, which was becoming more and more well-known and widely regarded as one of a handful of good English-language sources about Saudi Arabia available online.

The blog that I started with the intention of having fun and improving my command of the English language had claimed a life of its own and in many ways had become central to my own life. When I would meet someone for the first time at a party, the conversation usually went something like this:

"What do you do?"

"I'm a blogger. Have you heard of a blog called "Saudi Jeans"?"

"Oh yeah, I know that blog!"

I would smile, and then add: "I am Saudi Jeans."

I was among the first to have a blog in Saudi Arabia. Back in 2004, the blogging community was small and made up mainly of young people who found in blogging a great medium. All of those early bloggers quit after a while. For some reason, I'm the only one of that original community who continued to actively blog.

since then, the Saudi blogosphere has grown rapidly, and today there are more than ten thousand Saudi blogs out there. These blogs offer a lot of diverse content, and they reflect a more authentic image of the country than what is usually available in the local media, which is heavily censored, or in the international media, which typically fails to understand the complexities and culture of Saudi Arabia.

Soon after I started blogging I was introduced to a much wider community of Arab bloggers. I began reading blogs from Egypt,

Jordan, Lebanon, Tunisia, and Morocco. Less than two years after I started "Saudi Jeans" I was being asked for interviews by media outlets around the world and getting invited to speak at conferences about my experiences as an "Arab blogger." In these conferences I had the chance to meet fellow bloggers from almost every other Arab country, many of whom are still my friends and colleagues today.

I will never forget meeting Wael Abbas for the first time in Beirut back in late 2007. We were invited to speak on the same panel at the Second Arab Free Press Forum. I had been reading Wael's blog for some time, but meeting him in person and listening to him talk about dealing with repeated crackdowns by the Egyptian government was awe-inducing for me. Wael is a blogger and human rights activist who is most widely known for documenting videos of police brutality in Egypt. His work and actions led to the prosecution of some Egyptian police for torture, long before the uprisings in 2011 occurred. His YouTube account, which included videos of police brutality, voting irregularities, and protests, was famously shutdown by YouTube in 2007. Over the years Wael, myself, and many other Arab bloggers have formed a loosely connected network through which we keep tabs on each other online and meet occasionally at events once or twice a year.

While most bloggers in the Middle East preferred to hide behind a pseudonym to protect their identity, I was one of the first Saudi bloggers to use my real name and photo on the web. I realized early on that the credibility I would gain from using my true identity would outweigh such protection. Anonymity has its appeal, but it is certainly not foolproof.

Using your real name involves a significant risk, especially if the government frowns upon what you write. That's what happened with my friend and fellow blogger Fouad al-Farhan, who got arrested in December 2007 after he wrote about political prisoners in Saudi Arabia.

I worked with other bloggers both inside and outside the country, like Tunisian Sami Ben Gharbia and Mauritanian Nasser Weddady, to launch a successful online campaign calling for al-Farhan's freedom.

I played the role of the unofficial spokesman of the campaign, talking to CNN, BBC, Al-Hurra, and other channels, newspapers, and websites about the case and defending the blogger's right to free speech.

Appearing on international television to criticize the government is even more risky than blogging, but I did it because I believe that freedom of expression is an essential human right. Some people saw what I did as brave. Other people saw it as foolhardy. For me, I did it because I thought that it was the right thing to do.

Fouad's detention helped bring the blogging community together in Saudi Arabia. But while he was still in detention, another tragic event happened. Hadeel al-Hodaif, one of the early female bloggers in the country, entered a coma from which she never woke up. She passed away shortly after, but not before leaving a legacy that still lives with us to this day. Her brave writings, her defense of free speech, even for those she disagreed with, and then her sudden departure are things we will always remember fondly. When my blog was briefly blocked in summer 2006, she was one of the first people to call for lifting the block, despite all the attacks she received for defending me, "a liberal Shi'a."

Fouad's detention was a turning point for me but also for blogging in general in Saudi Arabia. Some bloggers were intimidated because they feared that they would face a similar fate if they continued, and so they opted to quit blogging altogether. But not everyone was silenced. Another group of bloggers felt empowered by what had happened because they felt that the government was finally starting to take bloggers seriously. This encouraged some of them to start using their real names instead of pseudonyms.

Authorities began to harass bloggers more often. Many bloggers were forced to shut down their blogs, but I got away with a lot of things that I said because I was blogging in English, so there were fewer monitoring capabilities and less censorship.

The authorities eventually came after me, but indirectly. They went to my family and let them know that they were displeased with my work. My family was understandably terrified. At the time, I was in Riyadh at school, and they were at home. My brother called and asked me to come home. I took the first train home, and as soon as I arrived I was met by my mother with tears in her eyes, asking me to quit blogging. My mom was very scared that I was going to be thrown in jail.

I was upset that authorities had gone to my family and scared them. But I was not surprised. I knew I was being watched, and this is a tactic that they use with a lot of bloggers and young activists. The authorities know how important family is in our society, and that if there is anyone you would listen to, it is your family. Instead of coming after you, they threaten your family so they will put pressure on you.

I told my mother that there was no reason to be scared. "I'm not doing anything illegal," I told her. But she was unconvinced. "I don't know and I don't care what you do," she said. "But I'm your mom, and I'm asking you to stop."

"I can't quit blogging now," I told her, "because if I quit that means they won." I was not going to let them silence me. She knew I was stubborn; she was the one who raised me. She called my uncle hoping he could make me change my mind. I did not want my uncle to get involved, but surprisingly he was more reasonable than my mother about the situation.

"You are an adult now," my uncle told me. "We cannot control you. We cannot make you do something you don't want to do. But we are your family, and we are concerned for your safety. You are not stupid. and you seem to know what you are doing. All we are asking is that you be more careful, for the sake of your mom and little brothers. who will suffer if you go to jail. They deserve at least this from you."

It was clear that they realized they could not stop me and that all they could do was to pray for my safety. I promised to be careful and to inform them if I felt threatened, but I told them that quitting was not an option.

Being a blogger in a place that doesn't respect freedom of expression is certainly not easy. You have to walk a fine line between saying what you think and the possible consequences of what you say. Unlike outsiders who struggle to understand the intricacies of debates in Saudi Arabia, I was born and raised in this country. I know what the red lines are. I know when to stay away from them. I know when to dance around them and maybe get close but without touching them. And I know when to cross them. Yes, these red lines may appear blurry sometimes, but as someone who lived his whole life in Saudi Arabia, I think I have a good sense for how to deal with them.

While blogging in this part of the world can be risky, it can also be very rewarding. Blogging has given me opportunities to travel, to learn and do things I would otherwise never have gotten to do.

Shortly after I started my blog, I was invited by Ethan Zuckerman to contribute to Global Voices Online, an international community of bloggers who report on blogs and citizen media from around the world. I was traveling from one country to another to speak at conferences about blogging and social media, and I was asked to write for mainstream news organizations. In April 2009 I participated in G20Voice, a citizen media initiative supported by several British NGOs to cover the G20 Summit in London, and in June of the same year I wrote an op-ed for the *New York Times* about President Barack Obama's historic Cairo speech.

In the fall of 2010, I moved to New York to study journalism at Columbia University. I don't think I would ever have been admitted to such a prestigious school if it wasn't for my blog. On the sixth anniversary of my blog "Saudi Jeans," I wrote this:

> It has been a great journey. Like a roller coaster, full of ups and downs, turns and twists, joy and fear. Sometimes fast, sometimes slow. Sometimes nice, sometimes nasty. But always, always interesting.

> Some argue that although I say the goal of this blog is to push for change in Saudi Arabia, little has changed in the country, and this little has nothing to do with "Saudi Jeans" or blogging. That could be true, and I'm okay with it. Changing a nation is too great of an endeavor for a humble blog like mine to meet.

But for me, the question is not if blogging has changed (or can change) Saudi Arabia or not. The question I keep asking myself is: is it worth trying? And my answer is absolutely yes.

I know that I aim too high. That's just me. I can't settle for less, I want everything. I'm greedy like that, but I don't accept injustice and I believe that we, as people, deserve better. My dreams are big and wild, but I will never suppress them. You can share those dreams, or laugh at them, but you can't stop me, and you can't shut me up.

I wrote these words without realizing that later that year something larger than I had ever imagined was going to happen. In December 2010, a Tunisian fruit seller named Mohammad Bouazizi immolated himself in frustration, and things could never be the same again.

From my new home in New York, I was, like the rest of the world, watching the events unfolding in the Middle East—first in Tunisia, and then in Egypt, Libya, Bahrain, Yemen, and Syria. However, I wasn't just "watching" these events; I was living them, despite the distance and time difference. I have Tunisian friends who fought the oppression of Ben Ali's regime for years. I have Egyptian friends who slept for days in Tahrir Square until Mubarak stepped down, and I have Bahraini friends who were detained and had to go into hiding to escape unfair trials and long jail sentences.

I'm not Tunisian or Egyptian or Bahraini, but I felt personally invested in their revolutions. I felt that these uprisings were mine as much as they were theirs.

Which brings me back to my home country and the question that many people have been asking since the beginning of the "Arab Spring": When are we going to see a revolution in Saudi Arabia?

My answer: Don't hold your breath, but don't close your eyes.

Many of the underlying causes that led to the uprisings in other parts of the Arab world exist in Saudi Arabia. Factors like the youth bulge, high unemployment, and the lack of freedom and justice are present in the Kingdom. Some people might even argue that such problems are even more oppressive there than in other countries that experienced unrest over the year 2011.

However, we must remember that, unlike many other Arab countries, Saudi Arabia has the resources by which the government can afford to delay dealing with these problems. The keyword here is "delay." Money can buy the government time, but it is a finite resource, and sooner or later, they will have to deal with these issues. The only way to deal with them is by initiating true political and social reform.

So far, the government has not shown a great desire to do that. They don't seem to realize that they are standing on the wrong side of history, and they don't seem to understand that the status quo is unsustainable. Change is inevitable.

# Domino Theory Cartoon
## by Carolos Latuff

This illustration documents the domino effect that swept through the region, which began with Tunisia's government, led by former president Ben Ali (depicted by the first domino). Tunisia's revolution was followed by Egypt, depicted by the second domino with former Egyptian president Hosni Mubarak's exasperated face. Activists used social media and other online platforms to connect and mobilize to spread the spirit of revolt from Tunisia across North Africa and to the Gulf.

# Domino Effect
## by Omar Offendum

Omar Offendum is a Syrian American hip-hop artist born in Saudi Arabia, raised in Washington D.C., and living in Los Angeles. He has been featured on several major news outlets, toured the world to promote his ground-breaking music, helped raise thousands of dollars for various humanitarian relief organizations, and lectured at a number of prestigious academic institutions. Most recently he has been involved in creating several critically acclaimed songs about the popular democratic uprisings throughout the Arab world. Omar is currently hard at work on his second studio album while continuing to tour to promote his 2010 solo release, affectionately dubbed "SyrianamericanA." You can view his work at http://offendum.bandcamp.com/

For far too long
a middle eastern
freedom song was

considered improbable
or not even optional
that arabi youth
were too irresponsible
religion an obstacle
but it was inevitable to the conscious folk

who knew what was possible
conditions were optimal
the domino effect they all neglected was unstoppable

ripples spill to waves
quick as martyrs fill the graves
no lament
whatever it takes
our soldiers are spent
but "these are the breaks"
we're told as men
to never mistake
a brother's kindness for a weakness
the same applies to tyrants
thinking their pride's a sign of greatness

humpty dumpty sat on a wall
put up by masons
so he would fall
flat on his face
and give him the spoils
weapons contracts and oil . . .
oil?
ha!
what you cookin?
betting that they could keep getting away with the dough
when nobody was looking

their hubris wouldn't
let them believe
they ever could leave
that everyone needed them
please

that's bout as naive
as thinking that Palestine will not be free'd
It ain't up to you
Mr Despot
or shall I say Desperate?
shutting down the internet
is just making us all the more restless

you just don't get it—do you?
it's bigger than Facebook
bigger than Twitter
No this is the sum of years
of living in fear
while you got the glitter
but it wasn't gold
when citizens' hopes were sold to the highest bidder
go cry us rivers
your crocodile tears are bitter

sweet surrender
send 'em off
kicking & screaming
with an agreement
that their lenders cut them off at the knees
and get to freezing bank accounts
in whole amounts for what they stole amounts to treason
till (all) these clowns start stepping down or skipping town
it's hunting season

(INHALE)

the air is clear we're finally breathing

(EXHALE)

I just can't tell you what it means to me when

hearing millions of my people chant for peace & freedom
souls rebelling overwhelming
wishing my father'd lived to see them

Tunisia – Egypt – Libya
Yemen – Oman – Bahrain
Soomal – Sudan – Algeria
Iraq – Maghreb – Libnan
Kuwait – Jordan – Sa'oodia
UAE – Mauritania
Djibouti – Qatar – Comor
Sooria
Falasteen

Tunis – wa Misr – wa Leebya
Yemen – 'uman – Bahrain
Soomal – Sudan – Jazaair
3iraq – Maghreb – Libnaan
Kuwait – 'urdun – Su'oodiyeh
Emarat – Mauritan(ia)
Djibouti – Qatar – Qumur
Sooria
Falasteen

# Afterword

## by Maytha Alhassen and Ahmed Shihab-Eldin

We would be remiss not to mention the challenges of editing this book, ones that poignantly reflect the very challenges taking place in the region. This anthology was originally conceived in the summer of 2011 as a two-month project that would collect twenty narratives from activists on the ground and immersed in the digital realm from five "Arab Spring" countries. In the midst of what eventually transformed into a year of work, we were challenged to confront our own predisposed notions and stereotypes.

We also recognized that developments on the ground were moving too rapidly that to try to capture or highlight all the relevant or revolutionary milestones would be done in vain.

This book does not, and more importantly, could not reflect the competing coalitions and narratives that materialized as young Arabs challenged their leaders. Among the many narratives, the emerging dominance of the long-repressed Muslim Brotherhood as a popular political movement in Tunisia, Egypt and elsewhere in the region cannot and should not be ignored.

Although political platforms with Islam at their core, such as the Muslim Brotherhood, would eventually dominate both parliaments and political discussions after sitting dictators were ousted, they were not central in the early mobilization of civil unrest and revolt.

During the editorial and logistical process of publishing this book, these groups had yet to fill the political and economic vacuum created by the uprisings themselves. The significance of their successes, namely Mohamed Morsi being named Egypt's (and the Arab world's for that matter) first democratically elected president, are not fully included in these stories. Although representatives of these organizations are not present in this book, references to their relevance in these revolutions can be found within some of the essays.

## "Arab Spring"

Finding a comprehensive name for these regional movements presented an unexpected challenge. Adopting the Western "prose du jour" to describe the social movements in MENA, we provisionally titled this book "Youth Voices from the Arab Spring." As we began to solicit essays from high-profile figures and grassroots activists, we discovered that our call for stories for a book on the "Arab Spring" fell on deaf ears.

Our prospective contributors, rather than fervently objecting to this Western-conceived nomenclature, were confused by it. They had no idea what we were talking about. One contributor asked, "Is it called the 'Arab Spring' because Tunisia's revolution is called the 'Jasmine Revolution'?" Another agreed to sign on but with reservation, "I do like the sound of this book, but what is the 'Arab Spring'?"

Fascinated by the overwhelming response of puzzlement to this phrase, we implored contributors to provide us with a phrase or phrases they use or hear more commonly used to describe the regional movements. We also did some investigative research into the origins of the phrase "Arab Spring." There were those who favored "uprisings" and others who declared these events a moment of "Arab awakening." Some acknowledged that the Arabic translation of "Arab Spring" was becoming more standard in Arabic press. We learned that the terms more widely used among the people were *thawra* (revolutions) and *harakat al-thawrat* (revolutionary movements), We also learned that the unifying theme across all these revolutions was *karama*, dignity.

Obviously, then, we changed the book's title to *Demanding Dignity*. Just as the contributors to this book contest the repression of their agency in their respective states, by choosing this title we contest the dominant Western narrative that embodies and imagines their struggles in two words that enjoy uncritical media ubiquity: "Arab Spring."

## Revolution

Although we use the term "revolution," which suggests that the process of change is complete, by doing this we do not mean to suggest that the work to transform these countries is done. This book's contributors continue to put pressure on their governments and to object to their exclusion from the very movements they started or participated in. A former member of Bahrain's parliament tirelessly works to document Human Rights abuses by the government, while a Tunisian activist recently helped to organize a "Rock the Vote" type of concert tour in anticipation of the country's first-ever elections.

## Danger

Perhaps naïvely on our part, we did not foresee the challenge of receiving pieces from contributors who were still intricately entangled in revolutionary movements. For some, the fact that the movement is ongoing meant periods of disconnection from the Internet. (Yemeni activists have had to deal with two hours a day of Internet access.) For others this meant they had to drop out of the project.

In the most drastic cases, potential contributors dropped out because of the threat of indefinite detention. Multiple Bahraini and Syrian activists who were initially enthusiastic about contributing to the project eventually bowed out, after realizing their family's and their own security could potentially be jeopardized by telling their story. Razan Ghazzawi, a Syrian activist who initially agreed to contribute, was detained by the Syrian government on December 4, 2011 on the Syrian and Jordanian border as we were still finalizing revisions to her essay. Unsurprisingly, we woke up to this news on our Twitter timeline. She was released from prison two weeks later, and several months after, detained once more. (NOTE: Razan's essay has been withheld from this book due to our inability to get her final approval to publish it.)

Another Syrian blogger who initially expressed interest in contributing to the book later mysteriously ignored our inquiring replies. We found out the reason why through a newspaper story: He was detained by Syrian authorities for his blogging activities.

## Communication Barriers

For many of our contributors, writing about their experiences, reliving them as they wrote, was an emotional, cathartic process. For some it was their first time recounting the vivid details of their torture.

Because this book engages stories from contributors residing in and traveling through multiple continents, rather than residing in the United States like previous I Speak for Myself book, the editing process called for creative communication strategies, using a variety of languages and technology. We found ourselves communicating with contributors who juggled work during the day and organized activities at night, which led to many late night Skype calls and Twitter DM's.

One of our contributors was invited to Sweden to receive the Edberg Award for her courageous use of social media in Egypt. But upon arriving, news broke of the latest deadly confrontation between her fellow revolutionaries and military soldiers, forcing her to travel back home, where she also shuttled back and forth to visit a parent with a terminal illness. Between blackberries, iPads, and the unreliability that came with her nomadic lifestyle and spotty Internet access, we somehow managed to complete her story.

A contributor from Bahrain, in addition to making revisions on her essay, was juggling meetings with Oslo's Freedom Forum, U.S. Secretary of State Hillary Clinton, and the U.S. Congress in a bid to keep her sister, and by extension all her countrymen, from being arrested again. Several of her family members had been detained or gone missing. Her father was on a hunger strike to protest his own arrest and that of others. Certain that she would never be allowed to leave if she ever returned to Bahrain, she, like others, was forced into exile.

Finally, while Internet access may have enabled communication with the contributors, government surveillance often meant that links we wanted to send as resources to our contributors were blocked. It is worth mentioning that the Syrian government used technology made by a U.S. company (Blue Coat Systems) to censor and target Internet users. Whether enabling or thwarting communication, the Arab revolutions' relationship with the Internet did underscore a new emerging dimension to transnational movement breaking and building.

# About the Editors

**MAYTHA ALHASSEN** was born to Syrian parents in the suburbs of Southern California. She was raised in the San Gabriel Valley on a cul-de-sac completely inhabited by her father's family. She is a doctoral student in American Studies & Ethnicity at University of Southern California. Her work bridges the worlds of social justice, academic research, media engagement, and artistic expression.

Alhassen writes and performs poetry and has worked as a performer and organizer for the play "Hijabi Monologues." In 2005 she became the first female blogger for Arab-American themed blog Kabobfest (www.kabobfest.com). Because of her blogging experience with the site, an unexpected foray into hosting and broadcast journalism began in 2007 with the Arab American TV variety show "What's Happening" (www.artwhatsup.com) on Arabic station ART.

Alhassen has appeared on Al Jazeera English's "The Stream" (stream.aljazeera.com) as a guest co-host and a substitute co-host/digital producer. She also shared what it means to be a US-born woman practicing Islam with CNN. Her essay on the same topic was published in May 2011 in the first book of the "I Speak for Myself" series. Alhassen's writings have appeared in CNN, Huffington Post, Counterpunch and in academic journals and her work has been featured in the *Los Angeles Times*, *Miami Herald*, and *The Nation*.

She received her B.A. in Political Science and Arabic and Islamic Studies with honors from University of California, Los Angeles (UCLA) and a master's in Anthropology from Columbia University. While at Columbia, she researched Malcolm X's connections to the Arab world for the Malcolm X Project and worked with arts-based social justice organization Blackout Arts Collective.

Alhassen has worked with the online educational children's travel series "Project Explorer" (www.projectexplorer.org) and travels nationally and internationally conducting workshops and lecturing. Her writings can be read on www.mayalhassen.com

**AHMED SHIHAB-ELDIN** is a storyteller, social-media addict and is currently hosting and producing HuffPost Live, a disruptive and ground-breaking online network. In 2011, Ahmed created, produced and co-hosted Al Jazeera English's Emmy-nominated social media show, "The Stream." Before joining Al Jazeera English he worked as a reporter and producer for The Doha Film Institute and helped launch the inaugural Doha Tribeca Film Festival. Ahmed worked as a multimedia producer at PBS's award-winning documentary series Wide Angle, and as a news producer for the *New York Times*. Working as a freelance reporter, he has reported from in New York, Boston, Michigan and across the United States and Arab world, including Lebanon, the UAE, Kuwait, Qatar, Egypt and Jordan.

Soon after graduating from the Columbia University Graduate School of Journalism, Ahmed began teaching digital media as an adjunct professor. He also advises master's projects and serves as a digital media consultant for News21, a collaboration of 12 journalism schools under the Carnegie-Knight Initiative on the Future of

Journalism Education. Ahmed has been blogging for the Huffington Post since 2008. He also worked on special projects as a videographer for the Rockefeller Foundation and FRONTLINE/WORLD. In 2008, his master's digital media project earned him a Webby Award for "Defining Middle Ground: The Next Generation of Muslim New Yorkers." Since the Arab uprisings began in 2011, Ahmed has been invited to speak about the democratization of media and the Arab world at media and technology conferences in the USA, Arab world and Europe, including the 2011 Google Zeitgeist Conference.

Born in California, Ahmed spent most of his formative years in Kuwait, Austria and Egypt, where he lived for nearly a decade. His parents were both born in Palestine.

# Acclaimed Books on Islam
# from White Cloud Press

**I SPEAK FOR MYSELF** *American Women on Being Muslim*

edited by Maria Ebrahimji & Zahra Suratwala

**Selected as a Huffington Post "Top Religion Book for 2011"!**

$16.95 / Islam / ISBN: 978-1-935952-00-8

"These are the voices of mothers, daughters, sisters and neighbors we can all identify with representing an honest effort to allow American-born Muslim women to change the narrative of American Islam—in their own words." Deepak Chopra, author of *MUHAMMAD*

**ALL AMERICAN** *45 American Men on Being Muslim*

edited by Wajahat Ali and Zahra T. Suratwala

$16.95 / Islam / ISBN: 978-1-935952-59-6

A unique collection of stories shattering the misconceptions surrounding American Muslim men through honest, accessible, personal essays.

**THE MUSLIM NEXT DOOR**
*The Qur'an, the Media, and that Veil Thing*

by Sumbul Ali-Karamali

$16.95 / Islam / ISBN: 978-0-9745245-6-6

"A beautiful book. For anyone who truly wants to know what Muslims believe, this is the perfect book." Reza Aslan author *NO GOD BUT GOD: THE ORIGINS, EVOLUTION, AND FUTURE OF ISLAM*

**APPROACHING THE QUR'AN** *The Early Revelations*

by Professor Michael Sells

$21.95 / Islam / ISBN: 978-1-883991-69-2

"The best version of Muslim scriptures available in English ... An important and illuminating work, one that will be welcomed by scholars, students, believers, and all who seek to better understand Islam and its sacred scripture." Carl Ernst, Professor of Islamic Studies, University of North Carolina, and author of *THE SHAMBHALA GUIDE TO SUFISM*

WHITE CLOUD PRESS
www.whitecloudpress.com / ph. 800-380-8286